The Creative Curriculum® for Preschool, Sixth Edition

Volume 1: The Foundation

Diane Trister Dodge; Cate Heroman;
Laura J. Colker, EdD; Toni S. Bickart;
Kai-leé Berke; and Heather Baker

TeachingStrategies® · Bethesda, MD

Editorial: Kimberly Maxwell and Dana Wood
Layout/production: Jeff Cross and Abner Nieves
Illustrations: Jennifer Barrett O'Connell
Cover design: Propellor-id.com

Teaching Strategies, LLC
4500 East West Highway, Suite 300
Bethesda, MD 20814

www.TeachingStrategies.com

978-1-60617-698-6

Library of Congress Control Number: 2016934946

Printed and bound in the United States of America.

2020   2019   2018   2017   2016
10   9   8   7   6   5   4   3   2   1

Contents

Volume I: The Foundation

Foreword

More than 35 years ago, Teaching Strategies was founded by Diane Trister Dodge, one of the most visionary advocates for the field of early childhood education. At that time, Diane and Teaching Strategies made a commitment: to always provide the most effective resources to support the critical work of those who teach and care for our youngest learners. Over the years, those resources have taken different forms as our knowledge of research and best practice has expanded, but what's stayed consistent across the organization's history is that commitment. We continually evolve our resources and our thinking to uphold our commitment and ensure that we're always giving teachers just what they need to be successful.

This sixth edition of *The Creative Curriculum® for Preschool* is a continuation of the legacy of commitment to the early childhood field that originated with Diane and has been carried out by Teaching Strategies for more than 30 years. It builds off the work of some of the foremost thinkers and talented educators in early childhood education: Diane Trister Dodge, Cate Heroman, Toni Bickart, Diane Burts, and others, who have truly led the field in the development of forward-thinking, innovative resources and strategies for supporting early childhood educators. The sixth edition takes Teaching Strategies' unique approach to teaching and learning and expands upon it to include objectives for development and learning that span the whole of the early childhood years, from birth through third grade. It includes new resources that place even more emphasis on science and technology, social studies, and the arts, in keeping with what we know is most important for children's learning based on current research and best practice for early childhood education.

On the following pages, you'll have the opportunity to learn more about the history and evolution of *The Creative Curriculum® for Preschool* and understand how the exploration and discovery that's the hallmark of every *Creative Curriculum®* classroom will help you teach children to become creative, confident learners with the critical thinking skills that are so important for their future success, in school and in life. You'll also learn about the *Daily Resources* and understand the ways that they can support you throughout your day, even as you bring your own expertise and creativity to your planning. And throughout these six volumes, you'll find support for building your professional knowledge; strategies for working with every type of learner; current research that will help build your understanding of best practice; and guidance for building the kind of high-quality teacher-child relationships that are truly the foundation for all learning.

Thank you for your commitment to our youngest, most vulnerable learners. We are honored to be your partners in this critically important work.

Kai-leé Berke

Kai-leé Berke
Chief Executive Officer
Teaching Strategies, LLC

Introduction

Over the years, *The Creative Curriculum® for Preschool* has grown and changed along with the early childhood field as we learn more from research and gain new insights about what teachers need to know in order to teach effectively. *The Creative Curriculum®* now has a long, rich history. It has evolved from single volumes that used room arrangement as a teaching strategy to a rich collection of foundational and daily practice resources that help build teachers' knowledge and manage every moment of their days. Each new edition reflects our commitment to respond to the needs of early childhood educators.

History of *The Creative Curriculum®*

The first (1978) and second (1988) editions of *The Creative Curriculum®* helped teachers organize their rooms into interest areas and use them effectively. It began with four interest areas (Blocks, House Corner, Art, and Table Toys) and then added Library, Sand and Water, and Outdoors in the second edition.

The third edition (1992) explained the philosophy and theories behind *The Creative Curriculum®*, included goals and objectives for children's learning, and offered guidelines for teaching and working with families. Three more interest areas were included (Cooking, Music and Movement, and Computers).

In the years between the third and fourth editions (1992–2002), scholarly research and reports such as *Eager to Learn* (2001); *From Neurons to Neighborhoods* (2000); *A Good Beginning: Sending America's Children to School with the Social and Emotional Competence They Need to Succeed* (2000); *Preventing Reading Difficulties in Young Children* (1998); and the *National Panel Reading Report* (2000) helped to advance the field. With the new developments, it was clear that more guidance was needed about appropriate teaching strategies.

The fourth edition of *The Creative Curriculum® for Preschool* rested on a firm foundation of research and responded to new requirements for addressing academic content. While keeping the original environmentally-based approach of earlier editions, it defined more clearly the vital role of the teacher in connecting content, teaching, and learning for preschool children. It added a discussion of the research and theory on which *The Creative Curriculum®* is based; an overview of child development; guidance on the teacher's role in addressing content in literacy, math, science, social studies, the arts, and technology; and one new interest area (the Discovery area).

Between 2003 and 2009, new reports were published, including *Developing Early Literacy: Report of the National Early Literacy Panel A Scientific Synthesis of Early Literacy Development and Implications for Intervention* (2009); *Early Childhood Assessment: Why, What, and How* (2008); and *Mathematics Learning in Early Childhood: Paths Toward Excellence and Equity* (2009). In response, Teaching Strategies continued to offer new materials. A number of resources were developed to expand *The Creative Curriculum®*. These included *Literacy: The Creative Curriculum® Approach* (2004), *Mathematics: The Creative Curriculum® Approach* (2007), and *Study Starters: A Step-by-Step Guide to Project-Based Investigations in Science and Social Studies, Volumes I and II* (2005 and 2006). Attention was also focused on building capacity within programs. To clearly show what all aspects of teaching and learning look like in classrooms that implement *The Creative Curriculum®*, a DVD was developed, *The Creative Curriculum® for Preschool in Action!* (2007). An Implementation Checklist was also published (2003) as well as *The Coach's Guide to The Creative Curriculum® for Preschool: A Step-by-Step Resource for Individualizing Professional Development* (2009).

In 2010, we created *The Creative Curriculum® for Preschool,* 5th Edition. For the first time, the curriculum included both the foundational volumes that helped to build teachers' professional knowledge of best practice, as well as *Daily Resources,* which offered teachers detailed guidance on what to do each day. Also for the first time, both *The Foundation* and the *Daily Resources* were rooted in 38 newly-developed objectives for development and learning that were created based on what research showed was the most critical for children's success in school. To us, the decision to begin including daily practice resources was very much in line with what we'd always done historically, which was evolving our thinking in order to support the needs of the field. We recognized that most teachers have limited time to plan the range of experiences that make their classrooms the positive and exciting environments that all children deserve. Our daily support has given teachers everything they need to organize and manage their days intentionally and effectively.

The Creative Curriculum® for Preschool, Sixth Edition

Today, the sixth edition of *The Creative Curriculum® for Preschool* continues to help teachers build foundational knowledge of child development and best classroom practices and provide day-to-day, moment-to-moment support for helping every child to succeed. It includes a brand-new volume on Science and Technology, Social Studies, and the Arts, further enhancing our longstanding focus on these important content areas and recognizing the increased role that technology plays in our evolving society. It retains the 38 objectives for development and learning that research has shown to be most important for children's success in school, but expands those objectives through third grade, helping preschool teachers to see the critical role they play in laying the foundation for children's later learning and growth.

The Creative Curriculum® for Preschool, Volume I: The Foundation

This resource begins with an overview of the research and theory that underlie *The Creative Curriculum® for Preschool.* We explain the influence of research and theory on our understanding of child development and on the recommendations we make to teachers. Volume 1 has five chapters, each of which presents one of the central components of teaching preschool children effectively. They are

- Chapter 1, "How Children Develop and Learn"
- Chapter 2, "The Learning Environment"
- Chapter 3, "What Children Learn"
- Chapter 4, "Caring and Teaching"
- Chapter 5, "Partnering With Families"

The figure below shows how these five components form a framework that is applied in each of the classroom interest areas and outdoors.

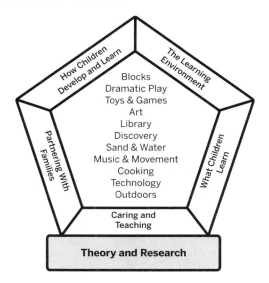

The Creative Curriculum® for Preschool, Volume 2: Interest Areas

In this volume, we explore the 10 classroom interest areas (Blocks, Dramatic Play, Toys and Games, Art, Library, Discovery, Sand and Water, Music and Movement, Cooking, Technology) and the Outdoors and describe the materials appropriate for each area. We demonstrate how *The Creative Curriculum®* objectives help teachers plan for, guide, and assess children's learning. Letters to families explain the value of children's play in each area and ways to support children's learning at home.

The Creative Curriculum® for Preschool, Volume 3: Literacy

This volume describes the latest research on early literacy learning, provides detailed explanations of the seven important components of literacy, and offers specific guidance on planning meaningful literacy experiences in each interest area and throughout the day. It also includes an expanded section on supporting English-language acquisition.

The Creative Curriculum® for Preschool, Volume 4: Mathematics

This volume summarizes the research related to early mathematics learning, describes five components of mathematics and five mathematical process skills, and offers suggestions for incorporating mathematics learning into each interest area and into routines. It also incudes guidance on planning meaningful math experiences throughout the day.

The Creative Curriculum® for Preschool, Volume 5: Science and Technology, Social Studies & the Arts

This volume offers guidance and support for teachers planning project-based investigations through studies of science and social studies and arts topics. It expands on information provided in *The Creative Curriculum® for Preschool, Volume 1: The Foundation*, showing in detail the ways that the classroom can be a rich environment for the areas of science and technology, social studies, and the arts. It discusses how to make these subject areas a part of children's everyday learning through teacher-child interactions, changes to the interest areas, and family and community involvement.

The Creative Curriculum® for Preschool, Volume 6: Objectives for Development & Learning: Birth Through Third Grade

The last volume provides teachers with detailed information about each objective. It presents the research related to each objective, explains why the objective is important, shows the developmental progression for each objective, and includes classroom strategies related to each objective to help teachers develop and learn. The objectives describe the knowledge, skills, and behaviors that are most predictive of school success. The objectives span the whole of the early childhood years, birth through third grade, highlighting the critical importance of foundational skills and how they build upon each other to support children's development and learning through the early elementary grades.

The first 36 objectives are organized into nine areas of development and learning:

- Social–Emotional
- Physical
- Language
- Cognitive
- Literacy
- Mathematics
- Science and Technology
- Social Studies
- The Arts

A tenth area, English Language Acquisition, helps you follow a child's progress in acquiring both receptive and expressive skills in English.

Curriculum Resources for Daily Practice

In addition to the six volumes of *The Creative Curriculum® for Preschool*, Sixth Edition, the curriculum includes a number of resources for daily practice. These resources provide teachers with detailed guidance on what to do each day. The resources include:

- Six **Teaching Guides** that provide daily support for the entire school year, offering comprehensive, detailed plans that each span several weeks and guide teachers moment-by-moment through the day

- **Intentional Teaching Cards**™ that provide playful and engaging activities with directions to help teachers individualize each activity to meet the unique needs of every learner.

- **Mighty Minutes®** that help teachers turn every minute of the day into learning opportunities, intentionally promoting language, literacy, math, science, social studies, and physical skills during "in-between" times

- **The Teaching Strategies® Children's Book Collection**, which features beloved classic tales, contemporary works by award-winning authors and illustrators, and original nonfiction titles for use during high-quality read-alouds.

- **Book Discussion Cards**™ that explain how to read and talk about selected books in the Teaching Strategies® Children's Book Collection, helping teachers make the most of repeated, interactive read-alouds with children.

- **The Teaching Strategies® Children's eBook Collection** (DVD), which features English and Spanish titles in the Children's Book Collection that have been adapted for the eLearning environment.

Making the Curriculum Your Own

The Creative Curriculum® for Preschool resources are designed to support teachers at all levels of experience in planning and implementing a high-quality developmentally appropriate program. Their effectiveness in helping children acquire social competence and the skills they need to succeed as learners can be achieved best if the resources are implemented as intended. Like an architect's blueprint, they exist only on paper until they are interpreted and used to build your program. This does not mean that every program using *The Creative Curriculum®* will look the same. To make *The Creative Curriculum®* work for you, incorporate your own interests and teaching style as well as information about the children you teach and their families.

Implementing any curriculum requires a commitment to learn it and to use it to guide the decisions you make each day. This sixth edition gives you a comprehensive picture of a high-quality program and the strategies you can use to bring it to life in your classroom. We hope you will use *The Creative Curriculum®* to create a classroom where you can teach effectively and where children thrive.

References

Bowman, B. T., Donovan, M. S., & Burns, M. S. (Eds.). (2001). *Eager to learn: educating our preschoolers.* Washington, DC: National Academy Press.

National Early Literacy Panel. (2009). *Developing early literacy: Report of the National Early Literacy Panel: A scientific synthesis of early literacy development and implications for intervention.* Washington, DC: National Institute for Literacy.

National Institute of Child Health and Human Development. (2007). *Report of the National Reading Panel: Teaching children to read: An evidence-based assessment of the scientific research literature on reading and its implications for reading instruction* [NIH Publication No. 00-4754]. Washington, DC: U.S. Government Printing Office.

National Research Council. (2008). *Early childhood assessment: Why, what, and how* (C. E. Snow & S. B. Van Hemel, Eds.). Washington, DC: The National Academies Press.

National Research Council. (2009). *Mathematics in early childhood: Paths toward excellence and equity* (C. T. Cross, T. A. Woods, & H. Schweingruber, Eds.) Washington, DC: The National Academies Press.

National Research Council and Institute of Medicine. (2000). *From neurons to neighborhoods: The science of early childhood development* (J. P. Shonkoff & D. A. Phillips, Eds.). Washington, DC: National Academy Press.

Peth-Pierce, R. (2000). *A good beginning: Sending America's children to school with the social and emotional competence they need to succeed* [Monograph]. Bethesda, MD: The Child Mental Health Foundations and Agencies Network and National Institute of Mental Health.

Snow, C. E., Burns, M. S., & Griffin, P. (Eds.). (1998). *Preventing reading difficulties in young children.* Washington, DC: National Academy Press.

Theory and Research Behind *The Creative Curriculum*®

Theory and Research Behind *The Creative Curriculum*®

Until the 20th century, little scientific attention was given to studying how children develop and learn. In the past 75 years, however, research has provided a wealth of information about childhood as a separate and distinct stage of life with its own characteristics. That research informs developmental and learning expectations for young children in early childhood education programs.[1]

One of the major influences guiding the field of early childhood education over the last 20 years has been the position statement on developmentally appropriate practice of the National Association for the Education of Young Children (NAEYC). It was last updated in 2009 in response to the changing contexts in which early childhood programs operate and to reflect new research about child development, learning, and effective teaching.[2]

Developmentally appropriate practice means teaching in ways that match the way children develop and learn so as to promote their optimal development and learning. Early childhood professionals make decisions about the education of children on the basis of information about

- child development and how children learn
- the individual strengths, needs, and interests of each child
- the cultures of each child's family and community

The Creative Curriculum® *for Preschool* is based on five fundamental principles. They guide practice and help us understand the reasons for intentionally setting up and operating preschool programs in particular ways. These are the principles:

- Positive interactions and relationships with adults provide a critical foundation for successful learning.
- Social–emotional competence is a significant factor in school success.
- Constructive, purposeful play supports essential learning.
- The physical environment affects the type and quality of learning interactions.
- Teacher–family partnerships promote development and learning.

This section summarizes the major theories and research that helped us identify these principles. We tell how each influences our understanding of child development and learning and how each informs the recommendations we make to teachers.

Teacher–Child Interactions and Relationships

American educator, philosopher, psychologist, and theorist John Dewey explored education as a social process.[3] He thought that children learn best when they interact with other people in a rich environment.[4] Through the responses they receive from others, children attach value and social meanings to their activities. Dewey urged that the classroom be organized as a community in which children learn in collaboration with each other and with their teachers.

Russian psychologist Lev Vygotsky also explored social interaction and concluded that it is crucial to children's learning.[5] He found that children need to talk about problems in order to solve them and talk about concepts in order to understand and apply them. In his theory, thought and language are intertwined. Vygotsky used the term *zone of proximal development* (ZPD) to describe the range of a child's learning about a particular experience. The lower limit of the zone represents what a child can do independently; the upper limit is what a child can do with the help of others who have more advanced skills.

The process of helping a child build knowledge and understanding is called *scaffolding.* Just as a scaffold helps a builder reach a high roof, scaffolding helps a child perform skills at a higher level than he or she could by working independently. Teachers' verbal directions, physical assistance, and probing questions help children figure out how to approach learning tasks, improve skills, and acquire knowledge. As a child discusses a problem or task with an adult, the adult supplies language to assist the child. The child gradually internalizes that language and more mature thinking. Vygotsky taught that teachers need to be expert observers of children, understand their levels of learning, and find ways to extend their learning.

Newer research also shows the importance of teacher–child relationships.[6] Children's ability to form positive relationships with adults is important to their social development and academic success.[7] We now know that relationships do not just provide a context for learning; they actually affect the physical structure of the brain.[8] Nurturing and positive interactions release chemicals that promote brain development. The quality of these relationships predict children's social–emotional competence, persistence, enthusiasm for learning, and academic success.[9] High-quality social interactions benefit all children, regardless of family or economic background, and they are associated with the positive development of literacy and other academic skills.[10] Warm, supportive relationships encourage children's motivation, engagement, self-direction, cooperation, and positive attitudes toward school.[11]

Supportive relationships with teachers and other adults can also help children overcome the challenges associated with living in circumstances that put them at risk developmentally, and they help children whose early relationships have not been positive.[12] Since the 1970s, research on resilience has focused on children who develop well despite hardships. Perhaps the most significant result of this work has been to challenge the assumption that children who grow up under the threat of disadvantage and hardship are doomed to a life of problems. Research has shown that children can develop the strengths and skills necessary to deal positively with adversity.[13] This research has also begun to provide information about the kind of help that children who are threatened by harmful conditions need in order to thrive. Not surprisingly, the research notes the importance of teachers.

Relationships with primary caregivers and teachers also affect children's relationships with their peers.[14] Close teacher–child relationships seem to encourage the development of children's prosocial skills.[15] Children who have secure attachment relationships with primary caregivers and teachers have an easier time interacting with peers, forming positive relationships, and being a part of a group.

Your Teaching Practice

Relationships are built on personal knowledge and interactions over time.[16] For optimal learning and development to occur, children need secure, consistent relationships with responsive adults.[17] The absence of warm, secure relationships can be devastating to children.[18] Teachers use these strategies to build these important relationships with children:

- Get to know each child well. Frequently interact with each child one-on-one in order to develop a warm, positive relationship.

- Demonstrate respect for children's ideas and efforts to solve problems.

- Validate children's efforts by acknowledging what they did and how they did it.

- Provide learning experiences that are challenging enough to promote children's learning but not so challenging as to frustrate them.

- Model self-talk that supports children's thinking. Offer ideas about how to approach tasks successfully.

- Observe children purposefully and regularly, and document what you see and hear. Use this information to understand each child's development and learning better.

Social–Emotional Competence

Well-known psychologist Erik Erikson explored the cultural and social aspects of development that influence a person's actions and interactions throughout life.[19] Erikson's psychosocial theory, called the "Eight Ages of Man," begins at birth and continues through old age. Each stage builds on the resolution of conflict during earlier stages. During the first 6 years, children are challenged by the conflicts of *trust vs. mistrust* (infancy), *autonomy vs. shame and doubt* (ages 1–3), and *initiative vs. guilt* (ages 3–6). Erikson described what adults need to provide at each stage in order to help children meet the challenges they face.

Trust develops when the child's experiences show that the world is safe, reliable, and responsive to his or her needs. Infants who receive consistent and loving care learn to trust. Infants who get inconsistent responses when they cry, who are not always fed when they are hungry, and who are not comforted when they are hurt, develop mistrust. *Autonomy*, or independence, is acting with will and control. It involves a sense of one's power that is built on the foundation of trust described in Erikson's first stage of development. Children develop autonomy when adults give them a chance to do things on their own. When adults make excessive demands or criticize in ways that devalue children's efforts, children learn to doubt their abilities. Developing *initiative* means responding positively to challenges, taking on responsibilities, enjoying accomplishments, and becoming purposeful. In this stage, children direct their energy toward tasks and begin to develop a sense of future possibilities. Children with initiative are eager to try new materials and ideas. Guilt can set in when adults belittle children and their work.

Newer research has established compelling links between social–emotional development, behavior, and school success.[20] Emotional understanding is critical to positive social relationships and peer acceptance.[21] Children who can interpret emotional signals accurately are more likely to respond appropriately to others and are less likely to become angry and aggressive.[22] The more adults acknowledge children's emotional reactions and explain emotional signals, the better children become at interpreting them.[23]

Kindergarten teachers rank self-regulation, the ability to control one's emotions and behavior and to resist impulses, as the characteristic most necessary for school readiness. They indicate that over half of their children lack effective self-regulatory skills.[24] Children who regulate their emotions positively do better in school and have an easier time getting along with peers.[25] Children tend to develop stronger self-regulation skills when they are in adult-supported, rather than adult-directed, play situations. Supporting, rather than directing, their behavior gives children the best chance to develop their own regulatory skills.[26]

Social competence, the ability to build positive relationships with others, affects school adjustment and academic success.[27] Some children's interactions put them at risk for developing negative relationships with peers and psychological difficulties.[28] Once children develop negative reputations, they are likely to be rejected by their peers unless adults intervene.[29] Teachers play a very important role in helping children develop positive peer relationships. Creative learning activities such as dramatic play, block play, and open-ended art activities provide opportunities for children to build positive relationships with peers.[30]

Early prosocial behaviors, such as cooperating, consoling, helping, and sharing, have been found to predict later academic achievement.[31] Children are more likely to use prosocial behaviors when their teachers use positive guidance strategies and a curriculum that emphasizes the value of community.[32]

Your Teaching Practice

Young children's social–emotional development involves learning how to understand their own and others' feelings, regulate and express their emotions appropriately, build relationships with others, and behave prosocially in groups.[33] These crucial skills have been found to predict successful kindergarten transition, early school success, and even later accomplishments in the workplace.[34] Teachers can guide the development of social–emotional competence by using these strategies:

- Provide play materials that support and challenge children's abilities. Promote problem solving and appropriate risk taking.

- Provide appropriate responsibilities and meaningful jobs in the classroom.

- Encourage children to see tasks through to completion. Offer support as needed.

- Help children express their feelings and resolve conflicts in constructive ways.

- Support children who need assistance in finding play partners. Teach them positive strategies for entering and participating in group activities.

- Support children as they interact with one another. Make modifications as necessary so that shy children or children with disabilities can engage in meaningful interactions with adults and peers.

- Offer opportunities for children to work together and to learn social skills. Pair more advanced learners with less advanced peers.

- Help children detect and interpret cues about how other people feel.

- Read stories to children about various emotions. Discuss why the characters look, feel, and act the way they do.

- Use positive strategies to guide children's behavior and help them learn how to cooperate with others.

- Teach turn taking and sharing, and model cooperation.

Constructive, Purposeful Play

Jean Piaget, a Swiss psychologist and developmental theorist, recognized the importance of play and its role in the development of logical thinking.[35] According to Piaget, play serves many purposes and provides an excellent vehicle for learning. By handling many different materials, children learn to observe, compare, sort, and sequence. Their knowledge grows as they experiment, make discoveries, and modify their current thinking to incorporate new insights. Supporting Piaget's theory that play is linked to learning, a recent study found that, when 4-year-olds were provided opportunities to engage in high amounts of child-initiated, free-choice activities supported by a variety of equipment and materials to explore, those children performed better on cognitive and language tasks at age 7 than did their peers who did not have such opportunities.[36]

Lev Vygotsky examined the social aspects of children's play and theorized that children think in complex ways.[37] As children play, they make rules, use symbols, and create narratives. Vygotsky thought that adults and more knowledgeable peers enhance a child's ability to learn through play because they model and encourage more advanced skills. He found that children talk to each other during social play about what they want to do and how they are going to play. He thought that such talk enhances self-regulation.

Newer research supports Vygotsky's theories. Complex sociodramatic play is linked to the development of self-regulation and may be particularly beneficial for children who are impulsive or who are less advanced in self-regulatory development.[38] Private speech, or self-talk, is an important part of developing self-regulation skills. Krafft and Berk found that the private speech of 3- to 5-year-olds was more likely to occur during open-ended activities, especially dramatic play, than in closed-ended tasks with predetermined goals.[39] Smilansky and Shefatya found that children who engaged in high levels of sociodramatic play in preschool performed better in later school years than peers whose preschool play was less mature.[40]

Researchers have found that, in addition to being linked to self-regulation skills, constructive, purposeful play is associated with other positive outcomes.[41] Play can support memory development. As children act out real-life scenarios in their play, they discover meaningful connections among the information to be remembered. Children's play with toys can aid their effective use of recall strategies as they organize the toys into meaningful groups based on their play.[42] Playing with story-related dolls during children's enactment of stories was found to aid narrative development and narrative recall.[43]

Play is also associated with children's positive social skills and approaches to learning. Researchers Fantuzzo and McWayne found that the peer-play competence of preschoolers was associated with their motivation to learn, task persistence, autonomy, and prosocial behavior.[44] Literacy-enriched sociodramatic play centers encourage children to help each other and are effective in supporting collaborative literacy learning.[45]

Play also provides the context for foundational learning in the content areas.[46] Through play, children explore mathematical ideas and construct literacy understandings. They develop understandings about science and technology and learn fundamental process and inquiry skills. Play is also an important avenue for learning in social studies and the arts.

Children's language and literacy development is facilitated by important characteristics of sociodramatic play, such as varied vocabulary, extended discourse, and explanatory talk.[47] Play is linked to oral language development,[48] learning decontextualized language,[49] and symbolic thinking.[50] Playing with words, or word play, supports children's phonological awareness.[51] Dramatic play contributes to children's development of abstract thinking, imagination, and language skills, and it supports their school adjustment.[52] When adults enter children's play thoughtfully, they can scaffold children's learning and promote more advanced levels of cognition and language.[53]

Infants and children from all socioeconomic backgrounds and cultures play.[54] Culture and family background, previous experiences, and the presence of a disability are factors that influence what children play, how they play, and with whom they play.[55] Children are more comfortable with what is familiar, and they hesitate to play if nothing in the classroom resembles their home environment.[56]

In addition to being linked to self-regulation skills, studies have found that purposeful and productive play is positively related to

- memory development[57]
- symbolic thinking[58]
- positive approaches to learning[59]
- positive social skills[60]
- language and literacy skills[61]
- math skills[62]

Your Teaching Practice

Purposeful, engaging play is an important vehicle for children's learning. When they play in meaningful ways, children learn about themselves, other people, and the world around them. As they play, children acquire language, learn to solve problems, learn to control their behavior and feelings, and explore social roles.[63] The interactions between teachers and children during play are critical to their learning. Teachers facilitate this learning as they carefully observe children's play to determine the most appropriate levels and types of support to offer.

- Provide children with opportunities to engage in different types of play. Describe what is happening, offer suggestions, and include children with disabilities.

- Match play materials and props to the cultural and developmental characteristics of the children. Realistic props are good for very young children, but encourage preschoolers to use more abstract props or to make believe without props.

- Observe children's interests and build on them. Talk with children about what they are doing. Ask probing questions that stretch children's thinking (e.g., "How else might you…?" and "In what ways is this similar to…?" and "How can you solve that problem?").

- Encourage children to engage in make-believe play with other children. Encourage play with peers who are more advanced as well as those who are at the same or a less advanced developmental level.

- Invite children to create play scenarios. Encourage them to make their own props to support their play.

- Help children plan their play. Encourage children to remind themselves and each other of what they decided to do and say as they enact a scenario.

- Provide at least an hour of free, unstructured play daily in a half-day program and more in a full-day program. Give children opportunities to make choices and decisions, solve problems, pursue their interests, build oral language and literacy skills, discover mathematical relationships, be scientists, and see themselves as competent learners.

Interacting With the Environment

Both Dewey and Piaget explored how the physical environment, including materials, affect children's learning. Dewey proposed that children learn best in a stimulating environment that is designed according to the interests and experiences of the children in the classroom.[64] Teachers must observe carefully in order to plan engaging educational experiences that help children develop new skills and learn more about the world.

Piaget theorized that children construct knowledge through action.[65] He thought that children's curiosity about the world around them drives their learning. As described by Piaget, learning is a dynamic process with a number of stages. In the *sensorimotor* stage, which begins at birth and lasts until about age 2, babies learn through simple motor behaviors and by reacting to what they experience through their senses. At about age 2, children enter what Piaget called the *preoperational* period. During this stage, which lasts throughout the preschool years, children begin to notice the properties of the objects they explore. However, their observations are limited to only one attribute of an object at a time.

Piaget explained that children must engage in tasks actively in order to develop and learn. Children seek and process new information on the basis of what they already know (assimilation). They also modify their thinking in order to make sense of new information and experiences (accommodation).[66] By handling materials of different sizes, shapes, and colors, children eventually learn to sort, classify, compare, and sequence. Their knowledge grows as they experiment, make discoveries, and modify their earlier way of thinking to incorporate new insights.

While more recent research has shown that child development is more fluid and more tied to specific content knowledge than Piaget's stages suggest, it confirms that learning takes place through positive interactions between and among children and adults as children interact in their physical environments. The way the physical environment is set up helps children know what is important, what they are to do, and how they might do it. It can support or undermine children's attention and persistence. It can contribute to children's self-regulation when it is arranged so that children can function independently as they select activities and obtain and put away materials.[67] High-quality physical environments may be especially important for children who experience social and economic risks and may serve as a protective factor for these children.[68]

Over the past 20 years, scientists have been able to study neurological aspects of how children learn. These studies have confirmed that early experiences affect brain development. Nurturing, stable relationships and linguistically and cognitively rich environments contribute positively to healthy brain development and learning.[69]

Your Teaching Practice

For children to excel in school, experiences and the environment should support all aspects of their development. Brain research shows that the cognitive, emotional, and social capabilities of children are intertwined.[70] Academic learning cannot be separated from social–emotional development. Children's physical and emotional well-being is closely linked to their ability to think and learn effectively in well-designed environments with appropriate materials.

- Set up the environment so that children can explore and easily find and return materials on their own.

- Build upon the interests of the children. Give children many choices and chances to investigate.

- Allow children time to explore and experiment with books, art materials, discovery items, music, dramatic play, sand and water, blocks, toys and games, cooking, technology, and the outdoors.

- Involve children in creating the classroom environment. Encourage them to share materials as they explore. Provide places for them to display their work.

- Teach the whole child. Remember that social–emotional, physical, cognitive, and language development are intertwined. Include plenty of physical activity and chances to explore literacy, math, science, social studies, technology, and the arts.

Partnerships With Families

Dewey wrote about how the values and cultures of children's families and communities extend into life at school.[71] To ensure continuity and give meaning to what is learned at school, teachers must become very familiar with children's everyday lives. Dewey thought that children's home lives must be considered when teachers plan their programs.

Developmental psychologist and theorist Urie Bronfenbrenner argued that children develop within a variety of interconnected systems.[72] These systems are dynamic and interactive, and each system has a powerful impact on a child's development. Important learning settings for a preschool child are the home, neighborhood, and early education program. Bronfenbrenner thought that the developmental potential of each setting is enhanced when there are supportive links and open communication among the people in those settings. Dewey's and Bronfenbrenner's research lend support for frequent family involvement and for communication between families and teachers.

Positive teacher–family relationships are reciprocal and characterized by mutual respect and the exchange of ideas.[73] Reciprocal relationships are crucial in helping families support their children's enthusiasm for and engagement in learning.[74] A positive relationship is particularly important when a family's home culture and socioeconomic background differ from that of the teacher.[75]

Family participation involves both formal and informal connections between families and their children's educational programs. Families are not likely to be open to parent education or other involvement unless teachers establish positive relationships and engage families in conversations that are supportive and culturally responsive.[76]

Theory and 4 decades of research underscore the importance of a strong partnership between each family and the early childhood program. Numerous studies have documented the academic benefits to children of a family–school–teacher partnership. When families are involved, children do better. These findings hold true regardless of the educational background or income level of the parents.[77] Indeed, successful partnerships can even overcome the negative effects of poverty. Moreover, these benefits are sustained over time.[78]

Family–school bonds can enhance children's problem-solving skills and social competency, and reduce aggression at home and at the educational program.[79] Strong family–school connections can be formed through family participation in preschool-based activities and regular communication between families and teachers. Participation might include attending family–teacher conferences, extended class visits, and helping with class activities. Such participation has been linked positively to child language; self-help; and social, motor, adaptive, and basic school skills.[80] The frequency of parent–teacher contact has also been found to have a positive effect on children's preschool performance.[81]

Family engagement in a child's early educational experience is important because it increases the parents' knowledge of their child's program and can demonstrate to the child the value they place on schooling.[82] Not only can strong family–school connections promote positive child gains during the preschool years, but research shows that the benefits extend well into the future.[83]

Research also underscores the need to reach out to fathers and other extended family members.[84] Participation by fathers is linked with both school readiness and children's emotional self-regulation.[85]

Your Teaching Practice

Children today have increasingly diverse family backgrounds.[86] For example, families vary in their cultures, ethnicities, belief systems, experiences, compositions, parenting abilities, and geographic locations. Positive relationships are the foundation for working effectively with diverse families.[87] Regular communication with families is critical to children's development and learning. When children receive consistent messages and support from both their families and their teachers, everyone benefits.

- Develop positive relationships with families, both formally and informally. Be a good listener and keep an open mind about different perspectives.

- Communicate with families regularly. Share information in person if possible. Share information by phone or e-mail, hold family conferences, and send home newsletters.

- Offer a variety of family involvement options. Invite family members to visit the classroom and share a special food, song, story, or experience with the children. Encourage families to volunteer in your program. Invite them to join field trips and eat meals with the children. Suggest things families can do at home to support their children's development and learning.

- Share positive information with families. Describe children's strengths and interests and discuss problems that need to be addressed.

- Reach out to all family members. Everyone who is special to a young child has an important role.

- Become familiar with local community services that are available to support children and families.

Summary

Our understanding of best practice in early childhood education is shaped by the researchers and theorists who laid the groundwork for our thinking about how children develop and learn. Their work is the foundation for defining high-quality early childhood education and care.

The research described in this chapter validates and expands our thinking. As a preschool teacher, you translate research and theory into practice every day. The ways you set up your program, plan your day, interact with children and families, and follow learning objectives for children are informed by this research. Being familiar with the research makes you a knowledgeable professional.

References

[1] Berk, L. E. (2009). *Child development* (8th ed.). Boston, MA: Pearson Education, Inc.

[2] Copple, C., & Bredekamp, S. (Eds.). (2009). *Developmentally appropriate practice in early childhood programs* (3rd ed.). Washington, DC: National Association for the Education of Young Children.

[3] Dewey, J. (1897). My pedagogic creed. In J. Dewey & A. W. Small, *Teachers manuals* (No. 25). New York, NY: E. L. Kellogg & Co.

[4] Mooney, C. G. (2013). *Theories of childhood: An introduction to Dewey, Montessori, Erikson, Piaget, & Vygotsky* (2nd ed.). St. Paul, MN: Redleaf Press.

Rushton, S., & Larkin, E. (2001). Shaping the learning environment: Connecting developmentally appropriate practices to brain research. *Early Childhood Education Journal, 29*(1), 25–33.

[5] Vygotsky, L. S. (1978). *Mind in society: The development of higher psychological processes.* Cambridge, MA: Harvard University Press. (Original work published in 1934)

[6] Rudasill, K. M., & Rimm-Kaufman, S. E. (2009). Teacher–child relationship quality: The roles of child temperament and teacher–child interactions. *Early Childhood Research Quarterly, 24,* 107–120.

[7] Bronson, M. B. (2006). Developing social and emotional competence. In D. F. Gullo (Ed.), *K today: Teaching and learning in the kindergarten year* (pp. 47–56). Washington, DC: National Association for the Education of Young Children.

Howes, C. (2000). Social–emotional classroom climate in child care: Child–teacher relationships and children's second grade peer relations. *Social Development, 9*(2), 191–204.

Paleromo, F., Hanish, L. D., Martin, C. L., Fabes, R. A., & Reiser, M. (2007). Preschoolers' academic readiness: What role does the teacher-child relationship play? *Early Childhood Research Quarterly, 22,* 407–422.

Pianta, R. (1999). *Enhancing relationships between children and teachers.* Washington, DC: American Psychological Association.

[8] Shore, R. (2003). *Rethinking the brain: New insights into early development Rev.* New York, NY: Families and Work Institute.

[9] Clifford, R. M., Barbarin, O., Chang, F., Early, D. M., Bryant, D., Howes, C., et al. (2005). What is pre-kindergarten? Characteristics of public pre-kindergarten programs. *Applied Developmental Science, 9*(3), 126–143.

Hamre, B. K., & Pianta, R. C. (2001). Early teacher-child relationships and the trajectory of children's school outcomes through eighth grade. *Child Development, 72*(2), 625–638.

Howes, C. (2000). Social-emotional classroom climate in child care: Child–teacher relationships and children's second grade peer relations. *Social Development, 9*(2), 191–204.

Pianta, R., Howes, C., Burchinal, M., Bryant, D., Clifford, R. M., Early, D. M., et al. (2005). Features of pre-kindergarten programs, classrooms, and teachers: Do they predict observed classroom quality and child-teacher interactions? *Applied Developmental Science, 9*(3), 144–159.

[10] Mashburn, A. J. (2008). Quality of social and physical environments in preschool and children's development of academic, language, and literacy skills. *Applied Developmental Science, 12*(3), 113–127.

[11] Birch, S. H., & Ladd, G. W. (1997). The teacher–child relationship and children's early school adjustment. *Journal of School Psychology, 35*, 61–79.

Howes, C., Burchinal, M., Pianta, R., Bryant, D., Early, D., Clifford, R., et al.(2008). Ready to learn? Children's pre-academic achievement in pre-kindergarten programs. *Early Childhood Research Quarterly, 23,* 27–50.

Pianta, R. C., & Steinberg, M. S. (1992). Teacher-child relationships and the process of adjusting to school. In R. C. Pianta (Ed.), *Beyond the parent: The role of other adults in children's lives*, 57, 61–80. Hoboken, NJ: Wiley/Jossey-Bass.

[12] Masten, A. S., Best, K. M., & Garmezy, N. (1990). Resilience and development: Contributions from the study of children who overcome adversity. *Development and Psychopathology, 2*, 425–444.

Howes, C. (2000). Social–emotional classroom climate in child care: Child–teacher relationships and children's second grade peer relations. *Social Development, 9*(2), 191–204.

[13] Paleromo, F., Hanish, L. D., Martin, C. L., Fabes, R. A., & Reiser, M. (2007). Preschoolers' academic readiness: What role does the teacher-child relationship play? *Early Childhood Research Quarterly, 22*(4), 407–422.

[14] Howes, C., Hamilton, C. E., & Matheson, C. C. (1994). Children's relationships with peers: Differential associations with aspects of the teacher-child relationship. *Child Development, 65*, 253–263.

Katz, L., Kramer, L., & Gottman, J. M. (1992). Conflict and emotions in marital, sibling, and peer relationships. In C. U. Shantz & W. W. Hartup (Eds.), *Conflict in child and adolescent development* (pp. 122-149). New York, NY: Cambridge University Press.

[15] Paleromo, F., Hanish, L. D., Martin, C. L., Fabes, R. A., & Reiser, M. (2007). Preschoolers' academic readiness: What role does the teacher–child relationship play? *Early Childhood Research Quarterly, 22*, 407–422.

[16] Hyson, M. (2008). *Enthusiastic and engaged learners: Approaches to learning in the early childhood classroom*. New York, NY: Teachers College Press.

[17] Copple, C., & Bredekamp, S. (Eds.). (2009). *Developmentally appropriate practice in early childhood programs* (3rd ed.). Washington, DC: National Association for the Education of Young Children.

[18] National Scientific Council on the Developing Child (NSCDC) (2004). *Young children develop in an environment of relationships: Working paper No. 1*. Retrieved December 28, 2009, from http://www.developingchild.harvard.edu

[19] Erikson, E. H. (1950). *Childhood and society*. New York, NY: W. W. Norton and Company.

Erikson, E. H. (1994). *Identity and the life cycle*. New York, NY: W. W. Norton and Company.

Hamre, B. K., & Pianta, R. C. (2001). Early teacher-child relationships and the trajectory of children's school outcomes through eighth grade. *Child Development, 72*(2), 625–638.

[20] Raver, C. C. (2002). Emotions matter: Making the case for the role of young children's emotional development for school readiness. *Social Policy Report, 16*, 3–18.

Zins, J. E., Bloodworth, M. R., Weissberg, R. P., & Walberg, H. J. (2004). The scientific base linking social and emotional learning to school success. In J. Zins, R. Weissberg, M. Wang, & H. J. Walberg (Eds.), *Building academic success on social emotional learning: What does the research say?* (pp. 3–22). New York, NY: Teachers College Press.

[21] Denham, S., Warren, H., von Salisch, M., Benga, O., Chin, J-C., & Geangu, E. (2013). Emotions and social development in childhood. In P. K. Smith & C. H. Hart (Eds.), *The wiley-blackwell handbook of childhood social development* (2nd ed.) (pp. 413–433). Oxford: Blackwell.

Eisenberg, N., Fabes, R. A., Shepard, S. A., Murphy, B. C., Guthrie, I. K., Jones, S., et. al. (1997). Contemporaneous and longitudinal prediction of child's social function from regulation and emotionality. *Child Development, 68*, 642–664.

Hubbard, J. A., & Coie, J. D. (1994). Emotional correlates of social competence in children's peer relationships. *Merrill-Palmer Quarterly, 20*, 1–20.

Hyson, M. C. (2004). *The emotional development of young children: Building an emotion-centered curriculum* (2nd ed.). New York, NY: Teachers College Press.

[22] Webster-Stratton, C., & Herbert, M. (1994). *Troubled families—Problem children: Working with parents: A collaborative process*. Chichester, England: Wiley.

[23] Berk, L. E. (2006). Looking at kindergarten. In D. F. Gullo (Ed.), *K today: Teaching and learning in the kindergarten year* (pp. 11–25). Washington, DC: National Association for the Education of Young Children.

Denham, S. A., & Kochanoff, A. T. (2002). Parental contributions to preschoolers' understanding of emotion. *Marriage and Family Review, 34*, 311–343.

[24] Rimm-Kaufman, S. E., & Pianta, R. C. (2000). An ecological perspective on the transition to kindergarten: A theoretical framework to guide empirical research. *Journal of Applied Developmental Psychology, 21*(5), 491–511.

[25] Bronson, M. B. (2000). *Self-regulation in early childhood: Nature and nurture*. New York, NY: Guilford Press.

Ponitz, C. E. C., McClelland, M. M., Jewkes, A. M., Conner, C. M., Farris, C. L., & Morrison, F. J. (2008). Touch your toes! Developing a direct measure of behavioral regulation in early childhood. *Early Childhood Research Quarterly, 23*, 141–158.

[26] Berk, L. A., Mann, T. D., & Ogan, A. T. (2006). Make-believe play: Wellspring for development of self-regulation. In D. G. Singer, R. M. Golinkoff, & K. Hirsh-Pasek (Eds.), *Play = learning: How play motivates and enhances children's cognitive and social-emotional growth* (pp. 74–100). New York, NY: Oxford Press.

[27] Ladd, G. W., Birch, S. H., & Buhs, E. S. (1999). Children's social and scholastic lives in kindergarten: Related spheres of influence? *Child Development, 70*, 1373–1400.

Riley, D., San Juan, R. R., Klinkner, J., & Ramminger, A. (2008). *Social and emotional development: Connecting science and practice in early childhood settings.* St. Paul, MN: Redleaf Press.

National Research Council and Institute of Medicine. (2000). *From neurons to neighborhoods: The science of early childhood development* (J. P. Shonkoff & D. A. Phillips, Eds.). Washington, DC: National Academy Press.

Wentzel, K. R., & Asher, S. R. (1995). The academic lives of neglected, rejected, popular, and controversial children. *Child Development, 66*, 754–763.

[28] Buhs, E. S., Ladd, G. W., & Herald, S. L. (2006). Peer exclusion and victimization: Processes that mediate the relation between peer group rejection and children's classroom engagement and achievement? *Journal of Educational Psychology, 98*(1), 1–13.

Ladd, G. W. (2006). Peer rejection, aggressive or withdrawn behavior, and psychological maladjustment from ages 5 to 12: An examination of four predictive models. *Child Development, 77*, 822–846.

[29] Black, B., & Hazen, N. L. (1990). Social status and patterns of communication in acquainted and unacquainted preschool children. *Developmental Psychology, 26*, 379–387.

Kaiser, B., & Rasminsky, J. S. (2012). *Challenging behavior in young children: Understanding, preventing, and responding effectively* (3rd ed.). Boston, MA: Allyn & Bacon.

[30] Wishard, A. G., Shivers, E. M., Howes, C., & Ritchie, S. (2003). Child care program and teacher practices: Associations with quality and children's experiences. *Early Childhood Research Quarterly, 18*, 65–103.

[31] Caprara, G. V., Barbaranelli, C., Pastorelli, C., Bandura, A., & Zimbardo, P. G. (2000). Prosocial foundations of children's academic achievement. *Psychological Science, 11*, 302–306.

[32] DeVries, R., Haney, J., & Zan, B. (1991). Socio-moral atmosphere in direct-instruction, eclectic, and constructivist kindergartens: A study of teachers' enacted interpersonal understanding. *Early Childhood Research Quarterly, 6*, 449–471.

Schmidt, H. M., Burts, D. C., Durham, R. S., Charlesworth, R., & Hart, C. H. (2007). Impact of developmental appropriateness of teacher guidance strategies on kindergarten children's interpersonal relations. *Journal of Research in Childhood Education, 21*, 290–301.

[33] Rubin, K., Bukowski, W., & Parker, J. (1998). Peer interactions, relationships, and groups. In W. Dunn, & R. Lerner (Eds.), *Handbook of child psychology, Vol. 1: Theoretical models of human development* (5th ed., pp. 619–700). New York, NY: Wiley.

[34] Peth-Pierce, R. (2000). *A good beginning: Sending America's children to school with the social and emotional competence they need to succeed* [Monograph]. Bethesda, MD: The Child Mental Health Foundations and Agencies Network and National Institute of Mental Health.

[35] Piaget, J. (1972). *Play, dreams, and imitation in childhood*. London: Routledge and Kegan Paul. (Original work published in 1945)

[36] Montie, J. E., Xiang, Z., & Schweinhart, L. J. (2006). Preschool experience in 10 countries: Cognitive and language performance at age 7. *Early Childhood Research Quarterly, 21,* 313–331.

[37] Shore, R. (2003). *Rethinking the brain: New insights into early development* (Rev.). New York, NY: Families and Work Institute.

[38] Elias, C. H., & Berk, L. E. (2002). Self-regulation in young children: Is there a role for sociodramatic play? *Early Childhood Research Quarterly, 17,* 216–238.

[39] Krafft, K. C., & Berk, L. E. (1998). Private speech in two preschools: Significance of open-ended activities and make-believe play for verbal self-regulation. *Early Childhood Research Quarterly, 13,* 637–658.

[40] Kim, S. Y. (1999). The effects of storytelling and pretend play on cognitive processes, short-term and long-term narrative recall. *Child Study Journal, 29*(3), 175–191.

[41] Bergen, D. (2002). The role of pretend play in children's cognitive development. *Early Childhood Research and Practice, 4*(1). Retrieved May 27, 2007, from http://www.ecrp.uiuc.edu/v4n1/bergen.html

[42] Newman, L. S. (1990). Intentional and unintentional memory in young children: Remembering vs. playing. *Journal of Experimental Child Psychology, 50,* 243–258.

[43] Kim, S. Y. (1999). The effects of storytelling and pretend play on cognitive processes, short-term and long-term narrative recall. *Child Study Journal, 29*(3), 175–191.

[44] Fantuzzo, J., & McWayne, C. (2002). The relationship between peer-play interactions in the family context and dimensions of school readiness for low-income preschool children. *Journal of Educational Psychology, 94,* 79–87.

[45] Stone, S. J., & Christie, J. F. (1996). Collaborative literacy learning during sociodramatic play in a multiage (K–2) classroom. *Journal of Research in Childhood Education, 10,* 123–133.

[46] Fantuzzo, J., & McWayne, C. (2002). The relationship between peer-play interactions in the family context and dimensions of school readiness for low-income preschool children. *Journal of Educational Psychology, 94*, 79–87.

Steglin, D. A. (2005). Making a case for play policy. Research-based reasons to support play-based environments. *Young Children, 60*(2), 76–85.

[47] Dickinson, D. K., & Tabors, P. O. (Eds.). (2001). *Beginning literacy with language: Young children learning at home and school.* Baltimore, MD: Paul H. Brookes.

[48] Davidson, J. I. F. (2015). Language and play: Natural partners. In D. P. Fromberg & D. Bergen (Eds.), *Play from birth to twelve and beyond: Contexts, perspectives, and meanings* (3rd ed.) (pp. 107–118). New York, NY: Garland.

[49] Howes, C. & Matheson, C. C. (1992). Sequences in the development of competent play with peers: Social and pretend play. *Developmental Psychology, 28*, 961–974.

O'Reilly, A. W., & Bornstein, M. H. (1993). Caregiver–child interaction in play. *New Directions in Child Development, 59*, 55–66.

Sigel, I. (2012). Educating the Young Thinker model from research to practice: A case study of program development, or the place of theory and research in the development of educational programs. In J. L. Roopnarine & J. E. Johnson (Eds.), *Approaches to early childhood education* (5th ed.) (pp. 315–340). Columbus, OH: Merrill/Macmillan.

[50] Charlesworth, R. (2008). *Understanding child development* (7th ed.). Clifton Park, NY: Thomson/Delmar Learning.

Kim, S. Y. (1999). The effects of storytelling and pretend play on cognitive processes, short-term and long-term narrative recall. *Child Study Journal, 29*(3), 175-191.

[51] Fernandez-Fein, S., & Baker, L. (1997). Rhyme and alliteration sensitivity and relevant experiences among preschoolers from diverse backgrounds. *Journal of Literacy Research, 29*(3), 433–459.

[52] Fantuzzo, J., & McWayne, C. (2002). The relationship between peer-play interactions in the family context and dimensions of school readiness for low-income preschool children. *Journal of Educational Psychology, 94*, 79–87.

Levy, A. K., Wolfgang, C. H., & Koorland, M. A. (1992). Sociodramatic play as a method for enhancing the language performance of kindergarten age students. *Early Childhood Research Quarterly, 7*, 245–262.

[53] Gmitrova, V., & Gmitrova, G. (2003). The impact of teacher-directed and child-directed pretend play on cognitive competence in kindergarten children. *Early Childhood Education Journal, 30*(4), 241–246.

Levy, A. K., Wolfgang, C. H., & Koorland, M. A. (1992). Sociodramatic play as a method for enhancing the language performance of kindergarten age students. *Early Childhood Research Quarterly, 7*, 245–262.

[54] Trawick-Smith, J. (2012). *Early childhood development: A multicultural perspective* (6th ed.). Upper Saddle River, NJ: Pearson.

[55] Berk, L. E. (2009). *Child development* (8th ed.). Boston, MA: Pearson Education, Inc.

Charlesworth, R. (2008). *Understanding child development* (7th ed.). Clifton Park, NY: Thomson/Delmar Learning.

[56] Heisner, J. (2005). Telling stories with blocks: Encouraging language in the block center. *Early Childhood Research and Practice, 7*(2). Retrieved May 27, 2007, from http://ecrp.uiuc.edu/v7n2/heisner.html

Levy, A. K., Wolfgang, C. H., & Koorland, M. A. (1992). Sociodramatic play as a method for enhancing the language performance of kindergarten age students. *Early Childhood Research Quarterly, 7,* 245–262.

Trawick-Smith, J. (1998). Why play training works: An integrated model for play intervention. *Journal of Research in Childhood Education, 12,* 117–129.

[57] Levy, A. K., Wolfgang, C. H., & Koorland, M. A. (1992). Sociodramatic play as a method for enhancing the language performance of kindergarten age students. *Early Childhood Research Quarterly, 7,* 245–262.

[58] Davidson, J. I. F. (2015). Language and play: Natural partners. In D. P. Fromberg & D. Bergen (Eds.), *Play from birth to twelve and beyond: Contexts, perspectives, and meanings* (3rd ed.) (pp. 107–118). New York, NY: Garland.

Kim, S. Y. (1999). The effects of storytelling and pretend play on cognitive processes, short-term and long-term narrative recall. *Child Study Journal, 29*(3), 175–191.

[59] Levy, A. K., Wolfgang, C. H., & Koorland, M. A. (1992). Sociodramatic play as a method for enhancing the language performance of kindergarten age students. *Early Childhood Research Quarterly, 7,* 245–262.

[60] Corsaro, W. (1988). Peer culture in the preschool. *Theory into Practice, 27*(1), 19–24.

Levy, A. K., Wolfgang, C. H., & Koorland, M. A. (1992). Sociodramatic play as a method for enhancing the language performance of kindergarten age students. *Early Childhood Research Quarterly, 7,* 245–262.

[61] Berk, L. E. (2009). *Child development* (8th ed.). Boston, MA: Pearson Education, Inc.

Kim, S. Y. (1999). The effects of storytelling and pretend play on cognitive processes, short-term and long-term narrative recall. *Child Study Journal, 29*(3), 175–191.

Levy, A. K., Wolfgang, C. H., & Koorland, M. A. (1992). Sociodramatic play as a method for enhancing the language performance of kindergarten age students. *Early Childhood Research Quarterly, 7,* 245–262.

[62] *Ibid.*

[63] Krafft, K. C., & Berk, L. E. (1998). Private speech in two preschools: Significance of open-ended activities and make-believe play for verbal self-regulation. *Early Childhood Research Quarterly, 13*, 637–658.

[64] Clifford, R. M., Barbarin, O., Chang, F., Early, D. M., Bryant, D., Howes, C., et al. (2005). What is pre-kindergarten? Characteristics of public pre-kindergarten programs. *Applied Developmental Science, 9(3)*, 126–143.

Hamre, B. K., & Pianta, R. C. (2001). Early teacher-child relationships and the trajectory of children's school outcomes through eighth grade. *Child Development, 72(2)*, 625–638.

[65] Davidson, J. I. F. (2015). Language and play: Natural partners. In D. P. Fromberg & D. Bergen (Eds.), *Play from birth to twelve and beyond: Contexts, perspectives, and meanings* (3rd ed.) (pp. 107–118). New York, NY: Garland.

Hamre, B. K., & Pianta, R. C. (2001). Early teacher-child relationships and the trajectory of children's school outcomes through eighth grade. *Child Development, 72(2)*, 625–638.

[66] Krafft, K. C., & Berk, L. E. (1998). Private speech in two preschools: Significance of open-ended activities and make-believe play for verbal self-regulation. *Early Childhood Research Quarterly, 13*, 637–658.

[67] Mooney, C. G. (2013). *Theories of childhood: An introduction to Dewey, Montessori, Erikson, Piaget, & Vygotsky* (2nd ed.). St. Paul, MN: Redleaf Press.

[68] Mashburn, A. J. (2008). Quality of social and physical environments in preschool and children's development of academic, language, and literacy skills. *Applied Developmental Science, 12(3)*, 113–127.

[69] Black, B., & Hazen, N. L. (1990). Social status and patterns of communication in acquainted and unacquainted preschool children. *Developmental Psychology, 26*, 379–387.

[70] Howes, C. (2000). Social-emotional classroom climate in child care. Child–teacher relationships and children's second grade peer relations. *Social Development, 9(2)*, 191–204.

[71] Clifford, R. M., Barbarin, O., Chang, F., Early, D. M., Bryant, D., Howes, C., et al. (2005). What is pre-kindergarten? Characteristics of public pre-kindergarten programs. *Applied Developmental Science, 9(3)*, 126–143.

Hamre, B. K., & Pianta, R. C. (2001). Early teacher-child relationships and the trajectory of children's school outcomes through eighth grade. *Child Development, 72(2)*, 625–638.

[72] Bronfenbrenner, U. (1979). *Ecology of human development.* Cambridge, MA: Harvard University Press.

Bronfenbrenner, U. (Ed.). (2005). *Making human beings human.* Thousand Oaks, CA: Sage.

Bronfenbrenner, U., & Morris, P. A. (2006). The bioecological model of human development. In Damon & R. M. Lerner (Eds.), *Handbook of child psychology: Vol 1. Theoretical models of human development* (6th ed., pp. 793-828). New York, NY: Wiley.

[73] Copple, C., & Bredekamp, S. (Eds.), (2009). *Developmentally appropriate practice in early childhood programs* (3rd ed.). Washington, DC: National Association for the Education of Young Children.

[74] Mooney, C. G. (2013). *Theories of childhood: An introduction to Dewey, Montessori, Erikson, Piaget, & Vygotsky* (2nd ed.). St. Paul, MN: Redleaf Press.

[75] Ray, A., Bowman, B., & Brownell, J. O. (2006). Teacher-child relationships, social-emotional development, and school achievement. In B. Bowman & E. K. Moore (Eds.), *School readiness and social-emotional development: Perspectives on cultural diversity.* Washington, DC: National Black Child Development Institute, Inc.

[76] Mooney, C. G. (2013). *Theories of childhood: An introduction to Dewey, Montessori, Erikson, Piaget, & Vygotsky* (2nd ed.). St. Paul, MN: Redleaf Press.

Kelly, J., & Barnard, K. (1999). Parent education within a relationship-focused model. *Topics in Early Childhood Special Education, 19*(3), 151–157.

[77] Henderson, A. T., & Berla, N. (Eds.). (1994). *A new generation of evidence: The family is critical to student achievement.* Washington, DC: National Committee for Citizens in Education. (ERIC Document Reproduction Service No. ED 375968)

[78] Weiss, H. B., Caspe, M., & Lopez, M. E. (2006, Spring). Family involvement in early childhood education. *Family involvement makes a difference, 1.* Retrieved December 5, 2009, from http://www.hfrp.org/publications-resources/browse-our-publications/family-involvement-in-early-childhood-education

[79] Ou, S. (2005). Pathways of long-term effects of an early intervention program on educational attainment: Findings from the Chicago longitudinal study. *Applied Developmental Psychology, 37*(4), 379–402.

[80] Marcon, R. A. (1999). Differential impact of preschool models on development and early learning of inner-city children: a three-cohort study. *Developmental Psychology, 35*, 358–375.

[81] Izzo, C. V., Weissberg, R. P., Kasprow, W. J., & Fenrich M. (1999). A longitudinal assessment of teacher perceptions of parent involvement in children's education and school performance. *American Journal of Community Psychology, 27*(6), 817–839.

[82] Mooney, C. G. (2013). *Theories of childhood: An introduction to Dewey, Montessori, Erikson, Piaget, & Vygotsky* (2nd ed.). St. Paul, MN: Redleaf Press.

[83] Barnard, W. M. (2004). Parent involvement in elementary school and education attainment. *Children & Youth Services Review, 26*(1), 39–62.

Clements, M. A., Reynolds, A. J., & Hickey, E. (2004). Site-level predictors of children's school and social competence in the Chicago Child–Parent Centers. *Early Childhood Research Quarterly, 19,* 273–296.

Graue, E., Clements, M. A., Reynolds, A. J., & Niles, M. D. (2004, December 24). More than teacher directed or child initiated: Preschool curriculum type, parent involvement, and children's outcomes in the Child-Parent Centers. *Education Policy Analysis Archives, 12*(72). Retrieved December 5, 2009, from http://epaa.asu.edu/epaa/v12n72/

Mantzicopoulos, P. (2005). Conflictual relationships between kindergarten children and their teachers: Associations with child and classroom context variables. *Journal of School Psychology, 43*, 425–442.

Miedel, W. T., & Reynolds, A. J. (1999). Parent involvement in early intervention for disadvantaged children: Does it matter? *Journal of School Psychology, 37*, 379–402.

[84] McBride, B. A., Dyer, W. J., & Rane, T. R. (2008). Family partnerships in early childhood programs: Don't forget fathers/men. In M. M. Cornish (Ed.), *Promising practices for partnering with families in the early years: A volume in family-school-community partnerships*, (pp. 41–58). Charlotte, NC: Information Age Publishing.

[85] Dower, J. T., & Mendez, J. L. (2005). African American father involvement and preschool children's school readiness. *Early Education and Development, 16*(3), 317–340.

[86] Koralek, D. (Ed.) (2007). *Spotlight on young children and families.* Washington, DC: National Association for the Education of Young Children.

[87] Mooney, C. G. (2013). *Theories of childhood: An introduction to Dewey, Montessori, Erikson, Piaget, & Vygotsky* (2nd ed.). St. Paul, MN: Redleaf Press.

Henderson, A. T., & Berla, N. (Eds.). (1994). *A new generation of evidence: The family is critical to student achievement.* Washington, DC: National Committee for Citizens in Education. (ERIC Document Reproduction Service No. ED375968)

How Children Develop and Learn

How Children Develop and Learn

This chapter explains the first component of *The Creative Curriculum®* framework: how children develop and learn. That knowledge is one of the bases for planning your program, selecting materials, and guiding children's learning. Understanding how children develop and learn means understanding the widely held expectations for children at various levels of development as well as the differences you will certainly find among individual children.

This chapter is divided into two main sections:

"What Preschool Children Are Like" discusses their social–emotional, physical, language, and cognitive development, their use of process skills, and the typical characteristics of 3-, 4-, and 5-year-olds.

"Individual Differences" explains variations in gender, temperament, interests, learning styles, life experiences, culture, language learning, and special needs.

What Preschool Children Are Like

The preschool years (ages 3–5) are a special period in the lives of young children. During this time, they begin to trust people outside their families. They gain independence and self-control, and they learn to take the initiative and assert themselves in socially acceptable ways. They become keen observers who experiment to find out what happens when they interact with other people and manipulate materials. Their language skills surpass the limited vocabulary and sentence structure of toddlers.

Preschoolers use thousands of words and complex phrases and sentences to communicate. As they learn to understand others and express their ideas more effectively, their horizons expand. In addition, preschool children change physically, growing and gaining strength, agility, balance, and coordination.

Areas of Development

For the sake of discussion, child development is divided into four areas: social–emotional, physical, language, and cognitive. While the division is both necessary and useful, it is somewhat artificial. In reality, development cannot be categorized neatly. The four areas are closely related and often overlap. Development in one area affects and is influenced by development in all other areas. This reality requires teachers to pay attention to every area as they guide children's learning.

It is important to keep in mind that objectives for children's development and learning are interrelated. For instance, consider ways that literacy development depends upon other aspects of development. You promote language development when you talk to children and help them realize that print conveys messages. Social–emotional development is involved when you expect children to handle books independently and to work cooperatively with magnetic letters. Physical development is required for using writing tools such as chalk, pencils, and markers. You promote cognitive development as well as language and literacy development when you encourage children to act out the parts of a story in correct sequence.

The four areas of development and the 14 objectives that address them are identified below. Two additional objectives for English language acquisition are also presented. The purpose of the descriptions is to help you focus on particular areas while keeping the whole child and the interplay of development in mind. Critical process skills are also discussed. In chapter 3, "What Children Learn," the objectives for content learning in literacy, mathematics, science, social studies, the arts, and technology are identified.

Social–Emotional Development

Social–emotional competence is essential to children's well-being and their success in school and throughout life. With the current focus on readiness, accountability, and high standards, there is always a danger that programs will focus only on academic content and ignore aspects of development that are equally important for achieving long-lasting positive results.

Social–emotional development during the preschool years involves socialization, or learning social norms and customs and becoming a member of a community (Epstein, 2014). It includes learning how to interact with adults and children in ways that support all other areas of learning. Young children's social–emotional growth can be categorized into four general components of

- emotional self-regulation, which includes controlling strong emotions, delaying gratification, and a growing sense of overall self-awareness
- social knowledge and understanding, which is the ability to participate as a member of a group
- social skills, particularly as they relate to respecting and understanding differences in others as they learn to interact
- social dispositions, which includes both inherent temperamental traits as well as socially acceptable characteristics that are welcome in a community (Epstein, 2014)

The relationships children form with adults greatly influence their overall social–emotional development (Berk, 2013). When adults are responsive, when they express pleasure about children's accomplishments and discoveries, and when they create environments in which children can participate actively in daily routines and experiences, children know that adults consider them to be important, interesting and competent. Caring adults also reinforce acceptable behaviors, further helping children develop prosocial skills such as turn taking, sharing, and empathizing (Riley, San Juan, Klinkner, & Ramminger, 2008).

There are three objectives for social–emotional development and learning:

Objective 1. Regulates own emotions and behaviors

    a. Manages own feelings
    b. Follows limits and expectations
    c. Takes care of own needs appropriately

Objective 2. Establishes and sustains positive relationships

    a. Forms relationships with adults
    b. Responds to emotional cues
    c. Interacts with peers
    d. Makes friends

Objective 3. Participates cooperatively and constructively in group situations

    a. Balances needs and rights of self and others
    b. Solves social problems

Physical Development

Physical development includes children's gross-motor (large-muscle) and fine-motor (small-muscle) skills. Balance; coordination; and locomotion, or traveling, are part of gross-motor development. Children gain control of their bodies in a predictable sequence, from the center of their bodies and outward to their fingers and toes. For example, a child first catches a ball by trapping it against her whole body, then by holding her arms out to catch it, and finally by catching it with both hands. Similarly, fine-motor skills progress from the child's grabbing an object with his whole hand, picking up a small item with his thumb and index finger, and eventually controlling the hand muscles needed for writing.

Physical development is sometimes taken for granted in the early childhood classroom because it is often assumed that it happens automatically. Not only is this assumption ungrounded, but teachers need to remember that physical development is just as important to learning as every other area of development. Children need many opportunities to practice their gross-motor skills (e.g., pulling, climbing, running, kicking, throwing, and jumping) and fine-motor skills (e.g., cutting, drawing, and writing).

As their physical development advances, children master increasingly sophisticated tasks and take personal responsibility for meeting their own physical needs, such as dressing themselves. In addition, physical development promotes social–emotional development in many ways. As children learn what their bodies can do, they gain self-confidence. The more they can do, the more willing they are to try new and challenging tasks. Thus a positive cycle that affects overall learning is established.

The benefits of promoting physical development are well documented. Regular physical activity is linked not only to improvements in children's overall physical health, but also their social, cognitive, emotional, and physiological development (Martyniuk & Tucker, 2014). Physical education in the early grades supports children's academic achievement, general health, self-esteem, stress management, and social development. Research shows that increased physical activity correlates to increased student achievement, specifically in the areas of learning and memory function (Edwards, 2014).

There are four objectives for physical development and learning:

Objective 4. Demonstrates traveling skills

Objective 5. Demonstrates balancing skills

Objective 6. Demonstrates gross-motor manipulative skills

Objective 7. Demonstrates fine-motor strength and coordination
    a.   Uses fingers and hands
    b.   Uses writing and drawing tools

Language Development

Language is the ability to listen to, understand, and use words. Language learning is complex. It involves learning about the structure and sequence of speech sounds, vocabulary, grammar, and the rules for engaging in appropriate and effective conversation (Berk, 2013).

Language learning begins at birth, but many children do not have the ongoing experiences that support this learning. Especially with the increased exposure to media sources such as TV, computer programs, and apps aimed at young children, it is crucial that children experience language learning through interactions with others. Research shows that language is a "thoroughly social phenomenon" and although children may be exposed to language through media, it is critical that they have the interactions that help them acquire expressive and receptive language (Al-Harbi, 2015). Oral language, including grammar, vocabulary, listening comprehension, and speech, helps provide the foundation for ongoing support of literacy (National Early Literacy Panel, 2008; Strickland & Shanahan, 2004). Children use language to think and to solve problems, so language development is closely related to cognitive development.

Language is the principal tool for establishing and maintaining relationships with adults and other children. Children's desire to communicate with others motivates them to develop language (Epstein, 2007). Children with some disabilities and children who are English-language learners face particular challenges in learning to understand and use language effectively.

Teachers are very important in helping children develop strong language skills. Teachers influence language development through the language they use, the way they set up the environment, and the types of experiences they provide. The opportunities children have for sociodramatic play and the level of that play affects children's language development. Higher levels of play involve increased language use and more complex language structures (Heisner, 2005). The maturity of children's language skills also affects the complexity of their play.

There are three objectives for language development and learning:

Objective 8. Listens to and understands increasingly complex language

    a. Comprehends language
    b. Follows directions

Objective 9. Uses language to express thoughts and needs

    a. Uses an expanding expressive vocabulary
    b. Speaks clearly
    c. Uses conventional grammar
    d. Tells about another time or place

Objective 10. Uses appropriate conversational and other communication skills

    a. Engages in conversations
    b. Uses social rules of language

There are two additional objectives for English language acquisition:

Objective 37. Demonstrates progress in listening to and understanding English

Objective 38. Demonstrates progress in speaking English

Cognitive Development

Cognitive development, also called *intellectual development*, is influenced by the child's approach to learning, his or her biological makeup, and the environment. A child's background knowledge—what he or she already knows—also affects the child's ability to make sense of new information and experiences. Background knowledge influences the child's ability to process information, remember, classify, solve problems, acquire language, read, and understand mathematics (Bjorklund, 2012; McAfee & Leong, 1994).

The physical environment of the classroom and the kinds of interactions children have with adults and other children influence all aspects of their cognitive development, including the ways children approach learning tasks. Their increasing abilities to represent ideas and feelings, use symbols, and engage in sociodramatic play expand children's worlds beyond literal meanings and enable them to use materials and their imaginations to explore abstract ideas. They use objects in imaginative ways, for instance, making believe that a cup is a telephone or that a broom is a horse. A child might pretend to be mother or a firefighter. Children learn to present information through charts or pictures, for instance, graphing weather changes over time or drawing what happened to a story character. As children use logical thinking, they organize their world conceptually and gain a better understanding of how it works.

There are four objectives for cognitive development and learning:

Objective 11. Demonstrates positive approaches to learning

    a. Attends and engages
    b. Persists
    c. Solves problems
    d. Shows curiosity and motivation
    e. Shows flexibility and inventiveness in thinking

Objective 12. Remembers and connects experiences

    a. Recognizes and recalls
    b. Makes connections

Objective 13. Uses classification skills

Objective 14. Uses symbols and images to represent something not present

    a. Thinks symbolically
    b. Engages in sociodramatic play

Process Skills

Among the skills that extend across all areas of development and learning are process skills. These are the skills you use to learn. They include observing and exploring, connecting, problem solving, organizing information, and communicating and representing.

Observing and exploring involves noticing things and thinking about how, when, and why they change. As children observe and explore, they manipulate objects to understand their properties and how they work. For example, a child who notices that a car goes down a ramp faster if the ramp slopes more steeply might explore how fast the car travels when the ramp is tilted at different angles.

Connecting involves linking new learning to prior experience. There can be connections between the ways things are done at home and at school; between different areas of development (e.g., self-care tasks and fine-motor skills); and between and within content areas (e.g., math and science, and numbers and measurement). Connecting anchors new learning, puts it into a broader context, and enables children to apply it in a variety of situations. For instance, children might talk about their own bedtime routines after hearing the story *Bedtime for Frances*.

Problem solving involves identifying a problem, thinking of ways to solve it, and trying possible solutions. It involves generating ideas, using materials in different ways, and taking risks to try something new. For example, a group of children at the sand table might want to create a fence around their hill. They would decide which materials to use, guess how many they will need, and test their ideas.

Organizing information includes breaking an idea or problem into parts, classifying, and comparing. Organization makes gathering, tracking, and using information possible. For example, at group time, children create a graph by placing their names either by a picture of feet or by a picture of a car to show whether they walked or rode to school.

Communicating and representing involves sharing thoughts, ideas, and feelings with others in many different ways: through gestures, facial expressions, drawings, writing, and speaking. Communicating also includes using representations, such as drawings, dramatizations, graphs, or clay models. For example, a child might use clay to create a model of an imaginary class pet, a hedgehog.

In order for children to progress in the acquisition of skills and behaviors related to the objectives in each area of development, they must use process skills. For example, to learn to manage feelings or follow limits and expectations, children must notice, experiment, organize information in new ways, and try different ways of communicating. As children's gross-motor development improves, they must observe how to accomplish a task, solve the problem of how to make their bodies work in new ways, and analyze new tasks so they can try them one step at a time. As they increase their vocabularies, they must connect new words to previously learned concepts and language. Process skills are also an intrinsic aspect of all content learning.

Developmental Characteristics of Age-Groups

As you think about each of the four developmental areas (social–emotional, physical, language, and cognitive), it is also useful to consider examples of how 3-, 4-, and 5-year-olds typically behave. Preschool children usually act very predictably at each age. For example, you can anticipate that 3-year-olds will often find it difficult to share. Rather than trying to force a 3-year-old to give another child a turn with a favorite toy, it makes more sense to have duplicates of popular toys. As children learn to trust you and their school environment, you can set up systems for helping them take turns. Once children know that there are enough toys for everyone and that they will get a turn even if they have to wait, sharing becomes less of a problem for them.

Three-Year-Olds

Three-year-olds are often described as being in transition. They more closely resemble 4- and 5-year-olds than 2-year-olds. More than anything else, their expanded ability to express themselves and their ability to play in small groups set them apart from twos. These abilities expand their social worlds.

Social–emotional development: Three-year-olds are still learning to trust their family members, teachers, and other important people in their lives to take good care of them. Trust gives them the confidence to become more independent, and they feel competent when they brush their teeth and dress themselves as older people do. Three-year-olds want you to notice their newly acquired skills, for instance, setting the table or pedaling a tricycle. Although 3-year-olds become more socially competent, their emotional and behavioral regulation does not develop fully. Even very sociable 3-year-olds are still egocentric.

Physical development: The play of 3-year-olds is usually more sustained and focused than toddlers' play. Gross-motor activities, such as running, swinging, throwing and catching a ball, and dancing to music are great sources of pleasure for this age-group. So, too, is quiet play, such as using puppets and painting pictures. For some 3-year-olds, putting a puzzle together for the eighth time may be more fun than playing with a ball.

Language development: In this area, 3-year-olds develop skills at an astounding rate. While most 2-year-olds use only the basic language sounds, most 3-year-olds have mastered all sounds, perhaps with the exception (in English) of /f/, /l/ /r/, /s/, and /th/. Most 3-year-olds use plurals, talk in sentences, recite simple rhymes, and ask questions. They can tell you their first and last names. They love to share their thoughts with you and participate in conversations.

Cognitive development: Three-year-olds are exploding with thoughts and ideas. They use all of their senses to make sense of the world around them. However, they are only beginning to classify. They sort objects but usually by only one characteristic at a time. Their egocentricity generally keeps them from seeing another person's point of view, although this limitation may be affected by circumstances. Many show empathy, and you may see a 3-year-old bringing a special toy to a child who is upset.

Four-Year-Olds

Four-year-olds are working on many of the same developmental tasks as 3-year-olds, but they usually do so at a higher level. Because their language often seems fluent, you may assume that they understand more than they actually do. For instance, they often use the word *why*, creating the impression that they want an explanation. Often your explanation of why something happens is not nearly as important to the 4-year-old as the fact that you are giving the child your full attention.

Social–emotional development: Four-year-olds are a wonderful mix of independence and sociability. They like doing things on their own. They take great pride in imitating adult behaviors, and they also love playing with other children, especially in groups of two and three. Sharing becomes easier. Whether playing alone or in a group, 4-year-olds tend to be very expressive, using actions and facial expressions as well as words to get their points across.

Physical development: Four-year-olds are increasingly able to control their muscles. Most 3-year-olds go down steps by putting both feet on the same step before continuing down, but most 4-year-olds alternate their feet easily. The leg muscles of 4-year-olds enable them to maintain a rhythmic stride while running. They play enthusiastically on slides, swings, and other outdoor play equipment. Their fine-motor coordination improves dramatically as well. On their own, they can wash their hands, button their coats, and use Velcro® straps. Some are coordinated enough to cut intricate shapes with scissors, zip their coats, and attempt to tie their shoes.

Language development: Four-year-olds develop language skills rapidly. They usually understand and use positional words such as *in*, *by*, *with*, *to*, *over*, and *under*. They love to talk, be spoken to, and listen to books. Trying new words—including bathroom (potty) language—delights 4-year-olds. They like to use big words and deeply enjoy their ability to communicate.

Cognitive development: Four-year-olds are budding scientists. They are extremely curious about causes and effects and want to know why things happen. They approach the world with great curiosity and use their experiences to understand it. However, because separating reality from fantasy is hard for them, they sometimes have irrational fears. All of a sudden, the closet might be home to an unwelcome monster. They might also tell what many adults describe as lies. For example, after knocking over a glass of milk, a child might insist that she did not do so, truly believing that what just happened was beyond her control. Developmentally, 4-year-olds struggle with the differences between truth and fiction.

Five-Year-Olds

By the time children turn 5, they understand more about themselves, others, their relationships, and their abilities. This is a fascinating age-group.

Social–emotional development: Five-year olds are increasingly independent, self-sufficient individuals. They are dependable and responsible and enjoy having their reliability acknowledged. In many ways, they are model citizens: cooperative, eager to tend to their own personal needs, protective of others, interested in going to school, and usually polite and even tactful. Five-year-olds are also exceedingly social. They seek friends and usually have one or two special playmates. Curious about the outside world, 5-year-olds like taking trips and exploring the environment.

Physical development: Five-year-olds show more agility, balance, and coordination than 4-year-olds in both gross-motor and fine-motor movements. They can jump rope, ride bikes with training wheels, and stand on their tip-toes. Five-year-olds can control a paintbrush, weave, and write letters and numbers with increasing accuracy.

Language development: Five-year-olds show significant growth in their communication skills. They pronounce words more accurately, and their grammar is more conventional. They use more complex language structures, speaking and understanding paragraphs and stories as well as sentences. They ask relevant questions and carry on longer conversations. Five-year-olds also begin to extend their oral language skills to reading and writing.

Cognitive development: Five year-olds build understandings about concepts by experimenting. They make predictions and solve problems by observing the objects and people around them. They think in complex ways, relating new information and experiences to what they already know. They understand the concepts of color, size, and shape. They can also classify by two features, such as color and shape.

Your knowledge of the widely held expectations for children and of the usual behaviors of 3-, 4-, and 5-year-olds gives you a general basis for planning your program. However, it is crucial to understand that each child develops on an individual timetable and will respond to your program in his or her own ways. You must get to know each child well and appreciate each child's characteristics. The way you support one child's development and learning might not be the best way to meet the strengths and needs of another child.

Individual Differences

A critical aspect of knowing the children you teach is finding out what makes each child unique. No matter how much children resemble each other in their general patterns of development, every child brings particular interests, different experiences, and a learning style to your classroom. You therefore need a variety of strategies to help all children develop and learn.

Think about the children in your classroom. Perhaps you have a child who never seems to stop exploring, even during nap time. Perhaps you have a child who loves to dance. Maybe it seems as though she can only learn something if she is twirling while she listens.

Your understanding of individual differences will help you respond in ways that make every child feel comfortable and ready to learn. Perhaps the most obvious difference among children is gender. Children also have different temperaments, interests, learning styles, and life experiences. They are strongly influenced by their cultural backgrounds. Some are also learning English as a second language, and some have special needs.

Gender

As adults, each of us has ideas about what it means to be male or female. Children, however, are still learning what it means to be a girl or a boy. Teachers therefore need to create a classroom environment where children feel safe in exploring gender-related roles and taking part in activities that are related to those roles.

Gender stereotypes are not usually helpful, even when it seems easy to back them up with one's own limited observations. For example, many people assume that boys like gross-motor play and that girls are quite content to play with figurines of people and animals for extended periods of time. Many say that girls are more likely to make representational drawings and write their names at an earlier age than boys.

Researchers debate the role of biology in explaining what appear to be differences in the way boys and girls generally behave. The way adults treat them also plays a role in children's behavior. As Katherine Hanson (1992, p.15) noted,

In child care settings, with infants and children between 13 months and two years, research shows that child care providers respond to the children based on their own sex role beliefs, and they use the child's gender to guide their responses... Adults were more likely to respond when girls used gestures or gentle touches or talked, and when boys forced attention through physical means or cried, whined, or screamed...

Because temperament and experience as well as biology play a role, teachers should ensure that both boys and girls receive positive messages about gender roles and what individuals are capable of doing. You need to be conscious of your own beliefs and the assumptions that affect the way you teach.

Think about your own experiences growing up. What messages did you receive about how boys and girls were expected to behave? Do you expect boys' play to be "rough-and-tumble" and expect girls to be gentle? What are the implications of your expectations? Do you want to pass your attitudes along to the children you teach? You may hear children insist, "Girls can't build with blocks" or "Boys don't dress up." They are repeating messages they have heard from others.

Remember that during the early childhood years children learn and explore new ideas when they are given the benefit of a safe place. Play is one of the vehicles they use to work out new understandings. Teachers should encourage children to examine their ideas about gender as they play and to think more flexibly about what girls and boys may and may not do.

Teachers can help children challenge their own and others' expectations. You can create an environment that allows children to explore stereotypes and feel comfortable. Think about the pictures you display and the books you read to children. Are there strong female role models? Are men presented in nurturing roles?

As you get to know the children in your classroom, note how gender influences children's behavior and your own expectations. Help children understand that your classroom is a place to explore freely.

Temperament

Temperament refers to our basic way of responding to the environment. For example, some children have a positive approach to new experiences and are generally cheerful and friendly. Other children tend to withdraw. They approach new situations cautiously and often adapt slowly. Some children protest new situations by crying, becoming fearful, or acting out.

Research suggests that children are biologically disposed toward particular behavioral styles (Chess & Thomas, 1996; Rothbart, et al., 2000). This is important for teachers to understand. For example, knowing that Carlos is easily distracted, you can offer him a quiet place to look at books, and you can turn off the music when he is trying to concentrate. Similarly, realizing that Setsuko tends to be shy, you can invite her to enter a dramatic play episode by asking her to join you and another child at the table for "tea."

While research has shown that temperament is inborn, providing suitable support for children can promote their development and learning. An active child can calm down, and a child who is easily distracted can learn to focus his attention. No matter with what temperament children are born, you can help them be more socially and academically successful.

While people have a tendency to maintain the same temperament throughout their lives, environment and experience do have an impact. You should not be surprised if a child's temperament at home seems different from her temperament at school. Similarly, a child who likes to play actively with his peers might become quiet around adults.

Note each child's behavior in a variety of settings and at various times of day. Doing so will help you make appropriate decisions. Understanding how children are likely to react to people and events helps you be a more responsive and effective teacher.

Interests

People also demonstrate their individuality through their interests and preferences. Particular topics interest some children but not others, and children's interests change continually. One child may be fascinated by monkeys and another by helicopters or trucks. One child loves hip-hop music; another will not go anywhere without a baseball cap.

Children's interests motivate them to continue learning. For example, if a child is interested in monkeys, you can engage her in reading, listening, and talking by offering a book about monkeys to look at or read aloud together. You can involve a child who loves to dance by playing music in your classroom. You can supply your Dramatic Play area with a variety of baseball caps to encourage the child who wears caps to spend time there.

If a child in your group is difficult to engage or does not use speech to communicate, try to find something that really interests him. Use that interest to help him interact with others and develop verbal skills. For example, a child who is skilled at using the computer and a tablet can be encouraged to help other children with less technology experience. Teachers who are aware of the interests of their children have a basis for building a relationship with and motivating each child to learn.

Children's interests are also good possibilities for long-term study topics. If a housing development is going up across the street from your school and you've observed that Derek is fascinated by trucks and that Crystal is constructing towers with blocks, you might consider a long-term study about buildings. Knowing the related interests of other children will help you think of ways to extend the study and sustain it over time.

Whether or not you are able to incorporate individual children's preferences into long-term studies, make it a practice to nurture their interests. By doing so, you convey the message that you value what is important to them. You also help them gain new skills and confidence.

Learning Styles

Every person has a preferred way of learning. Some people are visual learners. Some learn better by listening, while others have to handle something physically before they can understand it. One style is not better than another; it's simply the way a particular person learns best.

You will probably observe at least three styles of learning in your group of children:

Auditory learners, or children who learn best by listening, are attuned to oral language and other sounds. They solve problems by talking about them. Auditory learners can follow oral instructions and explanations. You can build their knowledge by describing and explaining what they did: "When you added coffee grounds to the paint, it changed the way the paint feels when it dries." You can also ask open-ended questions to encourage children to verbalize their thoughts: "What are you making for the baby doll's breakfast?" The more opportunities you provide for auditory learners to hear and verbalize concepts, the better they will understand them.

Visual learners, or children who learn best by seeing, are drawn to color, shape, and motion. They seem to think in images or pictures. Visual learners benefit when you show them how things are done, rather than just tell them verbally: "Jonetta, Kate can show you how to put the interlocking blocks together so that you can build with them." Visual learners also remember ideas and concepts better when they are presented as an image: "Let's make a graph of the different types of shoes we're wearing today." Children who learn by looking need to make visual representations of their thoughts and feelings: "Zach, I know that you're sad that your daddy had to go away. Why don't you draw a picture about the way you're feeling?"

Kinesthetic learners, or children who learn best by moving, are generally well coordinated and confident about their bodies. Touching things and moving help them process and recall information, and build understandings.

Have you ever seen a preschooler twirl around as she tries to remember something? This twirler might be a kinesthetic learner. Something about moving helps her learn a concept or process other information. Kinesthetic learners benefit by knowing that it is all right to get up and move around. You can facilitate their learning by relating concepts to their bodies, "When I push down on your head, you can feel the pressure, Setsuko. That's what a vise does to a piece of wood. It holds the wood in place."

Because children do not all learn in the same way, teachers should take all styles of learning into account. Traditionally, schools have appealed primarily to auditory learners and, to a lesser extent, to visual learners. Kinesthetic learners have had to adjust their way of learning in order to do well in school. Rather than expecting children to adjust, teachers should make sure that they present information so that all children—listeners, lookers, and movers—can be successful learners. Moreover, brain research shows that the more ways children explore a concept, the more likely they are to remember what they learn. You can maximize learning by offering learning opportunities for children of all learning styles.

Life Experiences

In addition to other individual differences, varying life experiences contribute to the uniqueness of each child. Consider how each of these factors may affect the children you teach:

- family composition, including the number and gender of parents, guardians, and other family members who live with the child
- the presence of a chronic health problem or the disability of a family member
- exposure to violence, addiction, abuse, or neglect
- home language(s)
- the family's culture and child-rearing practices
- the community in which the child lives
- the kinds of work family members do
- the age at which the child's parents gave birth to or adopted their first child
- economic status
- living situation, including the family's history of moving
- parents'/guardians' level of education
- parents'/guardians' job history, including work-related travel
- special circumstances such as marital separation and divorce, the absence of a family member for reasons not directly related to marriage, the birth or adoption of a new sibling; and how many people and places the child experiences each day

Life circumstances affect a child's behavior and ability to learn. For example, a child with an alcoholic mother may feel that life is unpredictable and that trusting others is risky. In contrast, a child with a stable home life may be independent and confident.

Try to be aware of each child's life circumstances when he or she enters your program. Talking with family members and taking notes about what you learn is an important first step. Encourage families to communicate with you about anything new that is taking place in children's lives, and honor their styles of communication. This process will take time as you develop a trusting relationship with family members. Remember to respect the confidentiality of information that family members share with you. If a family shares information with you that you do not know how to handle, seek advice from your supervisor or an outside expert.

Culture

Culture involves the customary beliefs, values, and practices people learn from their families and communities through experience, observation, and sometimes direct instruction. Culture influences the way people think and interact with others. It affects an individual's choice of words, tone of voice, facial expressions, use of gestures, ideas about personal space, and reaction time. Cultures also have different norms for asking questions, responding to questions, and conversing. Some aspects of culture involve ethnic, racial, and religious identification. Others are specific to a geographic location or an economic level.

Here are some examples of how a family's culture affects behavior at preschool:

- A child may have learned to value reflection as part of learning. This child has been taught at home that thinking about what he is learning is more important than getting through a project quickly. If his teacher regards speed as an indication of mastery, the child will appear to be a slow learner, not the competent and thoughtful child he is.

- In some cultures, it is rude to look the teacher in the eye or to answer a question quickly. Children of these cultural groups may be uncomfortable when they are expected to make eye contact, and they may be startled if the teacher leaves very little time between asking a question and expecting a response.

- Some children are unfamiliar with questioning as a teaching technique. They may be confused because they think the teacher already knows the answers to the questions she asks. The children's lack of response might be interpreted incorrectly as a lack of knowledge or attention, rather than confusion about why questions are being asked.

Because culture—particularly child-rearing practices, beliefs, and goals—affects development and learning in important ways, you need to learn about, understand, and respect its influence on you and on the children you teach. This does not mean that you have to be fluent in every language children speak and an expert on all cultural practices. However, it does mean that you need to learn as much as you can about each child's family. Talk with parents and other family members to understand each family and to build partnerships. Keep in mind that every family is different and avoid assigning cultural labels to families. Rather than making assumptions about cultural influences, it is better to keep an open mind and consider the values behind each family's beliefs. Seek to discover information, keeping in mind that not all families will be comfortable about responding to direct questions.

Consider the children's family and community cultures as you plan meaningful learning experiences, select materials, choose study topics, and determine appropriate teaching strategies. By doing so, you give children the message that each and every child is important and worthy of respect. For example, a teacher who uses *The Creative Curriculum®* in rural Alaska might engage children in a study of salmon fishing and its influence on people's lives. A migrant Head Start teacher in Maine might highlight life in the camp of blueberry pickers. A military child development center in Sicily might have lots of materials and props related to shopping at the PX and living at the foot of a volcano. Because different groups of children find different experiences meaningful, no classroom in which *The Creative Curriculum®* is used is exactly like any other, and no one program is the same from year to year.

Including All Children

A critical aspect of best practice in early childhood education is the inclusion of all children. By incorporating the concept of Universal Design for Learning (UDL), *The Creative Curriculum®* shows how to implement a high-quality inclusive program. When teachers use UDL, they support the learning of all children, including English-language learners, advanced learners, and those with disabilities and developmental delays. By providing a variety of formats for instruction, learning, and assessment, teachers offer children multiple ways of acquiring knowledge and skills and of communicating what they know (DEC/NAEYC, 2007).

English- and Dual-Language Learners

The number of children who speak a first language that is not English has increased dramatically and continues to increase in the United States. The Census Bureau predicts that by the year 2050 Hispanic and Asian Americans will comprise 40 percent of the U.S. population (Cable News Network, 2008; U.S. Census Bureau, 2007). If not already, then in the future you will probably teach children whose home languages are not English. In *The Creative Curriculum®* we refer to these children as *English-language learners* (ELL). Some are learning English for the first time in the preschool setting, while others have developed various levels of English proficiency before starting preschool. We recommend using a combination of teacher observation, teacher judgment, and a home-language survey to determine which children are English-language learners.

Young children who are learning English already understand a lot about language and how to use it effectively. They are in the process of acquiring a second language (English), but they usually already know much about the vocabulary, grammar, and social rules of their home languages and are continuing to build skills and vocabulary in their home languages. They often know a lot about storytelling, too. For these reasons, many educators use the term *dual-language learners* (DLL). For these children, comparing and contrasting among their two languages promotes their ability to transfer what they know about language to their second language and contributes to their awareness of how language is used in the culture, e.g., literal meanings and implied meanings (Koda & Zehler, 2008), which in turn impacts their language and literacy development in both languages (Durgunoglu & Oney, 2000). Bilingual children have been found to develop this awareness earlier than monolingual children (Bialystok, 1997), as knowing two languages provides a comparison and contrast and increases their ability to detect linguistic patterns.

In order to make the most of their current knowledge while they are progressing toward full English proficiency, English-language learners need particular kinds of classroom support. The developmentally appropriate practices explained throughout this volume benefit all preschool children, but certain practices are of particular importance to children who are English-language learners. Current research and the experiences of successful programs show that specific teaching and assessment adaptations, important small-group and individual language interactions, and systematic support for the ongoing development of the children's home language skills are critical to the long-term success of young children whose home languages are not English (August & Shanahan, 2010; Escamilla et al., 2014; Goldenberg, 2012). For a discussion of the instructional and assessment strategies that optimize young children's acquisition of English and long-term academic success, see the section "Supporting English-Language Learners" in chapter 2 of *The Creative Curriculum® for Preschool, Volume 3: Literacy*.

A number of misconceptions about English-language learning can cause unnecessary anxiety for teachers and families. The following chart dispels some of these common misunderstandings (Genesee, n.d.; Snow, 1997).

Myths About Learning a Second Language

Myth	Reality
Children who are exposed to more than one language are at a clear disadvantage.	Children who speak more than one language are often very creative and good at solving problems. Compared to children who speak one language, those who are bilingual can communicate with more people, read more, and benefit more from travel. Bilingual people have an additional skill when they enter the workforce.
Learning more than one language confuses the child.	Children do not get confused, even when they combine languages in one sentence. Mixing languages is an expected part of learning multiple languages.
Learning two languages during the preschool years invariably slows children's readiness to read.	Actually, the opposite is often true. English-language learners usually learn to decode words well.
When children are exposed to two languages, they never become as proficient in either language as children who only have to master one language.	As long as they are exposed consistently to both languages, children can readily become proficient in both languages.
Only the brightest children can learn two languages without encountering problems. Most children have difficulty because the process is so complex.	Nearly all children are capable of learning two languages during the preschool years.

Research confirms the importance of supporting children's continued learning in their primary language while at the same time fostering their ability to learn to speak English (Tabors, 2008; August & Shananhan, 2006). Keep in mind these two very important findings:

- Children who develop a sound foundation in their first language are more efficient in learning a second language.
- Children transfer concepts and skills that they learn in their first language to their second language.

Having rich experiences in two languages is a definite asset. All children can benefit from learning another language.

Levels of English Language Acquisition

Early childhood teachers need to know about the process and stages of English language acquisition, methods to assess the overall language abilities of young English-language learners, and the influence of home culture and family values. As in all areas of development, children vary in their approaches to and rate of English language acquisition. Preschool children also vary in their readiness to use their new language to express what they know. There are many important differences among young English-language learners: the languages they speak at home, the social and economic resources available to their families, the amount and timing of their exposure to English, the timing and circumstances of the family's immigration to the United States, the family's literacy practices, similarities between a child's first and second languages, and so on. These factors influence the amount and type of instructional adjustment needed for children to learn the second language successfully (August & Shanahan, 2010; Snow et al., 1998). Teachers need to find out about each family's unique circumstances in order to design individualized approaches that build on the child's strengths and prior knowledge.

The following chart explains the typical developmental sequence of English language acquisition by describing what you might observe children doing at each level (adapted from Tabors, 2008).

Levels of Learning a Second Language

What You Might Observe

Home language use	Children continue to use their home language with teachers and other children, even if it is not understood.
Nonverbal/observational period	Children limit (or stop) the use of their home language as they realize that it is not understood by others. They use nonverbal methods to communicate, such as gesturing or pantomiming, usually to get attention, make requests, protest, or joke. Children listen to and learn the features, sounds, and words of the new language (receptive language skills) but do not yet use the new language to express themselves. This period of active language learning can last from a few months to a year.

Telegraphic and formulaic speech	Children begin using one- and two-word phrases in English and begin to name objects. They may use groups of words such as "Stop it," "Fall down," or "Shut up," although they may not always use them appropriately. The children repeat a phrase they hear others use to achieve social goals, even though they probably do not know the literal meaning of the words and are repeating familiar sounds because they are functionally effective.
Productive/fluid use of language	Children begin to use simple English sentences like those they hear in meaningful contexts. They begin to form their own sentences by combining words they have learned. Like all young children, they gradually increase the length of their sentences.

Special Needs

You may work with a child or children who have a documented disability or disabilities. We have to be very careful in thinking about special needs because labels such as *advanced learner* or *disabled* can obscure important information about children and often keep adults from considering the whole child. A child may be an advanced learner in some areas or have a particular disability, but rarely does either influence every aspect of development. For example, a child might be well ahead of her peers in reading but lack social skills. Similarly, a child may have a physical disability that prevents him from walking but have well-developed language skills. Labels do not help us understand the whole child; they interfere. Teachers should look at each child as an individual.

Advanced learners: Some children in your class may be developmentally ahead of their peers. You may notice that their language is more complex. They may have learned to read and write and always have books in their hands. They may solve puzzles quickly, ask questions about large numbers, surprise you by being able to add and subtract, or have interests that seem unusual for their age.

Children with strong skills are called *advanced learners*. We tend to think first about intellectual skills when we use that term, but children can demonstrate advanced skills in any number of areas. Gardner's work on different kinds of intelligences shows that people can be talented in at least eight different ways. For example, a child in your class may be athletically advanced, a logical thinker, a talented musician, or an incredible artist.

Even though cognitive, language, social–emotional, and physical development are all interrelated, a child is rarely advanced in all areas of development. In fact, advanced learners frequently have very uneven development, but their areas of strength help them practice skills in the areas in which they need more support. For example, some young children who have strong language skills approach physical tasks better when physical demonstrations are accompanied by verbal explanations of the steps involved (e.g., how to catch a ball).

Many adults have difficulty understanding why a child who is advanced in one area is not advanced in all. Why would a child who is mature enough to read still pick fights or have temper tantrums? Teachers must be careful to note areas in which the child needs extra support as well as to promote continued development of skills that the child has already strengthened.

Like all children, advanced learners need to be challenged or they will become bored and frustrated. The more the child feels challenged and stimulated—both at home and at school—the more confident he will be about taking risks and extending his skills.

The most important thing to remember is not to focus solely on a preschool child's particular skills or to single a child out. Rather, observe each child, follow his or her lead, and then create an environment where every child feels supported and challenged. Like all children, advanced learners need teachers to pay attention to their individual needs.

Children with disabilities: Approximately 9 percent of American children have a disability (U.S. Department of Education, NCES, 2015; OSEP, 2009). While there are many types of disabilities, most are described as developmental delays or as medical, emotional, or physical problems. Increasing numbers of preschool children are being identified as having autism.

Some children come to school already identified as a "preschool student with a disability" by their local school districts. The assigned disability category is different from the child's medical diagnosis. Most young children (ages 3–9 years) are identified under a broad disability category called *developmental delay*. This category includes children who have general delays in their social–emotional, cognitive, physical, or language development and who need special education and related services because of these delays.

Since 1976, special education laws and regulations have required that children with disabilities be allowed to attend the same educational programs and participate in the same daily activities as their peers. They also require that each child (ages 3–21) with a disability have an Individualized Education Program (IEP). This document answers basic questions about the nature of the child's disability and what must be done to meet his or her educational needs. It includes goals and objectives and a description of how the disability affects the child's access to the general curriculum. It also designates the types of special education and related services a child needs to access the curriculum.

If a child with a disability is enrolled in your classroom, you may initially feel overwhelmed. Without a special education background, you may not be familiar with the terms and processes of the special education field. To overcome any such discomfort, take a step back and reflect. Approach this child as you would any other child in your classroom. Think about the child's particular strengths and needs. What promotes or interferes with his learning? What adjustments could be made to the environment, daily activities, and teaching strategies to support this child's learning?

Seek out the child's family members and IEP team specialists (trained professionals such as occupational and physical therapists or speech-language pathologists) who work with the child. Ask them for helpful strategies and make decisions on the basis of the child's strengths, needs, interests, experiences, learning style, and temperament and on the basis of the unique nature of the classroom. Your common goal is to find ways for the child to participate in all aspects of the daily program.

A strategy or set of strategies that is effective for one child may not be appropriate for another child with a similar disability. Together with the child's family and other IEP team members, identify the supports the child needs. Individualized supports might include large-print books, communication devices, chairs with sides, or strategies such as giving a child more time to process information and respond.

Keep in mind that having a disability, like being an advanced learner, is only one characteristic of a child, not the whole child. Think of children with disabilities as children first. A child in your room may use a wheelchair or a hearing aid. Rather than defining these children by their disabilities—e.g., visually impaired, having Down syndrome, or having autism—think of them as preschoolers who are as curious about the world and as eager to learn as any other child.

Children with disabilities have a wide range of abilities and needs. For instance, some children with disabilities may also be advanced learners in some areas. Children with disabilities are not a homogenous group. Focus on what each child with a disability is able to do and then build on his or her strengths.

Whether you work with children with disabilities who are in a self-contained classroom or in an inclusive program, *The Creative Curriculum® for Preschool* is appropriate for all 3- to 5-year-old children. Its emphasis on organizing the physical environment to promote learning is especially important for children who require structure and predictability.

Throughout *The Creative Curriculum®*, references to strategies that help children with disabilities are made in relation to specific behaviors rather than to identified conditions. You should plan and individualize your program for these children as you would for every other child whom you teach.

The ultimate goal for children with disabilities is the same as for children without disabilities: to give them full access to the curriculum and to help them develop and learn as much as possible. This is what meeting individual strengths and needs is all about!

Conclusion

Knowing how preschool children develop and learn is critical to planning your program, selecting materials, and guiding children's learning. While all areas of development are interrelated, they are usually discussed in terms of four areas: social–emotional, physical, language, and cognitive. In addition to knowing how children generally develop and learn, teachers must also discover the unique qualities of each child and understand the significance of the child's gender, temperament, interests, learning style, life experiences, culture, language, and special needs. The more you know about each child, the better you are able to build the positive relationship that enables each to thrive. Knowledge of child development, individual children, and curricular objectives will also help you create an effective learning environment, which is the topic addressed in the next chapter.

References

Al-Harbi, S. (2015). The influence of media in children's language development. *Journal of Educational and Developmental Psychology, 5*(1), 1–5. doi:http://dx.doi.org.prox.lib.ncsu.edu/10.5539/jedp.v5n1p1

August, D., & Shananhan, T. (2006). *Developing literacy in second-language learners: Report of the National Literacy Panel on language-minority children and youth.* Mahwah, NJ: Lawrence Erlbaum Associates.

August, D., & Shanahan, T. (2010). Response to a review and update on *Developing literacy in second-language learners: Report of the National Literacy Panel on Language Minority Children and Youth. Journal of Literacy Research, 42,* 341–348.

Berk, L. E. (2013). *Child development* (9ᵗʰ ed.). Boston: Pearson.

Bialystok, E. (1997). Effects of bilingualism and biliteracy on children's emerging concepts of print. *Developmental Psychology, 33,* 429–440.

Bjorklund, D. F. (2012). *Children's thinking: Cognitive development and individual differences* (5th ed.). Belmont, CA: Wadsworth Thomson Learning.

Cable News Network. (2008, August 13). *Minorities expected to be majority in 2050.* Retrieved September 10, 2009, from http://www.cnn.com/2008/US/08/13/census.minorities/index.html

Chess, S., & Thomas, A. (1996). *Temperament: Theory and practice.* New York: Brunner/Mazel.

Division for Early Childhood. (2007). *Promoting positive outcomes for children with disabilities: Recommendations for curriculum, assessment, and program evaluation.* Missoula, MT: Author.

Durgunoglu, A.Y., & Oney, B. (2000). *Literacy development in two languages: Cognitive and sociocultural dimensions of cross-language transfer.* US Department of Education, Office of Bilingual Education and Minority Language Affairs (OBEMLA), Reading Research Symposium, Washington, DC.

Edwards, L. A. (2014). The learning brain: memory and brain development in children. *Harvard Educational Review, 84*(2), 265–274. Retrieved from http://search.proquest.com.prox.lib.ncsu.edu/docview/1541679065?accountid=12725

Epstein, A. S. (2014). *The intentional teacher: Choosing the best strategies for young children's learning.* Washington, DC: National Association for the Education of Young Children.

Escamilla, K., Hopewell, S., Butvilofsky, S., Sparrow, W., Soltero-González, l., Ruiz-Figueroa, O., Escamilla, M. (2014). *Biliteracy from the Start: Literacy Squared in Action.* Philadelphia, PA: Caslon, Inc.

Gabbard, C. (1998). Windows of opportunity for early brain and motor development. *Journal of Physical Education, Recreation & Dance, 69*(8), 54–56.

Genesee, F. (n.d.). *Bilingual acquisition.* Retrieved March 21, 2002, from http://www. earlychildhood.com/Articles/index.cfm?FuseAction=Article&A=38

Goldenberg, C. (2012). "Research on English Learner instruction." In M. Calderón (Ed.), *Breaking Through: Effective instruction & assessment for reaching English Learners* (pp. 39–61). Bloomington, IN: Solution Tree Press.

Hanson, K. (1992). *Teaching mathematics effectively and equitably to females.* New York: ERIC Clearinghouse on Urban Education Institute for Urban and Minority Education. (ERIC Document Reproduction Service No. ED348465)

Hart, B., & Risley, T. R. (2003). *The early catastrophe: The 30 million word gap by age 3.* Retrieved September 9, 2009, from http://www.aft.org/pubs-reports/american_educator/ spring2003/catastrophe.html

Heath, S. M., & Hogben, J. H. (2004). Cost-effective prediction of reading difficulties. *Journal of Speech, Language, and Hearing Research, 47,* 751–765.

Heisner, J. (2005). Telling stories with blocks: Encouraging language in the block center. *Early Childhood Research and Practice, 7*(2). Retrieved September 23, 2008, from http://ecrp. uiuc.edu/v7n2/heisner.html

Howes, C., & James, J. (2002). Children's social development within the socialization context of childcare and early education. In P. K. Smith & C. H. Hart (Eds.), *Blackwell handbook of childhood social development* (pp. 137–155). Oxford: Blackwell.

Jalongo, M. R. (2008). *Learning to listen, listening to learn: Building essential skills in young children.* Washington, DC: National Association for the Education of Young Children.

Kena, G., Musu-Gillette, L., Robinson, J., Wang, X., Rathbun, A., Zhang, J., Wilkinson-Flicker, S., Barmer, A., & Dunlop Velez, E. (2015). *The condition of education 2015* (NCES 2015-144). Washington, DC: National Center for Education Statistics, Institute of Education Sciences, U.S. Department of Education. Also available from http://nces. ed.gov/pubs2015/2015144.pdf

Koda, K. & Zehler, A. (Eds.). (2008). *Learning to read across languages: Cross-lingüistic relationships in first- and second-language literacy development.* New York, NY: Routledge.

Le, C. N. (2009). 14 important statistics about Asian Americans. *Asian-Nation.* Retrieved April 28, 2009, from http://www.asian-nation.org/14-statistics.shtml

Martyniuk, O. J. M., & Tucker, P. (2014). An exploration of early childhood education students' knowledge and preparation to facilitate physical activity for preschoolers: A cross-sectional study. *BMC Public Health, 14,* 727. doi:http://dx.doi.org.prox.lib.ncsu. edu/10.1186/1471-2458-14-727

McAfee, O., & Leong. D. (1994). *Assessing and guiding young children's development and learning.* Boston: Allyn & Bacon.

National Early Literacy Panel. (2008). *Developing early literacy: Report of the National Early Literacy Panel.* Retrieved January 2009, from http://www.nifl.gov/nifl/publications/pdf/ NELPReport09.pdf

Peth-Pierce, R. (2000). *A good beginning: Sending America's children to school with the social and emotional competence they need to succeed.* Bethesda, MD: The Child Mental Health Foundations and Agencies Network (FAN) and National Institute of Mental Health, Office of Communications and Public Liaison.

Pica, R. (1997). Beyond physical development: Why young children need to move. *Young Children, 52*(6), 4–11.

Robert, D. L. (1999). *The effects of a preschool movement program on motor skill acquisition, movement concept formation, and movement practice behavior.* (Doctoral dissertation, West Virginia University). Retrieved August 10, 2008, from http://eidr.wvu.edu/files/1193/Robert_D_Diss.pdf

Rothbart, M. K., Ahadi, S. A., & Evans, D. E. (2000). Temperament and personality: Origins and outcome. *Journal of Personality and Social Psychology, 78,* 122–135.

Rubin, K. H., Bukowski, W., & Parker, J. G. (1998). Peer interactions, relationships, and groups. In W. Damon & N. Eisenberg (Eds.), *Handbook of child psychology, Volume 3: Social, emotional, and personality development* (pp. 619–700). New York: John Wiley & Sons.

Sanders, S. W. (2002). *Active for Life: Developmentally appropriate movement programs for young children.* Washington, DC: National Association for the Education of Young Children.

Snow, C. E. (1997, November 1). The myths around being bilingual. *NABE News, 29,* 36.

Snow, C. E., Burns, M. S., & Griffin, P. (Eds.). (1998). *Preventing reading difficulties in young children.* Washington, DC: National Academy Press.

Son, S. H., & Meisels, S. J. (2006). The relationship of young children's motor skills to later school achievement. *Merrill-Palmer Quarterly, 52,* 755–778.

Strickland, D. S., & Shanahan, T. (2004). Laying the groundwork for literacy. *Educational Leadership, 61*(6), 74–77.

Tabors, P. O. (2008). *One child, two languages: A guide for early childhood educators of children learning English as a second language* (2nd ed.). Baltimore, MD: Paul H. Brookes.

U. S. Census Bureau. (2007). Hispanic Americans by the numbers: From the U.S. Census Bureau. *Information Please® Database.* Retrieved April 28, 2009, from http://www.infoplease.com/spot/hhmcensus1.html

U.S. Census Bureau, Population Division. (2000, January 13). *Projections of the resident population by age, sex, race, and Hispanic origin: 1999 to 2100* (NP-D1-A). Retrieved September 9, 2009, from http://www.census.gov/population/projections/nation/detail/d2001_10.pdf

U.S. Department of Education, Office of Special Education and Rehabilitative Services, Office of Special Education Programs. (2009). *28th annual report to Congress on the implementation of the Individuals with Disabilities Education Act, 2006, vol. 1.* Retrieved September 10, 2009, from http://www.ed.gov/about/reports/annual/osep/2006/parts-b-c/index.html

2

The Learning Environment

The Learning Environment

The second component of *The Creative Curriculum®* framework is the learning environment: the use and organization of the space in your classroom and outdoors, the structure you provide each day, and the plans you develop. A well-organized classroom helps children make choices, encourages them to use materials well, and teaches them to take increasing responsibility for maintaining the classroom. A consistent, well-balanced daily schedule gives children a sense of security, and your plans enable you to be prepared for each day. For these reasons, the learning environment is the starting point for implementing *The Creative Curriculum®*. We examine three aspects of the learning environment:

"Setting Up and Maintaining the Classroom" discusses the physical space of *The Creative Curriculum®* classroom. It is organized into 10 interest areas (Blocks, Dramatic Play, Toys and Games, Art, Library, Discovery, Sand and Water, Music and Movement, Cooking, and Technology), and the outdoors is also arranged intentionally. Interest areas offer multiple opportunities for children to explore, discover, and learn. The arrangement of furniture and materials involves children not only in learning but also in caring for the classroom.

"Establishing a Structure for Each Day" explains the importance of predictable daily events and a consistent schedule. When each day has a clear structure, children know what to expect and understand what is expected of them. With the assurance that their physical environment and daily schedule are familiar and predictable, they can attend to learning activities and function as part of a group.

"Planning Each Week" addresses decisions about the materials and experiences you will offer children at each time of the day. Preparing for each day helps ensure that children can make the most of their experiences in the program.

Setting Up and Maintaining the Classroom

The physical environment of your classroom has a profound effect on individual children, the group as a whole, and you. The physical environment includes the size of the room, the colors of the walls, the type of flooring, the amount of light, and the number of windows. Although you may have limited control over many of these features, you do have options about how to organize furniture, what materials to put out, and what you can bring outdoors to make the total space more interesting and functional.

A physical setting that is safe, attractive, comfortable, and well designed helps children engage in the activities you offer. Such an environment can support your goals for children and free you to observe and interact with them in positive ways that support their development and learning.

Establishing Interest Areas

A physical space divided into interest areas is an ideal setting for preschool children to explore, make things, experiment, and pursue their interests. Separate interest areas with varied materials offer children a range of clear choices. Sometimes children want to work quietly, either alone or with other children. Areas devoted to books, art activities, or toys and games provide several choices for quiet activities. Areas set aside for dramatic play, block building, woodworking, or large-muscle activities provide choices for more physical action.

Subdividing the classroom into spaces that accommodate a few children at a time addresses preschool children's preference for small-group settings. With a manageable number of other children, they feel comfortable and play more positively than in larger groups. In smaller well-defined spaces where they can concentrate on their work, children's play tends to be more complex.

The Creative Curriculum® classroom should always have defined areas for dramatic play, block building, toys and games, art, looking at books and writing, sand and water play, and a discovery table. If possible, places for children to engage in cooking activities, use musical instruments, and work with technology like a tablet or a computer should also be designated. When space is limited, computers and tablets can be located in the Library or Discovery area, and cooking equipment can be stored and brought out for an activity. Ideally, children should have daily access to musical instruments and equipment for making or listening to music, but this equipment can be brought from storage regularly if it cannot always be available.

Guidelines for Setting Up Interest Areas

To set up interest areas, note the location of electrical outlets, windows, doors, sinks, and storage space. See what movable furnishings are available for defining space (e.g., shelves, tables, freestanding easels, and dramatic play furniture). Take an inventory of the particular challenges in your room: built-in cabinets and shelves, columns, radiators, exposed pipes, the locations of doors that should not be blocked, and so on.

Here are some additional guidelines:

Establish traffic patterns for entering and leaving the room, putting belongings in cubbies, using the bathroom, and moving from one area to another.

Interest Areas

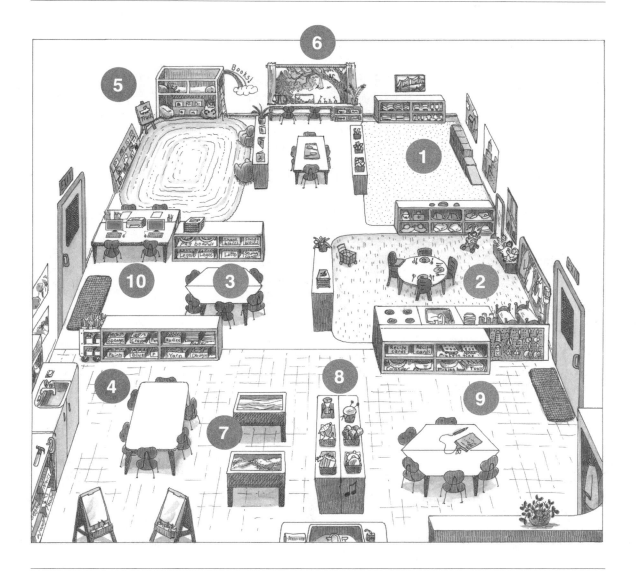

1. Blocks
2. Dramatic Play
3. Toys and Games
4. Art
5. Library

6. Discovery
7. Sand and Water
8. Music and Movement
9. Cooking
10. Technology

Clearly define areas that need protection by using walls and shelves (e.g., a block corner and a cozy library nook).

Locate interest areas that are relatively quiet, such as Library, Art, Technology, and Toys and Games, away from noisier ones, such as Blocks and Dramatic Play.

Decide which areas need tables and chairs (e.g., Toys and Games, Art, Library, Cooking, and Technology). Because young children use the floor and open spaces for much of their play, minimize the number of tables. Remember that you need just enough table space so everyone, including adults, can be seated at one time for snacks or meals. The tables should remain in the interest areas where they are usually located, not moved together as in a cafeteria.

Think about activities that are affected by floor coverings. Ideally, messy activities such as art, sand and water, and cooking should be in places with a washable floor. Also assess whether you will need drop cloths, pieces of vinyl, or a shower curtain. Blocks require a soft floor where children can sit or kneel comfortably.

Place interest areas near needed resources. Art, water play, and cooking activities should be near a water source; computers, CD players, and printers need electrical outlets.

Reserve areas with a lot of light as places where children look at books, write and draw, and care for plants.

Organize the room so you can see as much as possible from every location. Safety and child abuse prevention regulations require supervision of children at all times. That means always having children in full view.

Equipping Interest Areas

Interest areas work well when the materials you select are attractive, relevant to children's experiences and cultures, and challenging but not frustrating. The materials should introduce children to interesting content: pets and plants to observe and care for (science); collections to sort and graph (math); resource books for looking up information (literacy); gears and clocks to take apart (technology); and more.

In general, a good rule to follow in the beginning of the year is "Less is better." Too many new materials at the outset can overwhelm children. Start by showing them how to use and care for the materials. It is important to explain this strategy to families during the first days because they might be surprised by the limited supply of materials you have out.

To minimize sharing problems, provide duplicates of basic materials rather than a large selection of different items. Include familiar materials such as puzzles, stringing beads, and crayons. For guidance about selecting materials for each interest area, turn to the "Creating an Environment" sections of each chapter of *Volume 2: Interest Areas*.

Your Teaching Practice

Refer to your current *Teaching Guide* for changes to interest areas. It is a great resource for helping you decide which interest area enhancements to include. Remember that during a study, "less is better" can still apply. How do your interest areas currently reflect children's interests and explorations? Are there ways to simplify areas to encourage more hands-on investigation?

Displaying and Labeling Materials

Everything in your classroom should have a designated place. All children benefit from that kind of order, because children depend upon the consistency and predictability of their environment. When children know where things are and how and why they are grouped, they can work independently and constructively. They can also participate in cleanup and in caring for the classroom.

While you can be flexible about where children use materials during choice time (e.g., taking inch cubes from the Toys and Games area to decorate their block constructions), having a clearly marked place for everything makes it easier for children to return materials at cleanup time.

Labels should serve a purpose. To show children that everything has a place, label storage places. You can use photos, pictures of toys or equipment cut from catalogs or packaging, drawings, or shapes made from solidly colored adhesive paper (e.g., for blocks or woodworking tools) as labels.

Labels should have both pictures and words in lowercase letters. Use one color for English, and a different color for the second language that is predominant in your classroom. If several other languages are spoken by children in your classroom, include words from those languages in various places in the classroom so all children see their primary languages. Including a sample of the object (e.g., a bead or a marker) as well as a picture is especially helpful for a child with a visual impairment. Be careful not to have too many labels, particularly if you have labels in multiple languages.

Cover labels with clear adhesive plastic or laminate them so they will withstand messy fingers and being rotated. Tape labels on containers that hold materials and directly on the shelves. When you label materials in this way, cleanup becomes a matching and literacy game that helps children learn as they find the proper place for each object.

Here are additional guidelines:

Store materials that go together in the same place. For example, put pegs with pegboards, collage materials with glue and paper, and cars with the blocks.

Provide containers such as plastic dishpans, clear plastic containers, baskets, or shoe boxes to hold materials and toys with small pieces.

Use pegs, Velcro®, or a child-sized clothes tree for items that you want to hang up, such as dress-up clothes, utensils, smocks, etc.

Display materials so that children can see them easily. Place materials and toys on low shelves at children's eye level. Put books on a shelf with the covers facing out.

Store sharp items, such as graters and knives, and electric cooking **appliances** out of reach. Bring them out as needed and supervise their use carefully.

Other Considerations for Organizing the Classroom

In addition to establishing interest areas, there are other aspects of the physical setting to consider as you set up your room. You will need to identify a place for group time, places for displays, and storage areas for children's belongings and for materials children are not allowed to use on their own. Depending on children's needs, you may have to change your environment so all children have access to interest areas and materials. The classroom should be as comfortable and attractive as possible so children enjoy being there.

A Place for Group Time

Establish a place in your classroom where the whole group can gather to talk about the day, listen to books and stories, be introduced to new math and science materials, transition from one activity to another, and participate in music and movement activities. Many classrooms are not large enough to have an area devoted solely to whole-group activities. If your room has limited space, you can hold meetings in one of the large interest areas, for example, the Block area or Library area.

Here are additional guidelines:

Allow sufficient floor space to accommodate all of the children and adults in a circle.

Provide comfortable seating on the floor. If the area you select does not have a carpet or rug, you might use carpet squares so every child has a soft place to sit.

Display charts that you will discuss during group meetings, such as a job chart, the daily schedule, and charts for graphing activities.

Include an easel or chart stand so you can document group discussions or display a big book as you read to the class.

Choose a location near electrical outlets for audio equipment and **near shelves or cupboards** for materials such as tapes, CDs, scarves, and rhythm band instruments.

Classroom Displays

Most of the display space in your classroom should be saved for children's work. Some teachers make special places for each child's work on the walls and let children select the items they want to display. Large sheets of construction paper can serve as frames. Include the children's names (and perhaps photographs) to identify their work.

Invite children to tell you something about their artwork: what it is, how they made it, what they like about it, or what they learned by doing it. Record what they say on a card and include it in the display. Doing this is an oral language and literacy experience, and it conveys the important message to children that their work is valued. Displaying children's work also gives visitors an opportunity to see what you are teaching and what your group and individual children are learning.

Display children's work prominently and at their eye level. Keep displays simple. When the walls and all available spaces are filled with posters and artwork, children—and even adult visitors—are overwhelmed and find it hard to focus on any one thing. Change displays regularly. When children see the same things week after week, they cannot see their progress, lose interest, and begin to ignore what is displayed.

In the beginning of the year, display photos of the children with their family members. If you make home visits before school starts, take along a camera for this purpose. You can also take pictures as children and families arrive on the first day. Be sure to include your own picture and that of your co-teacher. As children get to know other members of the school community—the director, custodian, food service personnel, bus drivers, and nurse—add their photos as well. As the year progresses, take photos of children as they work in the various interest areas. Display these photos with a note about what children are learning. Children, family members, and administrators will be interested in these displays. They are an excellent way to share the learning that is taking place in your classroom.

Be sure that the purchased books and posters you display include respectful pictures of people from many ethnic backgrounds and of both genders. To convey the message that everyone has an important role, look for pictures that show people of all ages and abilities doing all sorts of jobs.

Consider the following places for displays:

- walls and bulletin boards
- pillars
- the tops and backs of shelves

- a clothesline and clothespins, or a net
- easels
- room dividers

You may need to be creative about displays if regulations or other licensing codes do not allow you to secure items to the walls. Hanging and freestanding bulletin boards are options.

Places for Storage

An orderly classroom requires storage space. Think in terms of three different types: open storage for materials you want to make accessible to children, secure storage for materials you want to control, and personal storage for children and adults.

Six to eight sturdy shelves that will not tip over are ideal for materials you want children to use independently. You can supplement open shelving by securing plastic milk crates together. If children will be taking naps, you also will need to find storage for cots or mats, blankets, and pillows.

To ensure children's safety, use secure storage for things like cleansers and knives. Secure storage is also useful for materials you do not want to use until later in the year. Organize and label what you store so you can find what you need easily.

For children's belongings, designate places that are easily accessed and clearly labeled with children's photos and names. Provide every child with a cubby or hook for a coat, hat, mittens, boots, backpack, and extra clothing. Labeled dishpans are useful for treasures brought from home and for work that children are to take home. Finally, set aside a place where adults––teachers, visitors, and family members––can store their belongings safely.

A Comfortable and Attractive Setting

Because you and the children spend a large part of the day in the classroom, it should be comfortable, attractive, and homey. Here are some suggestions:

Take advantage of natural light as much as possible. Mirrors reflect light and enable children to look at the environment from different perspectives. Table lamps and floor lamps add to the coziness of the classroom.

Incorporate softness into the environment wherever possible. Use soft chairs, a crib mattress or futon covered with an attractive sheet, pillows, area rugs, and stuffed animals.

Add a variety of textures to stimulate children's sense of touch (bumpy, smooth, rough, squishy, prickly, silky, and coarse).

Provide quiet spaces where children can be alone when they need some solitude. Consider a loft, a tent, an old bathtub or large box filled with pillows, a comfortable chair near a fish tank, and a CD player with headphones.

Include homey touches, such as a welcome mat at the door, fresh flowers in vases on tables, wicker baskets to hold plants and collections, curtains on the windows, lamps, tablecloths and place mats, photograph albums, colorful soaps by the sink, and magnets on a refrigerator (or any metal surface).

Bring living things into the classroom: plants and pets children can observe, care for, and cuddle. In the Discovery area include natural objects, such as bird nests, pinecones, shells, an empty beehive, and an ant farm.

Children With Disabilities

As you arrange furniture and choose materials, think about the abilities and needs of all children, including those with physical or sensory disabilities. How can you ensure that all children will be able to participate in all areas of the room? Consider safety, comfort, and the use of materials and equipment. A special education consultant can help you evaluate your classroom and outdoor areas to determine what changes, if any, are needed to encourage each child's full participation. Here are some suggestions:

Make sure that **traffic patterns and aisles** between interest areas will accommodate a wheelchair or walker. **Ramps and low toilets** may be needed to make facilities accessible.

Adjust tables so wheelchairs will fit underneath. Allow other children to stand at a raised table.

Provide wedges so children can play on the floor.

Allocate room to store adaptive equipment when children are not using it to stand, sit, or walk.

Offer materials with features that make them easy to use, such as puzzles with knobs and art tools with large handles.

Provide a variety of technology devices for children to use. Consider large keyboards, touch screen devices, and trackballs.

Use visual, auditory and tactile cues throughout the environment.

Be aware that being too close to the **sources of loud sounds** can interfere with hearing aids.

Caring for the Classroom and Children's Work

Classroom maintenance should be shared. By having children care for their space, they will learn to be responsible. They will also become competent and organized. Teachers need to provide ways to protect children's work and to identify jobs so everyone shares in the necessary chores.

A System for Classroom Jobs

Because the room belongs to everyone, taking care of it is a shared responsibility. Everyone helps with some daily jobs, for example, cleaning up during choice time, putting away personal belongings, scraping dishes and throwing out trash after meals. Other classroom jobs can be rotated each week: watering the plants, feeding pets, putting out cots, wiping tables, cleaning paintbrushes, setting the tables for snacks and meals, and so on. You may want to talk informally with young preschoolers about jobs. Older preschoolers can handle a more formal system.

One way to introduce caring for the classroom as a shared responsibility is to create a job chart. You can discuss the different jobs and explain to the children how to refer to the chart to find out and remember which job they have. If children do not yet recognize their names in print, you can make name cards that include a photo as well as the child's name. In addition to words, jobs can be listed with symbols (e.g., a drawing of a watering can) or photos of children engaged in the various tasks.

Talk with children about what needs to be done to keep the classroom in order. Generate a list of jobs, but do not expect children to come up with a complete list. You may have to ask leading questions and make some suggestions. Here are some examples of what you might say:

"Our classroom looks clean and organized today. Let's think about what we need to do to keep it this way. What are your ideas?"

"What jobs do we need to do to keep the room neat? I'll write a list of your ideas."

"We know that plants need water to grow, so we must be sure that someone is in charge of them."

"Suppose there is food on the tables when we finish eating. What would we have to do to clean up?"

After this type of discussion, you can tell the children that you will make a job chart and that everyone will have a job each day. When you introduce the chart during a later meeting, review each job and talk about how many children will do it. To reinforce the idea that everyone is a member of the classroom community, include categories like "Day off" or "Substitute" so that each child's name appears somewhere on the chart. You never know when you will need a substitute because someone with a job is absent!

Strategies for Protecting Children's Work

Children's work is tangible evidence of what they are learning and their competence as learners. Protecting children's work shows respect for their efforts.

Being as flexible as possible about time and materials has a positive effect on children's work habits, enables them to complete projects, and conveys the consideration you give to every child's needs. When teachers ask children to dismantle something they have worked hard to create—a carefully balanced block structure or a complex design made with pattern blocks—the children may think that their work is not valued. Similarly, ending a work period when many children are totally engaged in their activities sends the message that the work children do is not as important as the schedule. Here are some ways to protect children's work and convey respect for their efforts.

Provide physical boundaries. Give children a concrete way to know where their work spaces begin and end. For instance, you can define work spaces in the Block area by providing sheets of cardboard on which children build, or you can use hula hoops, carpet squares, or masking tape to define each building area. A very large cardboard box with the top and bottom removed also can define a space in which one or more children can build (depending on the size of the box). When not in use, the boxes can be folded flat for easy storage. Similarly, in the Toys and Games area, you can provide cafeteria trays on which children can build designs or contain a set of beads. Clear designations help children understand the concept of work space.

Preserve unfinished projects. Because children may want to continue working on projects they have started, sometimes returning to them for several days in a row, you will need a way to preserve unfinished work. Plastic trays are excellent for holding and storing table blocks, construction toys, or incomplete art projects. Identify a shelf in the classroom to store these trays. A project may remain on the tray as long as a child wants to work on it. However, you need to keep other children's wishes in mind. A project should be kept only as long as a child is working on it, especially if it involves materials needed by others. If you find that particular materials are very popular, try to provide duplicates. Establish a rule that, if another child wants some materials that another child is already using, he or she should first ask the child who already started a project whether the materials are still needed. If so, help the child who is just starting a project to find something else that will work.

Take pictures. A digital camera is a valuable tool for preserving work. When a child has completed a project, you can take a picture before the child dismantles it and returns the materials to their places. This practice is especially useful for structures and designs made with blocks and other construction toys. Pictures let children share their work with the whole class and enable the class to be inspired by an individual child's work. In addition, a photo can be saved for a child's portfolio and shared with family members.

Invite children to share their work. When you gather children together after choice time, encourage them to talk about what they did. Do not require every child to talk. You can help reluctant children, however, by describing what you observed and by asking questions: "Alexa, Crystal, and Juwan, you did a lot of work on setting up our grocery store today. Will you tell us what you did?" "I saw Dallas working for a long time on our new puzzle. It's a challenging one, isn't it?"

Evaluating the Effectiveness of the Physical Environment

You will know that your classroom environment is well organized if children are able to act in these ways:

- **select activities and make other choices** on their own
- **use materials appropriately** and creatively once they enter an interest area
- **stay involved** with an activity for a sustained period of time
- **learn in meaningful ways** when they play
- **help care** for materials

Take time to evaluate the physical environment. Does it convey the messages you intend? Is it efficient? Is it interesting for the children? Are you experiencing any problems that might be addressed by changing the environment?

Conveying Positive Messages

Teachers who are aware of the power of the environment arrange their space purposefully to convey the messages they want children to receive. Use the following messages and strategies for sending them as a guide to assessing how well your room arrangement is working.

"This is a good place to be."

Furniture is clean and well maintained.

Wall decorations consist mostly of children's art, which is displayed attractively at their eye level and with large spaces of blank wall so as not to be overwhelming.

The room includes decorative touches, such as plants, displays of collections (e.g., shells, leaves, and stones), tablecloths or fabric-covered pillows, baskets, interesting artifacts, and framed artwork.

Bright colors are used selectively on neutrally colored walls to highlight interest areas or mark storage areas.

"You belong here."

Each child has a cubby or basket (marked with his or her name and picture) for keeping personal items.

Furniture is child-sized and in good condition.

Pictures on the walls, in books, and in other learning materials include people of different ethnic backgrounds and economic means, people with disabilities, nontraditional families, and women and men in a variety of jobs.

Each child's work is displayed and protected.

Materials, equipment, and furniture enable all children to be involved in all areas of the classroom.

Materials reflect the children's home lives and cultures.

Pictures of the children with their families are displayed.

"This is a place you can trust."

Equipment and materials are arranged consistently so children know where to find the things they need.

Shelves are neat and uncluttered, and materials are labeled so children can make choices easily.

A well-defined, illustrated schedule is prominently displayed so children learn the order of daily events and know what to expect.

Routines, such as eating, resting, and toileting, are consistent, and transitions are smooth.

"There are places where you can be by yourself when you want."

Small, quiet areas of the room accommodate one or two children.

A large pillow or stuffed chair in a quiet corner with minimal displays invites children to enjoy being quiet and alone.

Headphones for a CD player and other technology devices enable children to listen individually.

"You can do many things on your own here."

Materials are stored on low shelves so children can reach them without help.

Materials are located in the areas where they are to be used, and they are organized logically (e.g., drawing paper is near the markers and crayons, and pegs are near the pegboards).

Shelves are labeled with pictures and words that show children where toys and materials belong.

Labels and printed materials are in the home languages of the children as well as in English, if possible.

An illustrated job chart (for older preschoolers) shows that everyone in the classroom has a job every day.

Photographs of children doing interesting things in the classroom are on display.

"This is a safe place to explore and try your ideas."

Protected and defined quiet areas encourage small-group activities (e.g., a table with 3–4 chairs located in an area enclosed by low shelves containing toys and games).

Smocks are available for art activities and water play so children can explore them without worrying about getting dirty or wet.

Protected floor space for building with blocks is clearly defined and out of the way of traffic.

The outdoor area is fenced and protected.

Materials are displayed attractively, inviting children to use them.

Toys that have not been used for a long time are rotated frequently, and new things are added to keep children's interest.

Children who find changes unsettling are assisted when changes are introduced.

How Is It Working?

In addition to considering the messages your classroom conveys, take time each day to assess how well the physical setting is working for the children and you. Observe children systematically during transitions, during group times, and when they select their own activities during choice time. Your observations will tell you what materials children typically select, how they use these materials, what they are learning, and how they relate to their peers while working. With this information, you can make the appropriate changes to the physical environment. Here are some examples of questions that will help you focus your observations:

How do children select interest areas and materials?

Which interest areas and materials are most popular? Which are rarely used?

Do any children need help in making choices?

Does anyone need a more clearly defined work space?

Do the traffic patterns permit children to move easily about the room, play safely, and build without interference?

Are children able to find and return materials independently?

Do children show gender-related preferences for materials or toys?

How do children use materials?

Do children have the skills to use materials successfully?

Do children use materials appropriately and creatively?

Which types of materials seem to stimulate dramatic play? Other social play?

Which materials hold children's interest the longest?

Are there enough materials to keep children involved in meaningful play?

Is sharing a problem?

Are the materials reflective of children's backgrounds and home life?

Do children know how to care for materials?

How do children interact with others?

Are children able to play successfully near and with each other?

Are any children isolated from and rejected by their peers?

Which children play together most often?

Are children talking together about what they are doing?

How do children ask for help from adults? From peers?

Which play experiences foster social play? Individual play?

What Problems Might Be Related to the Physical Setting?

Even if you have organized the classroom and outdoor areas carefully, things don't always go according to plan. Children may fight over toys, wander about, become easily distracted, or use materials inappropriately. Although such behaviors can have several causes, the room arrangement may be a contributing factor.

If children's behavior is challenging, a few changes in your room arrangement can make a dramatic difference. You also can involve children in finding solutions to problems. For example, during a discussion at group time you might prompt, "I notice that block buildings are being knocked down as people walk by. I wonder how we can fix that problem." Children will probably be more cooperative if you involve them in coming up with a solution instead of choosing a solution, yourself. Involving children also conveys the message that they are competent to solve problems, that you expect them to take responsibility for doing so, and that the classroom belongs to everyone.

The following chart presents possible reasons for restless or disruptive behavior related to the environment and identifies strategies for rearranging the space to correct and prevent recurrences of the problem.

Challenging Behaviors	Possible Causes	Changes to the Environment
Running in the classroom	Too much space is open; the room is not divided into small enough areas; activity areas are not well defined.	Use shelves and furniture to divide the space. Avoid open spaces that encourage children to run.
Fighting over toys	Too many popular toys are one-of-a-kind; children are asked to share too often.	Provide duplicates of toys. Show children when it will be their turns (e.g., use a sand timer or help children create a waiting list for turns).
Wandering around; inability to choose activities	The room is too cluttered; choices are not clear; there is not enough to do.	Get rid of clutter. Simplify the layout of the room and materials. Add more activity choices.
Becoming easily distracted; trouble staying with a task and completing it	Areas are undefined and open; children can see everything going on in the room; materials are too difficult or children are bored with them.	Use shelves to define areas. Separate noisy and quiet areas. Assess children's skills and select materials they can use in interesting ways.
Continually intruding on others' work spaces	Space is limited; poor traffic patterns prevent children from spreading out.	Define work areas for children (e.g., use masking tape or sections of cardboard for block building, and provide trays or place mats for toys). Limit the number of areas open at one time to allow more space for each.
Misusing materials and resisting cleanup	Children do not know how to use materials appropriately; materials on shelves are messy; the displays are disorderly.	Make a place for everything. Use picture and word labels to show where materials go. Provide consistent guidance on how to clean up.

Children's behavior is a good indication of how well the physical environment of your classroom is arranged. Once you set up the classroom effectively, you can turn your attention to establishing the daily routines and schedule.

Establishing a Structure for Each Day

The second aspect of building an effective learning environment is establishing a structure for each day (a predictable sequence of events). When time is blocked out in an orderly and consistent fashion, children tend to feel secure and become increasingly independent. When children do not know when things will happen, classroom life can seem chaotic.

In defining a structure for the day, think about the different events that take place every day at a fairly consistent time. Organize these events as a daily schedule in which there is a good balance of active and quiet times as well as a range of child-initiated experiences and teacher-planned activities. You also need to develop plans for each week. You may use the *The Creative Curriculum®* teaching guides for various studies or record your own plans on a "Weekly Planning Form." Because the first 6 weeks of school are such an important time to help children learn to function well in a group setting, a good resource is *The Creative Curriculum® for Preschool Teaching Guide: Beginning the Year.*

Daily Events

Daily activities and routines in preschool programs typically include taking attendance, periods when you meet with all of the children in a large group or with a few children in a small group, choice times when children are free to go to interest areas and to use whatever materials they wish, read-alouds, outdoor time, mealtimes, and rest times. These periods of the day are described below. Note that reading aloud and outdoor play are not described here because they are covered in detail in *Volume 2: Interest Areas* and *Volume 3: Literacy.*

Taking Attendance

Keeping track of attendance is a program requirement. It can also be an opportunity for children to learn to read and write their own names and to recognize the names of their classmates. Here are two approaches to taking attendance that also support literacy and mathematics learning:

- **Keep an attendance chart in the meeting area.** Divide the chart into two sections: one that is headed "Home" and one that is headed "School." Make a card with each child's name. In the beginning of the year you may want to include the child's photo. Glue Velcro® on the back of each card and on both sections of the chart. Show children how to move their cards from one section at the beginning of the day to the other section at the end. During the morning meeting, you can talk with the children about who is at school and help them count those children. The cards for any children who are absent will still be displayed, a visual reminder that they are part of the classroom community.

- **Provide paper and large pencils so children can sign in each morning.** Include a model of each child's name to refer to when signing. You will find that children who could initially only scribble their names learn to write them clearly over time.

Large Group

Large-group meetings are most successful when the meeting time is kept short (usually 10–20 twenty minutes, depending on the age of the children and how interested they are in what is happening). When structured well, meetings that involve the whole class serve several purposes.

Perhaps most important, meetings provide an opportunity for children to experience a sense of belonging to a group. Children practice communication skills as they express their thoughts, ideas, and feelings and share the work they have been doing. Group time provides opportunities to talk about topics that interest the children and to solve problems that affect the whole group.

Most teachers plan a large-group time in the morning and again at the end of the day. In addition, you may want to gather the children together at other times, for example, to read a story before rest time, to discuss plans for the next activity, to solve a problem that occurred during choice time, or to welcome a special visitor.

The first meeting can set the tone for the day. Children are often eager to talk about a variety of topics: what happened at home, a new pair of shoes, or what they want to do at school. Start this meeting in a similar way each day, for example, by singing a good morning song or reciting a favorite fingerplay. The sameness gives the day predictability and consistency.

Reviewing the children's answers to the "question of the day" often leads to interesting discussions of content area concepts. Sometimes it makes sense to discuss the children's responses during the day's first large-group meeting. Sometimes you will want to wait until the end of the day.

Take the opportunity to teach math by having the children count how many persons are present each day. Teach science by discussing the weather and drawing children's attention to signs of the seasons. Address social studies by talking about the community, for example, a fire or neighborhood road repairs. You might introduce new materials in the interest areas or discuss a field trip, a special cooking activity, or a guest who will visit. At large-group meetings you also can talk about the day's schedule and lead a discussion about the study topic. Use this time to conduct a shared writing experience, recording children's ideas and questions as a group.

The Creative Curriculum® for Preschool Teaching Guides offer detailed information about how to make large-group meetings engaging and meaningful for children. They give specific ideas for "questions of the day," for discussions, and for activities related to a topic of study.

What about the calendar? Child development research indicates that children do not truly understand time concepts until the first or second grade, even though they may use words associated with time. For example, they may be able to memorize and chant the days of the week, but they lack a full understanding of what terms like *day, hour, minute,* or *second* really mean. Preschoolers are focused on the here and now. They are learning the concepts of before and after, later, and next. Not until age 5 do they usually begin to understand the concept of a day. Creating a consistent daily schedule—rest time, mealtime, outdoor time, choice time— fosters children's learning about time concepts.

If you want to introduce a calendar, use it as a tool to show children how to keep track of important events. Mark the days when you will have a visitor, school will be closed, or a site visit is planned. This approach helps children learn the purpose of calendars and how calendars can be useful to them personally.

A group time just before children go home encourages children to reflect on the day's events and provides closure. Briefly review with children the highlights of the day and what is planned for the next day. End with a closing ritual such as singing a good-bye song or reciting a favorite poem. You can use the last meeting of the day to discuss the calendar by making one with large empty squares. Fill in the squares by asking children, "What do we want to remember about today?" and having a child draw a picture in the relevant place. This activity turns the calendar into a record of classroom life. An added benefit is that children are more likely to have something to say when their families ask, "What did you do in school today?"

Small Groups

Teachers plan for and work with children in small groups every day. Small-group experiences are designed to meet particular instructional goals. Small-group times enable teachers to

- **introduce a new concept** or **new materials** to children
- **teach a specific skill** to children
- **encourage conversations and the sharing of ideas**
- **extend children's thinking** by asking questions and posing new challenges
- **focus observations** on individual children and document what children know and can do

Depending on the number of adults in the room, you may be able to engage all of the children in small-group activities at the same time. At other times, children who are not participating in a small-group activity can be given a specific task or asked to select from a variety of other quiet activities.

The length of time for small-group experiences is variable. A small-group activity designed to introduce new concepts or materials, teach a particular skill, or conduct a focused observation typically lasts about 10–15 minutes. Some small-group activities, such as cooking, engage children fully for a longer period and usually take place during choice time.

The makeup of small groups will not be the same every day. Sometimes you invite children to be part of a group when you want them to work on a particular skill. One day you might invite a group of children to explore an open-ended material, such as leaves, shells, or buttons. Another day, you might read rhyming books with several children to promote phonological awareness. In small-group settings, you can address multiple objectives with children at different levels.

To plan small-group times, think about each child's progress in terms of the curricular objectives and form groups on the basis of interests, strengths, and needs. *The Creative Curriculum® for Preschool Intentional Teaching Cards™* that complement the *Teaching Guides* give directions for meaningful, engaging small-group activities.

Choice Time

During choice time—sometimes called *center time* or *work time*—children choose the interest area in which they would like to work, with whom they want to work, and what materials to use. Choice time typically lasts for an hour or more. During this period, most interest areas are available to children: Blocks, Dramatic Play, Toys and Games, Sand and Water, Library, Art, and so on. When children are finished working in one area, they are free to move to another.

Teachers observe children actively during choice time. They notice what children are doing and decide whether to become involved. Sometimes children play independently of adults. At other times, teachers make thoughtful decisions to ask open-ended questions and make suggestions that extend children's play and support their learning. For example, when you see a group of children gathered in the Toys and Games area, you might invite them to join you in a board game such as "Chutes and Ladders™." Another time, you might lead a classification game with children who are playing with a collection of objects. You guide children intentionally because you know that these games will help them acquire math skills and learn directionality. (The teacher's role during choice time is explained in detail in chapter 4 and in each chapter of *Volume 2: Interest Areas*.)

Making choices is such an important skill that it requires a systematic approach, especially with young preschool children. At a meeting before choice time, you can talk about which activities will be available. A visual cue, such as a chart with pictures of which interest areas are open, can help children focus on the choices available to them. A planning board placed in each area gives children a concrete method for managing choice time. Give each child a name card to place on a planning board to indicate where he or she will work.

If you use planning boards, you will need to introduce them to the children. During a meeting, explain how the number of pegs, Velcro® strips, or pockets in a pocket chart shows the number of children who may be in an area at one time. Show them where to put their name cards and explain why they should take their cards with them when they decide to try other activities during choice time.

Once children become accustomed to the way the classroom operates, a planning board may not be necessary. The number of chairs, amount of materials, and available space all establish limits on the number of children an area can accommodate. If a problem arises, use it as an opportunity to lead children through a process of deciding how to handle it: "We seem to have a problem here. Too many children want to be at the woodworking table, and that's not safe. What shall we do? Does anyone have an idea?"

If children are involved in solving a problem (e.g., by having a waiting list, making more room at the table, or setting up another woodworking table outside), they will be more invested in making the solution work. Soon you will find that, on their own, children will move chairs, make room for others, or remove themselves when an area is too crowded.

You may wonder whether you should be concerned if a child always selects the same activity during choice time. Because there are many ways to expand on children's interests and teach concepts in each area, this problem is handled easily. First, ask yourself why a child restricts himself to the same activity. Perhaps the child particularly loves to explore art materials or build with blocks. Sometimes, however, a child is stuck and uneasy about trying something new. Try to make the child feel safe in a new activity by inviting him to join you or a friend in doing something special, like cooking or trying a new app or game on a tablet.

Transitions

Transitional times can be relaxed and provide opportunities for learning and reinforcing concepts and skills, but they also can be chaotic. If children do not know what is expected and have to wait with nothing to do, they will find something to occupy their time—and it probably won't be something you find desirable! Here are some ways to structure transitions so they go smoothly and encourage learning:

Give children notice. For example, 5 minutes before clean-up time, talk to the children in each interest area: "You have time for one more puzzle" or "There is just enough time to finish that painting but not to start a new one." Keep in mind that cleaning up some areas, such as Blocks, may require more time than others. You might encourage children who are involved in those activities to start a little earlier than the rest of your group.

Allow sufficient time. Treat transitions as valuable experiences in and of themselves, and allow enough time so children do not feel rushed.

Give children specific tasks. Children can help set up a snack or lunch, clean up after art, and collect trash after a meal. Be specific about what you want children to do. "Please put away the plates" is not as effective as, "Please scrape the food off each plate and into the trash can. Then stack the plates on the cart."

Be clear and consistent. Provide clear directions to children during transitions and be sure that your expectations of them are age-appropriate. Keep the same routine each day so children learn what to do and how to do it without a lot of adult guidance.

Be flexible. When possible, allow children extra time to complete special projects or activities in which they are particularly involved. For example, give some children time to complete their block city while others begin cleaning up the art materials or dramatic play props.

Meet individual needs. Try to avoid having all children move from one activity to another as a group or requiring children to wait around, doing nothing until everyone is finished. Give children who have completed their tasks something else to do, such as getting a book to read or straightening up a display, until everyone is ready to move to the next activity.

Use transitions as opportunities to teach. Think of how to move children from one activity to the next in ways that teach and reinforce skills. For example, invite all children who are wearing stripes (or a particular color or shoes with Velcro®) to go to the next activity. Alternatively, you might say, "If your name begins with the same beginning sound as *bike*, *banana*, *baseball*, and *boat*, you may choose an interest area now." It is not easy to come up with ideas on the spot, so keep a set of *Mighty Minutes*® cards with you. These little cards include many ideas for those moments of the day between activities.

Transitions can be especially hard for some children. If children are having difficulty, make sure you that you are allowing sufficient time for transitions and that the children know what is expected of them.

Mealtimes

Mealtimes are learning times when teachers sit with children, have them serve their own food, and carry on conversations. Good experiences at mealtimes help children to develop positive attitudes toward food and nutrition. Because food plays an essential role in family life and is part of many cultural traditions, take time to talk with families about their children's eating habits and food preferences. Find out whether any children have food allergies or other chronic health conditions that necessitate dietary restrictions, and make sure everyone in the program has that information. Here are additional suggestions:

Make mealtimes sociable. Establish a calm and pleasant atmosphere. A quiet activity, such as a story before lunch, helps to set a relaxed tone. Quiet conversation is one aspect of a comfortable atmosphere.

Be prepared. If you continually jump up from the table to get what you need, children will start doing the same. To minimize your need to leave the table, keep extra food on a nearby cart. Have extra napkins, sponges, and paper cups as well. A pair of scissors to open packets of condiments, such as ketchup, is also helpful.

Encourage children to help. Provide small plastic pitchers, baskets, and sturdy serving utensils so children can pour their own milk or juice and serve their own food. Give children time to practice with the pitchers during water play, and be tolerant of spills and accidents. Keep a roll of paper towels and a sponge handy. Children can assist by setting the table, wiping the table after eating, and emptying trash from their plates into a designated can.

Allow enough time. Some children are slow eaters. Mealtime should not be rushed. Make sure there is time for setting up, eating, and cleaning up without hurrying.

Never use food to reward or punish behavior. Threatening to withhold food or offering special food treats for doing a task contributes to unhealthy attitudes about food. If a child acts in a challenging way during a meal, the best response is to deal directly with the inappropriate behavior.

Consider setting up a self-service snack bar if you serve snacks as well as meals in your program. That way, children can help themselves independently and return to what they are doing.

Rest Time

In full-day programs, rest time is important for children and provides a much needed break for adults. The length of rest time varies. For children who attend 6 hours or more, rest rejuvenates children for the afternoon program. Younger children may need more rest than older preschoolers. Even in half-day programs, children benefit from a short quiet time or calm-down time.

Because naps are often associated with home, some children have a difficult time settling down at school. This response is to be expected. Follow a regular routine at rest time so children feel secure and so they can relax. Here are some suggestions for rest time:

Prepare children for resting. Plan a quiet activity for the group right before rest time: a story, fingerplay, or quiet song, or listening to other quiet music. Have children help set up the cots or mats as they finish eating, toileting, and brushing teeth. Allow children to bring comforting toys or special blankets from home.

Give children time to settle down at their own paces. Children have different sleeping patterns and different ways of falling asleep. Playing quiet music, rubbing a child's back, or just sitting on a cot near a restless child often helps.

Supervise rest time. Many teachers use rest time to complete observation notes and to plan. Doing paperwork is fine as long as enough adults are always supervising the children.

Plan for children who wake up early and for children who do not sleep. Allow wakeful children to get up after 15 minutes or so to engage in quiet activities. You might create "nap bags" with quiet activities such as magic slates, books, and small toys or games that children may bring to their cots or mats.

Allow children to wake up at their own paces. Children who regularly sleep longer than most of the other children may need more rest. If you place their cots away from the center of activities, they can get the amount they need. These children may need extra attention when they get up.

If you are having a particular problem with a child during rest time, consult the child's family. Perhaps they can offer some insights that will help you meet the child's needs.

We have discussed the basic activities and blocks of time in a preschool classroom: taking attendance, large- and small-group times, choice time, transitions, mealtime, and rest time. When you plan and follow a daily schedule, you establish a predictable sequence of classroom events.

The Daily Schedule

The daily schedule blocks out time and establishes a sequence for routines and experiences. When the daily schedule suits the children's individual and group needs, classroom life proceeds smoothly and is enjoyable for everyone. A good schedule for preschool children is balanced. It offers choices and a range of activities, some initiated by children and others planned by teachers.

A daily schedule establishes the consistency that helps young children predict the sequence of events and thus to feel more secure and more in control of events. They delight in reminding you, "Snack comes next," or telling a visitor, "Now we go outside." In addition, a schedule helps children begin to understand time concepts as they anticipate what comes first in the day, second, next, and last. Consistency does not preclude flexibility, responsiveness, or spontaneity. It also does not mean that the clock rules the day. A special occurrence can be reason enough to alter the daily routine. For example, an unexpected snowfall might inspire you and the children to pause in the middle of choice time, put on jackets and hats, and go outdoors. Similarly, on a day when children are particularly engrossed in their chosen activities, you may decide to extend choice time. Keep in mind what's most important: You want children to be excited about and engaged in what they are doing. Be flexible about time when children are playing well.

In deciding your schedule, start with the fixed times of daily events that cannot be changed. A fixed period might be lunch or the time when a shared playground is available for your class's use. Keep in mind the developmental abilities of your

Our Day

Arrival
Group Meeting
Choice Time
Snack
Small Groups
Outdoors
Read-Aloud
Lunch
Rest
Outdoors
Read-Aloud
Choice Time
Group Meeting
Home

children. Waiting should be minimized, and adequate time should be allotted for putting on coats and hats, eating meals and snacks, and cleaning up. Work periods should be long enough to give children a chance to select materials and activities, plan what they want to do, explore freely, and clean up afterward without feeling rushed.

Daily Schedule Guidelines

- Offer a balance of active and quiet activities throughout the day.
- Allow at least 60 minutes for each choice time, if possible, so children can become deeply involved in their play.
- Allocate 40–60 minutes for each outdoor period.
- Plan two or three read-aloud times every day.
- Include times for teaching literacy and math skills intentionally every day.

To give you an idea of how to organize a full-day program, we provide a sample all-day schedule (11 hours) with an explanation of what takes place during the estimated time periods. We also offer suggestions for designing a full-day (6-hour) schedule and a half-day (3-hour) program. These sample schedules may be adapted to suit your situation.

The schedule is more than your guide for each day. When used well, it is a valuable tool for promoting literacy skills and understandings about time and sequencing. Display the schedule at children's eye level. Illustrate it with drawings or photographs of the scheduled activities along with the word(s) for each period. Refer to it during the day and focus children's attention on the order of daily routines and activities. For example, you might say, "Let's look at our schedule to see what comes next. We just finished large-group time. Next we have choice time! Think about whether you want to build with blocks, draw or paint, examine our new collection of shells, use the computer or the tablet, or go to the Toys and Games area."

All-Day Schedule
7:00 a.m.– 6:00 p.m.

Preparation, arrival, and choice activities	*60 minutes*	Review the plans for the day. Conduct a health and safety check (e.g., refill bathroom supplies, remove any broken or torn materials, check outside for trash). Prepare interest areas (e.g., add new materials, mix paint, set out ingredients for a cooking activity, collect materials needed for small groups). Greet each family and child as they arrive. Help children store belongings; respond to the "question of the day"; and select an activity (e.g., play with toys and games, draw, continue to work on a project, look at books, listen to recorded stories, or use the tablet or the computer). Talk with individual children, and supervise a self-service breakfast.
Handwashing and breakfast	*30 minutes*	Sit with children as they eat breakfast and have conversations. If you set out a self-service breakfast, continue with the independent activities suggested above.
Group meeting	*20 minutes*	Give a signal to gather the group together. Start with a welcome song; discuss attendance and job charts; invite children to share news; discuss the "question of the day"; record children's ideas; lead a song or fingerplay; conduct an activity or discussion related to a study topic; discuss plans for the day; and introduce any new materials added to interest areas.

Choice time	*70 minutes*	Transition children gradually to choice time activities (e.g., say, "If you are wearing red, you may choose an interest area."). Guide children in selecting where they want to start and what they want to do. Observe and interact with individual children to extend play and learning. Work with children engaged in study activities. Read books to individual children and spontaneous small groups. Give a 5-minute warning before cleanup time and help children put materials away in each interest area.
Small groups	*20 minutes*	Gather children for small-group activities to introduce new concepts and reinforce skills children are developing. If one or more other adults are in the room, you may choose to conduct two or more small groups at once. Otherwise, invite children not currently participating in a small group to select a quiet activity (e.g., play with toys and games, draw, continue to work on a project, look at books, listen to recordings, or use the computer). An alternative is to continue choice time for an additional 20 minutes, conducting a small-group activity during that time. Detailed guidance for conducting small-group activities is provided in *The Creative Curriculum® for Preschool, Volume 3: Literacy* and *Volume 4: Mathematics. Intentional Teaching Cards*™ also offer ideas.
Handwashing and snack	*15 minutes*	Sit with children and lead discussions about what took place during choice time and small-group activities. Have conversations with individual children. Those who finish early may go to the large-group area and look at books while others are finishing.
Read-aloud	*15 minutes*	Focus children's attention by beginning with a song or fingerplay that ends quietly. Read a story or discuss a book related to the topic of the class's current study.

Outdoor choice time	*60 minutes*	Supervise children who are using the playground toys and equipment (e.g., swings, climbers, and slides). Observe and interact with children as they jump rope, play ball games, blow bubbles, explore nature, and so on. Lead activities related to a study or assist games and movement activities that promote large-muscle development. Help children put away or carry in toys and materials, hang up jackets, use the toilet, and wash their hands.
Lunch	*40 minutes*	Help children prepare the tables for lunch. Eat with the children to encourage conversations about the day's events, the meal, and other topics that interest them. Guide children in cleaning up after lunch, brushing teeth, setting out cots or mats, and preparing to rest.
Read-aloud	*15 minutes*	Introduce a new story or reread a familiar one, asking questions and involving children in the reading.
Rest time	*90 minutes*	Help children relax and get comfortable. Supervise the rest area at all times. Provide quiet activities for children who do not sleep. Adjust the length of rest time to suit the age of the group and the needs of individual children.
Snack, choice time, and small groups	*60 minutes*	Set up a self-service snack so children can serve themselves as they get up and transition to an activity (selecting an interest area or participating in a small-group activity). Give a 5-minute warning and help children clean up.
Read-aloud	*15 minutes*	Read or involve children in retelling a familiar story.
Outdoor choice time	*60 minutes*	Supervise children in independent activities, have conversations, and lead an activity (sometimes a neighborhood walk).

Group meeting	*15 minutes*	Lead a movement activity; teach children a fingerplay or an activity with musical instruments. Review the children's responses to the "question of the day." Invite children to talk about the day, including what they want to remember about it. Record highlights on the class calendar and talk about plans for the next day.
Limited choice time and departures	*75 minutes*	Involve children in quiet activities, such as hanging up their artwork and preparing for the next day. Greet families and involve children in sharing the experiences they had that day.
Planning and reflection	*As time allows*	Review how the day went and your observations about individual children (skills, needs, and interests). Work on portfolios and observation notes.

Full-Day Schedule

9:00 a.m.–3:00 p.m.

Arrival, preparation, and choice activities	*30 minutes (before and while children arrive)*
Group meeting	*20 minutes (9:00–9:20)*
Choice time	*60 minutes (9:20–10:20)*
Cleanup, handwashing, and snack	*20 minutes (10:20–10:40)*
Small groups	*20 minutes (10:40–11:00)*
Outdoor choice time	*40 minutes (11:00–11:40)*
Read-aloud	*15 minutes (11:40–11:55)*
Lunch	*40 minutes (11:55–12:35)*
Rest and quiet activities	*45 minutes (12:35–1:20)*
Outdoor choice time	*30 minutes (1:20–1:50)*
Read-aloud	*15 minutes (1:50–2:10)*
Limited choices and small groups	*30 minutes (2:10–2:40)*
Group meeting and departures	*20 minutes (2:40–3:00)*
Teacher planning time	

Half-Day Schedule

2 ½–3 hours

Preparation, arrival, and choice activities	*30 minutes (before and while children arrive)*
Group meeting	*20 minutes (9:00–9:20)*
Choice time	*60 minutes (9:20–10:20)*
Cleanup, handwashing, and snack	*20 minutes (10:20–10:40)*
Small groups	*20 minutes (10:40–11:00)*
Outdoor choice time	*30 minutes (11:00–11:30)*
Read-aloud	*15 minutes (11:30–1:45)*
Music and movement experience, group meeting, and departures	*15 minutes (11:45–noon)*

Planning Each Week

A weekly plan helps you manage implementation of *The Creative Curriculum*®, determine what will happen during group activities and in each interest area, prepare the environment for that week's activities, and allocate time. Daily and weekly plans are developed in conjunction with each other. Your weekly plan helps you integrate day-to-day teaching, and you plan and prepare for each day so that you can achieve your goals for the week. Both plans also help make everything more efficient for you and the children.

Decisions about the week are based in part on what topic the children are currently studying. For example, suppose you are studying shoes and planning to take a trip to a shoe store at the end of the week. On Monday, you might do an activity with children in which they take off and sort their shoes. On Tuesday, you decide to read the fairy tale, "The Shoemaker and the Elves" (the Brothers Grimm). On Wednesday, you could introduce a foot-measuring tool so children can use it in their dramatic play.

The best plans often need to be modified according to the way children respond. You plan for possibilities. Your observations will tell you whether the activities you have planned and the materials you have provided are promoting the desired outcomes. For example, were children able to come up with different categories for sorting their shoes? Do they know how to use the foot measure? Have they incorporated it in their play? Should other props be added? Answers to these questions enable you to adjust your plans as necessary.

The classroom teaching team should work together to create and review the weekly plan. Each member of the team will have observations of children to share and will have important suggestions for adjusting the plan. Refer to your assessment information and to *Volume 6: Objectives for Development & Learning* to guide your planning.

The Creative Curriculum® "Weekly Planning Form" gives you a structure for planning each week and preparing materials and activities ahead of time. It is included in the appendix of this volume, and the following illustration explains the various sections of the form. We also show a completed planning form to give you an idea of how a topic that children are investigating influences weekly planning. (Planning a long-term study of the topic we picked, sand, is explained in detail in chapter 3.)

Interest Areas: As you observe children, note whether materials are appropriate and children are using them constructively. In the course of a study, you may want to add new materials related to the topic. List new materials or materials you would like to highlight here. You may also want to record some open-ended questions to ask children as they use the materials, or you might note objectives and dimensions that will help you focus your observations as children interact with materials and people in interest areas.

Large Group: Write down what you want to prepare, such as stories, songs, games, and study-related materials you need to have ready for each group time. Record the focus of your discussion and shared writing with the large group (this is usually related to the study topic). Also record the "question of the day."

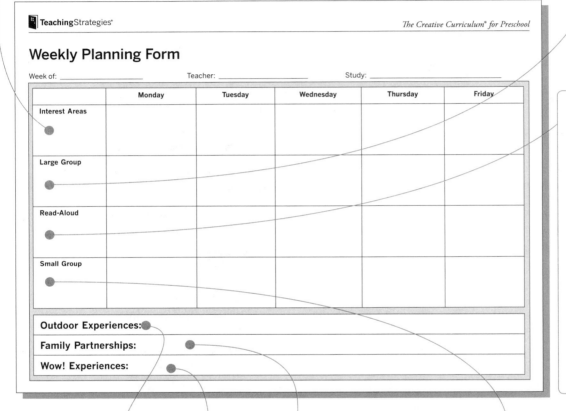

Read-Aloud: Record the titles of the books you plan to read to the whole group during the week. Review them and think of ways to make reading aloud interactive. (*The Creative Curriculum® for Preschool, Volume 3: Literacy,* explains strategies for conducting effective read-alouds.)

Weekly Planning Form

Week of: _____ Teacher: _____ Study: _____

	Monday	Tuesday	Wednesday	Thursday	Friday
Interest Areas					
Large Group					
Read-Aloud					
Small Group					

Outdoor Experiences:	
Family Partnerships:	
Wow! Experiences:	

TeachingStrategies®   *The Creative Curriculum® for Preschool*

Outdoor Experiences: Record special outdoor experiences you plan to offer this week. Consider your most recent checkpoint data and intentionally plan outdoor experiences that support children's gross-motor skill development.

Family Partnership: Include ways to involve children's families and community resources in the program. If you are using *The Creative Curriculum® LearningGames®*, write the names of the games here.

Wow! Experiences: List activities that require planning, such as field trips, site visits, celebrations, or an invited guest.

Small Group: List the experiences and materials you want to use during small-group times and the related objectives and dimensions. Use your most recent assessment information and current observation notes to make decisions about small-group experiences. If you are using *Intentional Teaching Cards™* or online activities, record the titles here.

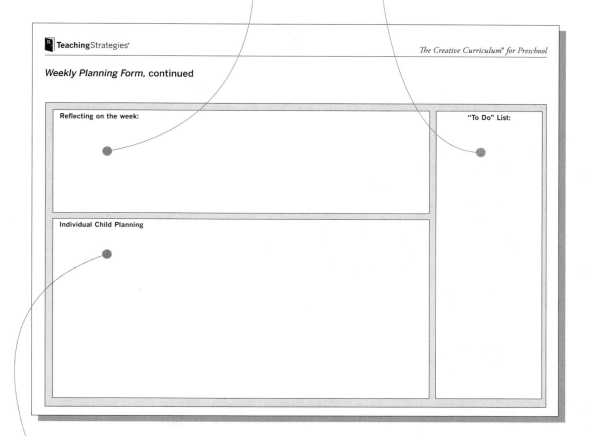

Reflecting on the Week: Use this space to record plans that worked well and changes you want to make in the future. Reflect on children's thinking and record considerations for next week's plan.

"To-Do" List: List arrangements to be made, materials to secure, and the coordination needed to implement your plans.

Individual Child Planning: Record plans for individual children and small groups of children. Base them on your most current assessment information and your observation notes. This planning might include supporting an individual child's development and learning; a small-group experience you want to offer to meet the needs of a particular group of children; or how you are going to adapt your daily small-group time to meet individual children's strengths, needs, and interests.

The Creative Curriculum® for Preschool

Weekly Planning Form

Week of: October 4   Teacher: Ms. Tory and Mr. Alvarez   Study: Sand

	Monday	Tuesday	Wednesday	Thursday	Friday
Interest Areas	**Discovery:** container of sand, folding fans, large straws, small brooms, dust pans, camera, photos of ripples and dunes	**Technology:** images or videos of dunes being created Focus observations on Objective 32	**Technology:** sand samples in closed containers, books showing sand of different colors, bookmarked images of beaches around the world	**Discovery:** magnifying glasses, materials to make sand specimens	**Library:** photos and books showing the wildlife that live or nest in the sand Focus observations on Objective 11
Large Group	**Movement:** "Traffic Jam" **Discussion and Shared Writing:** Sandy Beaches **Materials:** Mighty Minutes 114, "Traffic Jam"; photos of sand dunes	**Game:** "My Name, Too!" **Discussion and Shared Writing:** What Is a Sand Dune? **Materials:** Mighty Minutes 35, "My Name, Too!"; photos of ripples in the sand	**Movement:** "Bounce, Bounce, Bounce" **Discussion and Shared Writing:** Why Are There Different Colors of Sand? **Materials:** Mighty Minutes 30, "Bounce, Bounce, Bounce"; images beaches with interesting colors and textures of sand	**Game:** "Mr. Forgetful" **Discussion and Shared Writing:** Site Visit to Look for Sand **Materials:** Mighty Minutes 50, "Mr. Forgetful"; small containers; camera	**Movement:** "Action Count" **Discussion and Shared Writing:** Animals that Live in Sand **Materials:** Use Mighty Minutes 140, "Action Counting"; books about wildlife that lives in sand
Read-Aloud	*The Summer*	*Where the Wild Things Are* Book Discussion Card 51 (first read-aloud)	*Hello Ocean*	*Where the Wild Things Are* Book Discussion Card 51 (second read-aloud)	*Sand Dune Daisy*
Small Group	*Intentional Teaching Card* LL67, "Book Cover Memory Game" (Objectives 1a, 8b, 9a 11a, 12a, 17a, 18 a-c)	*Intentional Teaching Card* M30, "Buried Shapes" (Objectives 3, 7, 8, 9, 11, 18, 21, 34)	*Intentional Teaching Card* M89, "Dig It!" (Objectives 2c, 3a, 7a, 8b, 11b, 13, 20, 22a)	*Intentional Teaching Card* M45, "Picture Patterns" (Objectives 2, 7, 8, 9, 11, 19, 23, 26, 33)	*Intentional Teaching Card* LL64, "Will You Read to Me?" (Objectives 2a, 9a, 9b, 11a, 17a, 17b, 18 a-c)

Outdoor Experiences: Take ripple and dune-making materials, e.g., straws, fans, etc. outdoors to create ripples and dunes in the sandbox outdoors.

Family Partnerships: Invite family members to help prepare sandbags for the investigation next week by sewing simple sandbags out of cotton or lightweight vinyl fabric.

Wow! Experiences: Walk to look for sand samples in the playground down the street on Wednesday.

TeachingStrategies®

Teaching Strategies®

Weekly Planning Form, continued

Reflecting on the Week:

"To Do" List:

Call to confirm family volunteers to join us on the walk; ask Mrs. Reyes to buy contact paper; check out new sand books from the library; send home letters to families about sewing sandbags; get balance beam from storage closet

Individual Child Planning

Child: Shawna

Plan: Be available to help her enter play with other children during choice time, particularly in the Block area.

Child: Ben

Plan: Review *Intentional Teaching Card* SE03, "Calm Down Place"; observe Ben for signs that he's getting upset (stomping feet, raising voice) and encourage him to visit the cozy box.

Children: Setsuko, Kate, and Crystal

Plan: Bring balance beam outdoors.

Children: Jonetta, Kate, Setsuko, Hector, and Dallas

Plan: Use colored collage materials of various sizes and textures during "Picture Patterns" small group.

Conclusion

The learning environment is the starting point for implementing *The Creative Curriculum®*. The classroom needs to be a place where children feel safe and happy and where teachers look forward to coming to work each day. A well-organized environment helps children make choices, encourages them to use materials well, and teaches them to take increasing responsibility for maintaining the classroom. A well-balanced daily schedule and consistent routines enable children to know what to expect during each period of the day, and they support children's increasing independence. The plans you make and follow enable you to feel prepared and to be intentional about the many experiences you offer children every day. In a well-designed learning environment, teachers can teach and children learn. The next chapter explains what children should be learning in literacy, math, science, social studies, the arts, and technology.

What Children Learn

What Children Learn

The third component of *The Creative Curriculum*® framework addresses what preschool children learn in the content areas of literacy, mathematics, science and technology, social studies and the arts.

The emphasis on teaching content is greater today than in the past. Experts have developed standards that define what children should know and be able to do by certain grade levels. States and local school districts have adapted these standards. Teaching content in *The Creative Curriculum*® classroom is also guided by these standards.

This chapter describes the body of knowledge included in each content area and the process skills children use to gain that knowledge. It also explains how teachers integrate learning and make it meaningful to children by engaging them in studying topics of interest. Here are the components of the content areas that are addressed in this chapter:

Literacy—literacy as a source of enjoyment, vocabulary and language, phonological awareness, knowledge of print, letters and words, comprehension, and books and other texts

Mathematics—number and operations, geometry and spatial sense, measurement, patterns (algebra), and data analysis

Science—the physical properties of objects and materials, characteristics of living things, and Earth's environment

Social Studies—people and how they live, change related to people and places, and simple geography

The Arts—visual arts, music, dance and movement, and drama

Technology—tools and their basic operations and uses

Process Skills—observing and exploring; problem solving; and connecting, organizing, communicating, and representing information

Integrating Learning Through Studies—engaging children in exploring science and social studies by applying skills in order to answer questions that interest them

Literacy

Becoming literate does not just happen by itself. Teachers thoughtfully and purposefully interact with children and plan experiences that support emerging literacy. A print-rich environment that enables children to practice literacy skills in meaningful ways and explicit teaching of important concepts are the foundation of literacy learning in preschool. As children's excitement about their new reading and writing skills increases, teachers create many opportunities for continued literacy learning.

Components of Literacy

Over the past few decades, researchers and practitioners have studied how children learn to read, write, and understand written language (Snow, Burns, & Griffin, 1998; National Institute of Child Health and Human Development, 2007). They have identified the concepts children need to understand in order be competent, confident readers and writers. They have also identified the kinds of experiences that help children progress. On the basis of this research, we describe seven components of literacy for children ages 3–5:

- literacy as a source of enjoyment
- vocabulary and language
- phonological awareness
- knowledge of print
- letters and words
- comprehension
- books and other texts

Literacy as a Source of Enjoyment

First and foremost, children should experience the power and pleasures of literacy. Children eventually read because they are motivated to learn about things that interest them, to uncover the plots of stories, and to discover something that makes them laugh. The more they read, the better readers they become and the more motivated they are to continue reading. A child who finds literacy activities enjoyable will be more likely to participate during interactive read-aloud times, notice print in the environment, ask questions about the meaning of print, and use the books you display in the classroom. In the Library area chapter of *The Creative Curriculum® for Preschool, Volume 2: Interest Areas*, you can find many ideas for making that area inviting and attractive. In addition, you will find many ways to help children develop a love of reading.

Vocabulary and Language

When children are introduced to rich vocabulary, they learn the words they will need to read and write. Research has shown that children who have large vocabularies and lots of experience with using language are more successful in school (Hart & Risley, 2010). In *The Creative Curriculum®* classroom, children have many opportunities to develop their vocabularies, to listen, and to speak. These include

- informal conversations with peers and adults throughout the day
- songs, rhymes, fingerplays, and movement activities
- firsthand experiences and talking about what they are doing
- listening to and talking about books that are read aloud to them

Especially if you have children whose home languages are not English, you should know that a strong base in a first language promotes school achievement in a second language (Tabors, 2008). Children who are learning English as a second language are more likely to become readers and writers of English if they understand the vocabulary and concepts in their primary language first. These children need the special attention of adults to strengthen their vocabularies and other language skills. The long-term goal is for children to be able to understand, speak, read, and write in both their primary languages and English. You therefore want to support children's home languages as you help them acquire proficiency in English.

Phonological Awareness

Phonological awareness involves distinguishing the various sounds of spoken language. It includes the different ways oral language can be broken down into parts, for instance, words, syllables, and letter sounds. Recent research shows the importance of developing phonological awareness during the preschool years.

The skills that make up phonological awareness follow a developmental progression. The simplest level of phonological awareness is promoted by such strategies as playing with rhymes; calling children's attention to words that begin with the same sounds; and helping children clap out the individual words or syllables of a song, rhyme, or chant. Playing with speech sounds paves the way to phonemic awareness, which is the most advanced level of phonological awareness. Phonemic awareness is the ability to hear, identify, and manipulate the basic sounds—phonemes—of spoken words (National Institute of Child Health and Human Development, 2007). Phonemic awareness is typically addressed in kindergarten and first grade.

Phonological awareness is often confused with phonics, but they are not the same. Phonics is connecting a printed symbol with a sound, unlike phonological awareness, which is hearing and differentiating sounds. Phonics activities are appropriate for preschool children only if they understand that speech is made up of a sequence of sounds. The preschool teacher's role in promoting phonological awareness is to draw children's attention to the separate sounds of spoken language through playful songs, games, and rhymes.

Children who are learning English as a second language are also developing phonological awareness through the activities you do together. They may not say English sounds exactly as you do, however. These children are still learning to hear and discriminate the sounds of

English, so you need to acknowledge (rather than correct) their efforts while you continue to model correct English pronunciation.

Knowledge of Print

This component of literacy involves connecting print with meaning. Children acquire knowledge of print by seeing it in the environment and using it in their play. By drawing children's attention to the features of print, you help children to understand print concepts such as these:

- Print carries a message.
- Each spoken word can be written down and read, and every written word can be spoken.
- Print follows conventions (e.g., a left-to-right progression, upper- and lowercase letters, and punctuation).
- Books have common characteristics (e.g., front and back covers, authors, and illustrators).

Letters and Words

This component of literacy is more than being able to recite the ABC song. Really knowing about letters involves understanding that a letter stands for one or more language sounds, that these sounds and letters are grouped together to form words, that words are grouped in particular ways, and that writing has meaning.

To a child, the most important letters are those usually in his or her name, particularly the first letter. For example, Setsuko points to the "S" on a stop sign and says, "That's my letter!" Many children do not begin experimenting with spelling until they are 5 or 6 years old. You know a child has an understanding of beginning and ending sounds when he writes *PG* above his drawing of a pig. Some people call this stage *invented spelling, transitional spelling, temporary spelling, developmental spelling,* or *phonetic spelling.* Research has shown that early forms of spelling indicate that children are making important sound–symbol connections. Other stages of writing follow these early forms.

Comprehension

Comprehension refers to the understanding of spoken and written language. Children who comprehend what has been read aloud may ask questions or make comments about the story or act it out in their play.

The way you read to children is very important to their development of comprehension skills. Pausing at the end of a sentence to let children join in, asking open-ended questions, and helping children make connections to their previous experiences are all effective teaching strategies for promoting comprehension skills. *The Creative Curriculum® for Preschool, Volume 3: Literacy* discusses strategies for reading aloud to individuals and groups of children.

Books and Other Texts

Understanding books and other texts involves knowing how to read and write signs, menus, letters, shopping lists, newspapers, invitations, messages, journals, and books. Books have many forms: narrative storybooks, predictable books (books with language patterns like rhymes and refrains), informational books, counting books, alphabet books, and poetry books. You can help children learn about different forms of literature by offering a variety of books and calling children's attention to their particular characteristics. Storybooks offer particularly important learning opportunities. Through them, children discover many things. They learn that a story

- has a beginning, middle, and end
- has various characters
- takes place in a setting
- has a sequence of events
- might include conversations

Understanding books and other texts also involves learning how to handle books in particular ways, such as holding the book right-side up; progressing from front to back; and knowing book-related words such as *author* and *illustrator*.

Connecting Literacy Content, Teaching, and Learning

The chart on the following pages shows how to connect literacy content, teaching, and learning. The first column outlines the components of literacy for preschool. The second column shows some of the many ways teachers address this content effectively. The last column gives examples of what preschool children might do or say that shows their increasing understanding of each component of literacy.

Literacy Content	What Teachers Can Do	What Preschool Children Might Do
Literacy as a Source of Enjoyment (Enjoying being read to, reading, and writing)	Arrange the Library area attractively and include high-quality literature and soft, comfortable furniture. Read books to children and encourage them to talk about the stories and ideas. Place books about relevant topics in all interest areas. Add interesting materials to the writing area to encourage writing efforts: pencils, pens, markers, stationery, stamps, envelopes, etc.	Ask the teacher to read a favorite book. Join in saying the refrain as the teacher reads a predictable book. Scribble across the bottom of the page after finishing a picture and then tell the meaning of the caption. Listen to a story and ask questions about it.

Literacy Content	What Teachers Can Do	What Preschool Children Might Do
Vocabulary and Language (Acquiring new words and using them to communicate)	Engage in frequent one-on-one conversations with children. Provide children with many firsthand experiences and talk with them about what they are doing. Introduce new words by using various strategies: explaining, pointing to pictures, using facial expressions and other body language, or changing your tone of voice.	Point to a toy truck and say, "That's a frontloader. It picks up heavy things." Say at group time, "I'm going fishing with my dad tomorrow. We're going to bring fishing poles and a big net and catch 100 fish." Describe a scary dream as a *nightmare* after the teacher reads *There's a Nightmare in My Closet*.
Phonological Awareness (Hearing and distinguishing the separate sounds of spoken language; recognizing whether words or segments of words sound the same or different)	Lead children in singing, saying rhymes, reciting fingerplays, and playing language games. Talk about words and language sounds during daily activities (e.g., "Tasheen and Tyrone, your names both start with the same sound, /t/."). Read books that play with the sounds in words, such as those by Dr. Seuss.	Fill in the missing rhyming word in a phrase. Make up nonsense words or silly names (e.g., *Silly Willy* and *Funny Bunny*). Clap as designated words or syllables are said (e.g., clapping twice while saying the name *Kelly* during the recitation of a rhyme). Notice that several names or other words begin with the same sound (e.g., *Jonelle*, *Juwan*, and *Jonetta*).

Literacy Content	What Teachers Can Do	What Preschool Children Might Do
Knowledge of Print (Learning how print works)	Talk about features of print while writing with children (e.g., the top-to-bottom and left-to-right progressions). Occasionally run your finger under the words as you read a story. As you write with children, draw their attention to punctuation marks such as periods and question marks (e.g., "I'd better put a period here because it's the end of the sentence."). Post a sign with pictures and words about what to take for snack. Post sign-up sheets for activities.	Point to a shelf label and say, "Cars go here." Make a grocery list in the Dramatic Play area, writing from left to right and from top to bottom. Read a big book to a group of stuffed animals, pointing to the words and progressing from front to back.
Letters and Words (Identifying and writing some letters and words)	Display the alphabet at children's eye level and have alphabet cards available for children to use during play. Add materials such as alphabet puzzles, magnetic letters, foam letters, paper, and pencils to the interest areas. Draw children's attention to written letters and words in the context of meaningful everyday activities.	Use magnetic letters or other alphabet materials to form their names. Attempt to write a phone message in the Dramatic Play area. Say, "That's a *w*, pointing to the first letter of each word in *wishy-washy, wishy-washy.*

Literacy Content	What Teachers Can Do	What Preschool Children Might Do
Comprehension (Following and understanding a book, story, or conversation)	Add storytelling props to the Library area for acting out stories. Omit a word at the end of a sentence when reading a highly predictable book. Ask children open-ended questions while reading (e.g., "What do you think will happen next?" and "How would you feel if that happened to you?") Encourage children to recall the important events of a story (e.g., "Do you remember what happened when the wolf blew on the house of straw?").	Retell *The Very Hungry Caterpillar*, using felt fruit on the flannel board. Explain, "They ran away from the kids 'cause they were scared," after hearing the teacher read *Goggles*. Talk about their own experiences after hearing the teacher read *Ira Sleeps Over*. Act out the story *Caps for Sale*.
Books and Other Texts (Learning how to use a book and understanding the purposes of books; gaining a sense of story; learning about the uses of other texts, such as signs, menus, magazines, newspapers, etc.)	Model the proper handling and care of books. Help children use books and magazines to learn more about topics of interest. Add magazines, signs, pamphlets, telephone books, menus, and newspapers to the Dramatic Play area. Talk about the author and illustrator when introducing a story.	Retell *The Three Little Pigs* in correct sequence. Place a sign that reads, "Do not move!" on a design made with pattern blocks. Refer to a book about castles while building one with blocks. Ask for a book about butterflies so they can find the name of the one they saw. Draw a picture; write some letters on it; and say, "It's a letter for Grandma."

Objectives for Literacy Development and Learning

Objective 15. Demonstrates phonological awareness, phonics skills, and word recognition

    a. Notices and discriminates rhyme

    b. Notices and discriminates alliteration

    c. Notices and discriminates discrete units of sound

    d. Applies phonics concepts and knowledge of word structure to decode text

Objective 16. Demonstrates knowledge of the alphabet

    a. Identifies and names letters

    b. Identifies letter-sound correspondences

Objective 17. Demonstrates knowledge of print and its uses

    a. Uses and appreciates books and other texts

    b. Uses print concepts

Objective 18. Comprehends and responds to books and other texts

    a. Interacts during reading experiences, book conversations, and text reflections

    b. Uses emergent reading skills

    c. Retells stories and recounts details from informational texts

    d. Uses context clues to read and comprehend text

    e. Reads fluently

Objective 19. Demonstrates writing skills

    a. Writes name

    b. Writes to convey ideas and information

    c. Writes using conventions

(The objectives related to language were listed in chapter 1 of this Volume as part of the discussion of language development.)

Mathematics

Just as preschool teachers promote children's literacy intentionally, they use many opportunities during the day to help children build competence in math. When children give a cracker to each person at the table, pour water from one container to another, put all the big buttons in one pile and the smaller ones in another, or clap a rhythmic pattern, they are learning math. Everyday activities such as these provide the context and are necessary experiences for preschool children to progress in math. With adult guidance that promotes and extends children's mathematical thinking, children learn math facts and begin to understand math concepts.

Components of Mathematics

National standards in mathematics (NCTM, 2000) describe what children should learn in preschool. The components of math include

- number and operations
- geometry and spatial sense
- measurement
- patterns (algebra)
- data analysis

Number and Operations

Number concepts are the foundation of mathematics. Children's understanding of these concepts develops gradually over time as children explore, manipulate, and organize materials and as they communicate mathematical thinking with adults and peers.

Children are said to have number sense when they have intuitive understandings about numbers and their relationships. As children gain a sense of number they understand, for example, what *three* means in terms of quantity. They learn that "threeness" can be represented by the numeral *3*, the word *three*, and a set of three objects. They begin to explore the relationships among quantities and learn the meaning of *more*, *less*, *fewer*, and *the same*.

Counting is one of the number concepts that children understand earliest. That understanding begins with the development of verbal counting skills, or rote counting, sometimes as early as age 2. Rote counting is the memorization of a sequence of numbers. Rote-counting skills develop as children join in songs, fingerplays, and rhymes that involve numbers.

Understanding one-to-one correspondence follows rote counting. In terms of counting objects in a set, one-to-one correspondence means linking one, and only one, consecutive number with each item in the set. This technique should be modeled throughout the day in interest areas and daily routines, and it must often be taught directly. Sometimes children inadvertently count an object more than once. You can model strategies to help children keep track of what they are counting by showing them how to move each object to the side after they have counted it.

Understanding quantity, terms of comparison, and number symbols is also fundamental. Quantity involves the concept of an entire set (knowing that the last number named while counting a set tells the whole amount). If you ask a child to bring you three crayons and he brings you all three rather than just the third crayon counted, he probably has an understanding of quantity. A child who understands number order knows that it does not matter whether he counts a row of three crayons from left to right or counts them in a different order; the amount is the same. Making comparisons involves knowing the meaning of such terms as *more, fewer, bigger,* and *the same.*

Young children can learn the names of numbers and numerals without having any idea of what the symbols represent. Understanding a number symbol involves seeing a numeral (e.g., *3*) and associating that numeral with the corresponding quantity (e.g., three objects). Number symbols only have meaning for young children when they are introduced as labels for quantities. Rather than teaching children to recognize numerals (number symbols) in isolation, link them to their corresponding quantities.

Geometry and Spatial Sense

For young children, geometry involves recognizing and describing shapes in the environment. Children learn about and use their knowledge of two- and three-dimensional shapes when you give them opportunities to create designs with pattern blocks, draw, paint, cut shapes for in their artwork, sort blocks as they return them to the shelves, and identify shapes outdoors. First, children learn to recognize simple geometric figures like triangles, circles, and squares. Next, they learn to describe shapes verbally (e.g., "A square is a rectangle with four sides of the same length."). You support their understanding by describing the shapes that you see children create or locate.

Children gain spatial sense as they become aware of themselves in relation to other people and things. Through the experiences you provide, they learn about location and position (e.g., *on, off, on top of, under, in, out, behind, below*), direction (e.g., *backward, forward, around, through, across, up, down,* etc.), and distance (e.g., *near, far, next to*). As you give children opportunities to manipulate objects and shapes, they also learn to make predictions (e.g., "If I turn this shape upside down, it won't fit in the hole.").

Measurement

Developing an understanding of the principles and uses of measurement is the focus of measurement activities in preschool. Children develop understandings about measurement by using materials and participating in hands-on activities.

As a first step, children make comparisons without any measuring tools. Using the materials you provide, children learn concepts such as longer, shorter, heavier, lighter, faster, and slower. Next, children learn to use nonstandard tools, such as a shoe, a piece of string or ribbon, or even their hands, to measure objects.

Formal instruction in the use of standard tools such as clocks, rulers, scales, thermometers, and measuring cups comes later, typically toward the end of kindergarten and in the primary grades. However, if these measuring tools are made available to children, they explore and use them in their play and investigations.

Patterns (Algebra)

Patterns are regular arrangements of such things as objects, shapes, and numbers. As children learn to recognize regular repetitions of basic units, they figure out relationships among objects and eventually begin to generalize about numbers. That helps them learn to count and perform basic numerical operations.

Recognizing patterns is important to science and literacy learning as well as to mathematics. With guidance, preschoolers learn to recognize and analyze simple patterns, copy them, create them, make predictions about them, and extend them. Preschool children can recognize simple patterns easily. As you "read" a pattern of beads (e.g., red, blue; red, blue; etc.), children can join in. After recognizing simple patterns, they can copy patterns that they see or hear. To extend a pattern, children must figure out what comes next and continue the sequence.

Data Analysis

Data analysis includes collecting and organizing information and finding ways to represent it. In preschool this involves classifying, graphing, counting, measuring, and comparing. Instruction in each of these areas can build on children's interest in collections.

As part of collecting, children often begin to sort and make sets without a plan that they can explain. Then they sort more purposefully, for example, by properties such as identity, color, shape, or size. As children develop and refine their sorting skills, they sort by more than one attribute. This ability is strengthened when you encourage them to talk about their sorting rules (the criteria they use to define their categories).

Graphing is a direct extension of sorting and classifying. A graph presents information in a visually organized way that helps children understand relationships and make comparisons. Graphing enables children to show information in various ways. A simple graph of the kinds of shoes children are wearing could develop from a concrete representation to a symbolic one:

- concrete graph—made by using actual shoes with fasteners and shoes without fasteners
- symbolic graph—made by using pictures that represent shoes with and without fasteners

After children make a graph, they can use it to analyze and interpret the data. This step involves comparing, counting, adding, subtracting, and using terms such as *greater than*, *less than*, *equal to*, and *not equal to*. The graph on the right was made after the children in one classroom collected leaves on a walk.

To help children interpret this graph, a teacher might ask these questions:

- What does this graph tell us?
- Of which kind of leaf did we collect the most? …the least? How do you know that?
- Of which kinds of leaves did we collect the same number? How do you know that?

Connecting Math Content, Teaching, and Learning

In *The Creative Curriculum®*, math content is presented in ways that are meaningful to preschool children. The following chart shows how to connect math content, teaching, and learning. The first column outlines the components of math for preschool. The second column shows some of the many ways teachers address this content effectively. The last column gives examples of what preschool children might do or say that shows their increasing understanding of each component of mathematics.

Math Content	What Teachers Can Do	What Preschool Children Might Do
Number and Operations (Understanding numbers, ways of representing numbers, and relationships among numbers)	Teach children counting songs, rhymes, and chants (e.g., "One, two, three, four, five. Once I caught a fish alive."). Count during daily activities (e.g., the number of children who are present, the number of cups needed for each child to have one, or the number of paintbrushes needed so that there is one for each paint container). Encourage children to compare quantities: "Do we have more red caps or more blue caps?	Notice that it takes five scoops of sand to fill a cup. Predict that it will take 10 blocks to make a fence of a particular length; then count the blocks to see whether the prediction was correct. Count five children and then set the table with five plates, five napkins, and five forks.
Geometry and Spatial Sense (Recognizing, naming, building, drawing, describing, comparing, and sorting two- and three-dimensional shapes; recognizing and describing spatial relationships)	Talk about geometric shapes as children use unit blocks and pattern blocks. Provide empty boxes, tubes, and containers for children to use for constructions. Take children on a walk to look for shapes in the environment. Describe spatial relationships as children play (e.g., "You're putting the horse inside the fenced area you made.").	Use a geoboard to create geometric shapes with rubber bands. Explain, "I'm going to make my horse jump over the fence." Comment that bubbles are spheres. Use empty boxes, tubes, and containers to build an imaginary playground.

Math Content	What Teachers Can Do	What Preschool Children Might Do
Measurement (Using nonstandard units to measure and make comparisons)	Show children how to use common objects as measuring tools (e.g., "Look. This table is five blocks long.") Use a sand timer or kitchen timer to let children know that there are only 5 minutes left until cleanup. Ask open-ended questions during measurement activities (e.g., "What is the best way to measure the height of your pumpkin?"). Use words like *before, after, next, yesterday, today,* and *tomorrow* throughout the day (e.g., "Tomorrow is Leo's birthday.").	Realize that only a short time is left for cleaning up when the teacher turns the sand timer over. Measure a table by using a unit block. Count how many cups of sand it takes to fill a small bucket. Use a piece of ribbon to measure the length of a rug.
Patterns (Algebra) (Recognizing, copying, and extending patterns; making predictions about patterns)	Clap hands and then pat thighs in a pattern (e.g., clap, pat; clap, pat; etc.). Later move in a more complex pattern (e.g., clap, clap, pat; clap, clap, pat; etc.). Help children describe the "people patterns" that they make with their bodies (e.g., standing, sitting; standing, sitting; etc.) Draw children's attention to various patterns (e.g., "I see a pattern in your shirt today: red stripe, blue stripe; red stripe, blue stripe…"). Describe patterns you see children creating (e.g., "You made a pattern with the felt pieces: square, triangle; square, triangle…").	Beat a drum as the teacher does (e.g., loudly, softly; loudly, softly; loudly, softly; etc.). Line up small cars in a pattern of red, black; red, black; red, black; etc. Sponge paint a patterned border around a picture. Add interlocking cubes correctly to continue a pattern that they are shown (e.g., white, blue, green; white, blue, green; etc.).

Math Content	What Teachers Can Do	What Preschool Children Might Do
Data Analysis (Posing questions to investigate, organizing responses, and creating representations of data)	Pose a "question of the day" (e.g., "Do you like to wear your shoes during nap time?"). Show children how to make tally marks under the headings *Yes* or *No* on a chart of responses. Graph collections of objects found in the classroom, such as stickers, leaves, rocks, shells, buttons, etc. Have the children make a "people graph" in response to your question (e.g., "Do more children in our class have brown hair or blonde hair?"). Ask questions such as "How did you make your group?" and "Where does this one go?" and "How are these alike?"	Sort a collection of dolls into a group with shoes and a group without shoes. Make a graph of a sticker collection, sorting them by color. Make tally marks under the headings *juice* and *milk* on a piece of paper while surveying which beverage children prefer for snack. Draw a picture of each object that floats and each that sinks after testing them in the water table.

Objectives for Mathematics Development and Learning

Objective 20. Uses number concepts and operations

 a. Counts

 b. Quantifies

 c. Connects numerals with their quantities

 d. Understands and uses place value and base ten

 e. Applies properties of mathematical operations and relationships

 f. Applies number combinations and mental number strategies in mathematical operations

Objective 21. Explores and describes spatial relationships and shapes

 a. Understands spatial relationships

 b. Understands shapes

Objective 22. Compares and measures

 a. Measures objects

 b. Measures time and money

 c. Represents and analyzes data

Objective 23. Demonstrates knowledge of patterns

Science

Science content is more than isolated facts such as the stages in a butterfly's life. Scientific facts are important, but the way children learn to make meaningful generalizations on the basis of their firsthand observations is more significant. For example, learning about the development of a butterfly should lead to the big idea that many living things develop in a series of stages called a *life cycle*. Preschool children learn science by exploring the world around them. When you provide an environment with many varied materials, children manipulate them to see how they work. They experiment and ask questions. As they seek answers to their questions, they learn to enjoy, appreciate, and understand their surroundings. These are scientific activities.

Components of Science

To decide which concepts children should learn, observe children's scientific interests and what they say and do every day. Your observations will probably fall into the three categories that are the components of science (National Research Council, 2013):

- physical science
- life science
- Earth and the environment

Physical Science

Physical science concerns the physical properties of materials. By exploring materials, children learn about weight, shape, size, color, and temperature. They explore how things move and change. When children make a block ramp to race cars, look through a kaleidoscope, or pick up objects with magnets, they are learning about the physical properties of objects. Encourage children to think about questions such as these as you help them learn physical science:

- What does this look like? Is it big or little?...striped or spotted?...bright or dull?
- How does this smell: like perfume or like burned toast?
- How does this taste: sweet, salty, bitter, or bland?
- How does this sound: loud or soft?...fast or slow?
- How does this feel: slimy, squishy, hard, sharp, or tickly?
- How can you make this move? Can you roll it, twist it, blow it, swing it, or push it?
- How can you make this change? Can you mix it, pour it, smash it, or shake it?

It is not necessary to set up particular science experiments for children. You can create opportunities to learn about physical science in all interest areas.

Life Science

Life science involves living things. You are teaching life science when you give children opportunities to care for plants and animals. Children learn important information and process skills by exploring the immediate environment. A preschool in Louisiana might investigate crawfish while children in Alaska might learn about salmon or caribou. Children could learn about cacti in Arizona and corn in rural Nebraska. No matter what topics children study, these are some concepts to think about as you plan learning experiences:

- How do living things get food?
- What are the important characteristics of plants and animals?
- What do plants and animals need in order to grow?
- How do plants and animals depend on each other?
- How do living things change as they grow?
- Which animals lay eggs?
- What plants and animals live in our neighborhood?

Life science also includes learning about our bodies and how to stay healthy. These topics can be taught by exploring these big questions:

- How do our bodies grow and change?
- How do we use our senses?
- Why do we need different kinds of food?
- How do we stay safe and healthy?

Earth and the Environment

The component of science called "Earth and the environment" involves the natural world. In preschool, children learn by experiencing natural settings directly. The goal is for children to learn important ideas about those settings and develop respect for their natural surroundings. Think about how you might address the following questions:

- What is the land like in this community? Are there water, grass, sand, and rocks? Are there lakes, ponds, mountains, deserts, rivers, or fields? What are these things like?
- What can we see in the sky? How do those things in the sky affect the world around us?
- What is the weather here? How does it affect us?
- How can we take care of the world around us?

Connecting Science Content, Teaching, and Learning

In *The Creative Curriculum*® classroom, the content of science is taught by helping children explore the world around them in meaningful ways. The following chart shows how to connect science content, teaching, and learning. The first column outlines the components of science for preschool. The second column shows some of the many ways teachers address this content effectively. The last column gives examples of what preschool children might do or say that shows their increasing understanding of each component of science.

Science Content	What Teachers Can Do	What Preschool Children Might Do
Physical Science (Exploring the physical properties of common objects and materials by observing and manipulating them)	Provide tools such as magnets, magnifying glasses, balance scales, pulleys, and mirrors to encourage children's explorations. Use open-ended questions to extend investigations (e.g., "Why does this big toy boat float and the penny sink?"). Describe physical changes that children can observe (e.g., "When the blue paint ran into the yellow paint, it turned green!"). Include old, small appliances or broken toys on a "take apart" table to help children learn how things work.	Use a magnet to pick up metal objects buried in sand. Tilt block ramps more steeply to make cars go down faster. Use a pulley to lift a basket of books into the reading loft. Say, "Look! Blue paint dripped into the orange paint cup, and it all turned brown."
Life Science (Exploring living things, their life cycles, and their habitats)	Add living things, such as plants and pets, to the classroom and show the children how to care for them. Provide markers and paper so children can observe and record the growth of plants that they started from seeds. Talk with children about different kinds of animal homes, such as bird nests, beehives, anthills, etc. Observe and discuss the life cycles of animals such as butterflies and frogs. Help children learn about health and their bodies every day (e.g., "Can you feel your heart pounding after running so much?" and "The carrots you're eating are very good for you.").	Comment, "Our gerbil sleeps all day long. I wonder if it stays awake at night." Water plants after observing that their leaves are drooping. Notice that they breathe more deeply while running on the playground.

Science Content	What Teachers Can Do	What Preschool Children Might Do
Earth and the Environment (Exploring the properties of the world around them, notice changes, and make predictions)	Lead a discussion about things we do during the day and things we do at night. Paint the sidewalk with water and talk about why the water disappears. Talk about the seasons as children notice environmental changes (e.g., "I can tell that fall is here. The leaves are turning red, yellow, orange, and brown." Discuss the weather each day while preparing to go outdoors (e.g., "Jeremy, will you please check the outside temperature today? Do we need to wear sweaters?")	Play shadow tag. Talk about what they do during the day and at night. Add water to dirt while making mud pies. Paint with water on the sidewalk and notice that the picture soon disappears.

Objectives for Science Development and Learning

Objective 24. Uses scientific inquiry skills

Objective 25. Demonstrates knowledge of the characteristics of living things

Objective 26. Demonstrates knowledge of the physical properties of objects and materials

Objective 27. Demonstrates knowledge of Earth's environment

Technology

Technology involves the tools, machines, materials, techniques, and sources of power that make work easier and solve problems. Children learn about technology by exploring how things work. When they figure out what tools they need to build a structure with wooden scraps, they are solving technological problems. When children create colored lines on a computer screen by dragging a mouse or tap the icon on a touch screen to access a game, they are using tools. If you view technology from a broad perspective, you can see how it can be integrated into all aspects of the preschool classroom.

For children with disabilities, technology opens new avenues for learning. A child who is unable to speak can use communication devices to interact with others. A child who is physically impaired can use switches to control battery-operated toys. Special assistive devices enable children with disabilities to have equal access to the environment and learning opportunities.

Components of Technology

Standards in technology outline the skills, understandings, knowledge, and attitudes that children in preschool through grade 12 should acquire (International Society for Technology Education, 2007). The standards focus on both the basics of using computers and the uses of technology to communicate, learn new information, solve problems, and create. Equally important, the standards also stress social skills, such as working cooperatively with peers and using technology responsibly.

Four components of the technology standards apply to preschool children:

- awareness of technology
- basic operations and concepts
- tools and equipment
- people and technology

Awareness of Technology

For preschool children, technology involves knowing how tools are used at home, at school, and at various work sites. You can teach technology by asking children to name the tools and machines they use every day and to think about how tasks might be accomplished if this equipment were not available. You can also encourage children to find out how people use technology to do their jobs.

Basic Operations and Concepts

This component of technology includes the basics of using tools. For example, if children are using a CD player, they need to know how to insert a CD, turn the machine on and off, and use the play and stop buttons. The basics of using a tablet are using the touch screen, swiping up and down to navigate, and tapping to open an app or a game. The Technology area chapter of *The Creative Curriculum® for Preschool, Volume 2: Interest Areas* explains in detail how to introduce children to a variety of technology devices and tools. It also discusses ways to interact with children so they can learn about this technology.

Tools and Equipment

This component includes the different forms of technology, ranging from computers and digital cameras to wheels and shovels. By using various tools, children learn that each serves a different purpose. Explain,

"To draw a picture, we need paper and a crayon, a marker, or paint, or we need a computer drawing program."

"To write a story, we need paper and a pencil, pen, or marker, or we can use the computer's keyboard."

"To examine a tiny insect, we need a magnifying glass."

"To open up the app on the tablet, tap the icon on the touch screen twice."

People and Technology

This component involves using technology responsibly and safely, caring for equipment, and using it appropriately. Because technology is part of everyday life and is often taken for granted, it is important for children to understand that people, including themselves, control its design and use.

For example, children can control the way they navigate an app on a tablet, change the volume on a tape player, or flip a light switch. When children learn how to handle tablets and other mobile digital devices properly, how to swipe up and down on a touch screen to search through icons, and how to take care of a digital camera, they are controlling technology.

This component, "people and technology," also includes helping young children learn how people work together as they use technology. For instance, you can encourage a group of children to solve problems together on the computer. Help them realize that they can find a friend or adult to help them if they cannot figure out how to use a tool or piece of equipment, and they can share ideas about how to accomplish tasks.

Connecting Technology Content, Teaching, and Learning

In *The Creative Curriculum®*, teachers make learning about technology an appropriate part of the preschool program. The following chart shows how to connect technology content, teaching, and learning. The first column outlines the components of technology for preschool. The second column shows some of the many ways teachers can address this content effectively. The third column gives examples of what preschool children might do or say that shows their increasing understanding of each component of technology.

Technology Content	What Teachers Can Do	What Preschool Children Might Do
Awareness of Technology (Gaining awareness of tools and equipment for finding information, communicating, and creating)	Offer toy cell phones, cameras, and microphones for children to use during play. Point out how technology is used by people the children observe during site visits (e.g., "The computer helps firefighters see a street map so they can drive to the fire."). Take videos of children as they play. Watch the videos with the children and talk about the equipment involved.	Pretend to scan merchandise while playing store. Notice how computers are used at the fire station they visited. Suggest making a video of their trip to a grocery store.
Basic Operations and Concepts (Learning basic skills to operate tools and equipment; using appropriate terminology to communicate about technology)	Show children how to use a mouse, keyboard, track pad, or touch screen to operate a computer. Teach children about the icons on the tablet's screen and how to tap on them to access games and apps. Use technology terminology when showing children how to use the computer or the tablet (e.g., "I'm going to paste the picture here."). Teach children how to navigate the touch screen of the tablet.	Use a mouse, keyboard, or touch screen to operate the tablet or the computer. Use a drawing program to create a picture. Access a game on the tablet by tapping and swiping on the touch screen.

Technology Content	What Teachers Can Do	What Preschool Children Might Do
Tools and Equipment (Understanding that there are different kinds of tools and equipment and that they can be used in a variety of ways)	Encourage children to record their retelling of a story and ask others to listen. Set up a drawing program so children can create pictures to show what they have learned. Show children how to use a simple writing program to type their names and other words. Provide tools such as magnifying glasses, balance scales, and binoculars for children to use as they explore and investigate.	Tell a story into a mobile digital device and listen to it with another child. Use software to draw a flower for a get-well card. Use a simple counting program to match numerals and quantities. Watch birds at a feeder through binoculars.
People and Technology (Understanding that technology is controlled by people; using tools and equipment safely and responsibly; working collaboratively while using technology)	Show children that they can create a line by dragging the mouse as they use a painting program. Encourage children to work with each other to figure out how to navigate a learning game on the tablet. Develop rules with the children for using the tablet safely and properly.	Drag a mouse to create straight and wavy lines on a computerized painting. Say, "You shouldn't eat your snack next to the computer because crumbs can break the keyboard." Click on icons (picture cues) to navigate apps and games on the tablet.

Objective for Technology Development and Learning

Objective 28. Uses tools and other technology to perform tasks

Social Studies

Social studies are concerned with people: how they live today and lived in the past and how they work, get along with others, and solve problems. They also involve the ways people affect and are affected by their surroundings. Children begin learning social studies in infancy. They explore physical space by crawling, climbing, digging, and splashing. In preschool, board games and the challenge of riding around a tricycle path teach basic mapping skills. Children learn about time (history) from the predictable daily routines you establish, such as a story before rest time, large-group time after choice time, and outdoor play after lunch. When you set up a pretend grocery store and help children learn about jobs and about buying and selling, you help them learn economics. This learning continues as they visit the supermarket, the doctor, the hardware store, and the shoe store. Preschoolers begin to learn civics as you teach them to cooperate and to resolve differences in a classroom setting. Everyday experiences pertinent to children's lives are the foundation for learning social studies.

Components of Social Studies

Social studies standards focus on history, geography, economics, and civics. We organize the components of social studies for preschool into the following categories:

- people and how they live
- people and the environment
- people and the past
- spaces and geography

People and How They Live

"People and how they live" is the component of social studies that includes the physical characteristics of people; similarities and differences in habits, homes, and work; family structures and roles; and the exchange of goods and services. Preschool children can begin to explore these concepts by studying themselves and their families and by thinking about how classroom rules help children and teachers live together and get along.

These questions about people and how they live will help you design ways for children to learn these ideas:

- Who are the people in your family? What do they do?
- How do you make and keep a friend?
- What are the jobs of people in our community?
- How do people use money to get goods and services?
- What are some of the rules in your home, school, and community?

People and the Environment

"People and the environment" concerns the ways people change and protect the environment. For preschool children, this component includes such topics as building cities, making roads, building highways or dams, cleaning up a park, recycling, and preserving some green space. In preschool the method for teaching this content is to help children explore the areas around their homes and schools and to build on their ideas.

Here are some questions for children to think about as you help them explore the ways people affect and are affected by the environment:

- How can we respect and care for our world?

- What do people do that is bad for the environment? How do those things affect all of us?

People and the Past

"People and the past" concerns history. Preschool children focus on the here and now. They learn about chronological time in relation to themselves and begin to understand time concepts by noticing patterns in their daily schedules, what they did yesterday, and what they will do tomorrow.

Preschool children love to consider what they can do now that they could not do when they were babies. They can appreciate stories about other times and places if the topics are relevant to their own experiences. Consider these questions as you think about how to teach preschool children about people and the past:

- How do things and people change over time?

- How do we measure time?

- How do we talk about time? How do we talk about the past, present, and future (e.g., by using terms such as *this morning*, *after lunch*, and *tomorrow*)?

Spaces and Geography

Geography for preschool children includes the characteristics of the place where they live and the relationships between that place and other places. It also includes the physical characteristics of the children's world and mapping. This content is taught in the context of classroom and outdoor spaces by talking with children about how to navigate those areas. You can talk about mapping by discussing directions, e.g., how to get to the bathroom, the playground, and the carpool line. You can encourage children to build a model of their neighborhood in the Block area and to draw or paint maps of places they go. An important goal is for children to begin to understand that maps represent actual places.

These kinds of questions can help children understand spaces and geography:

- Where do you live? What is your community like?

- How do people move from one place to another?

- Where are you positioned in relation to other people and objects (e.g., near, far, next to, outside, or behind)?

- What is a map and how can it help us?

Connecting Social Studies Content, Teaching, and Learning

In *The Creative Curriculum®* classroom, teachers focus social studies instruction on the world of the children in their class: where they live and what they see around them. The chart below shows how to connect social studies content, teaching, and learning. The first column outlines the components of social studies for preschool. The second column shows some of the many ways social studies teachers address this content effectively. The last column gives examples of what preschool children might do or say that shows their increasing understanding of each component of social studies.

Social Studies Content	What Teachers Can Do	What Preschool Children Might Do
People and How They Live (Recognizing and respecting likenesses and differences among oneself and others, recognizing how people rely on each other for goods and services, learning social skills, and understanding the need for rules)	Create rules about getting along and cooperating in the context of real problems as they arise (e.g., "There was a problem at the sand table today. What rule can we make so everyone has enough room to play?") Provide paint, crayons, markers, and construction paper in various skin tones. Invite families to participate in the classroom and share aspects of their cultures. In the Dramatic Play area, introduce new props that focus on jobs (e.g., jobs in a flower shop, auto repair shop, restaurant, and grocery store). Visit different businesses in the neighborhood and discuss people's jobs.	Talk about family members and their roles. Describe their family members' jobs. Point out that their hair color is the same as someone else's. Use a toy cash register to pretend to sell shoes. Invite a child in a wheelchair to play catch with a ball.

Social Studies Content	What Teachers Can Do	What Preschool Children Might Do
People and the Environment (Learning how people affect the environment by changing it and protecting it; learning how people are affected by the environment)	Provide junk that can be used to create sculptures. Help children plant and observe trees in the schoolyard and collect trash. Talk about changes in the immediate environment (e.g., wind damage to a local building, fish that died as a result of pollution, or trees that were cut down to make way for a road or a parking lot). Set aside and sort plastic, paper, and metal for recycling. Recycle cardboard tubes and boxes by encouraging children to use them in the Block and Art areas.	Place trash in the classroom wastebaskets and playground garbage cans. Note, "If the tree on our playground is cut down, we won't have any shade."
People and the Past (Learning how people and things change over time)	Invite grandparents to talk about their lives as children. Ask children to bring in pictures of themselves as babies or to bring articles of their baby clothing. Discuss how the children have changed over time. Ask children questions that will help them recall the past (e.g., "What did you do yesterday when you got home?"). Explore toys from long ago. Teach children games you played as a child.	Hold up a baby shoe and say, "My foot used to be this little, but now it's big!" Say, "A long, long, long time ago I went to my Aunt Susie's house." Tell a friend, "I used to live in New York, but now I live here."

Social Studies Content	What Teachers Can Do	What Preschool Children Might Do
Spaces and Geography (Learning about the physical world and how we move about the world)	Provide board games like "Chutes and Ladders®" as a way of introducing beginning mapping concepts such as directionality and relative position. Create an obstacle course around and through which children can move. Show children how to mark the trees and swing set on a simple map of the playground. Encourage children to talk about the hills that they can see in the distance from the classroom.	Move a piece in the correct direction while playing a board game. Mold wet sand to make model mountains, hills, and valleys. Figure out how to maneuver around a tricycle path or an obstacle course. Use blocks to represent roads and buildings.

Objectives for Social Studies Development and Learning

Objective 29. Demonstrates knowledge about self

Objective 30. Shows basic understanding of people and how they live

Objective 31. Explores change related to familiar people or places

Objective 32. Demonstrates simple geographic knowledge

The Arts

Art involves designing, creating, and exploring. Children mix paints; pound and shape clay; build structures with blocks, boxes, and small plastic building blocks; dance; dramatize stories; clap rhythms; and sing chants and songs. Preschool children like to handle materials and move their bodies. Preschool teachers can introduce children to a wide variety of experiences in the arts throughout the day.

Components of the Arts

National standards for arts education include four components (Consortium of National Arts Education Associations, 1994):

• dance

• music

• theater or performing arts (which we call *dramatic play* in preschool)

• visual arts

You will find that these four components of the arts are discussed throughout *The Creative Curriculum*®. In addition to the ideas presented in this first volume, *Volume 2: Interest Areas* provides guidance on the visual arts, music, and movement (dance). Throughout the entire curriculum, emphasis is placed on the important role of symbolic and pretend play. Teachers address drama standards through activities in the Dramatic Play area, the Block area, the Library area, and the Music and Movement area. In addition, group activities are often opportunities for dramatizations. Here is how the standards for the arts apply to preschool.

Dance

When children dance, they use their bodies to express ideas, respond to music, and convey feelings. When you encourage children to vary their responses to different musical pieces, they learn more about how to move their bodies, and they use rhythm and space in many different ways.

Music

Music combines voice and/or instruments to create rhythms and melodies that express ideas and feelings. Children learn about music by listening and responding to many sounds. You should therefore provide children with opportunities to play musical instruments, learn and make up songs, listen to recordings, and talk about sounds. When preschool children listen to various kinds of music, explore instruments, create melodies, learn songs, and make up songs, they develop an appreciation for different kinds of music and become comfortable with different forms of musical expression.

Drama

Drama has a direct impact on other learning, including oral language development and literacy. In *Preventing Reading Difficulties in Young Children* (Snow et al., 1998) the authors report that children benefit from play-based instruction in which they invent dramatic play scenarios. This kind of sociodramatic play not only promotes oral language use and encourages children to practice storytelling skills, but it also offers a challenge for children to use language to negotiate their play. In turn, their oral language and cognitive skills support reading comprehension.

Visual Arts

For preschool children, the visual arts are painting, drawing, making collages, modeling and sculpting with clay or other materials, building, making puppets, weaving and stitching, and making prints and rubbings. Children benefit from opportunities to work with different kinds of paint and paper; draw with crayons, markers, and chalk; put things together with paste and glue; cut with scissors; mold play dough; and clean up with mops, sponges, and brooms. The more exposure you give children to all kinds of materials and the more you discuss different ways to use the materials, the more children become able to express their ideas and feelings through the visual arts.

The visual arts also promote an understanding of the world. Children learn to draw and draw to learn. Using markers, paint, paper, clay, collage, wire, and wood, children represent what they have learned about a topic. By doing so, they master art materials and learn about different perspectives, part–whole relationships, size, position, and the characteristics of people and things.

Connecting Content in the Arts, Teaching, and Learning

In *The Creative Curriculum*® classroom, the arts are addressed throughout the day. The following chart shows how to connect the content of the arts, teaching, and learning. The first column outlines the components of the arts for preschool. The second column shows some of the many ways teachers address this content effectively. The last column gives examples of what preschool children might do or say that shows their increasing understanding of each component of the arts.

Arts Content	What Teachers Can Do	What Preschool Children Might Do
Dance (Learning about the body's ability to move and using rhythm and space in different ways)	Offer children scarves and streamers to use as they dance to music. Invite children to move in different ways. Play different kinds of music that inspire children to move quickly (e.g., polkas) and slowly (e.g., lullabies). Teach new words, such as *smooth*, *jerky*, *gallop*, and *glide*.	Use scarves and streamers as they move to music. Imitate movements of animals they watched on a trip to a farm. Move quickly and slowly as the tempo of a march changes.
Music (Developing an awareness of different kinds of music and becoming comfortable with different forms of musical expression)	Set up an area where children can explore instruments, and listen to and create music. Introduce children to simple musical terms (e.g., *tune*, *melody*, *rhythm*, *beat*, *quickly*, *slowly*, *loudly*, *softly*). Teach children songs that are or might be familiar to their families. Make up songs or chants while pounding clay. Clap rhythms.	Make different sounds with musical instruments. Play musical games, such as "The Farmer in the Dell" and "Hokey Pokey." Say, "That music makes me think of a bee."

Arts Content	What Teachers Can Do	What Preschool Children Might Do
Drama (Communicating a message or story through action and dialogue)	Participate in and encourage children's pretend play. Gather props and invite children to act out familiar stories, such as *Caps for Sale*. Have children show you the facial expressions of people who are happy, sad, angry, tired, excited, or afraid. Provide puppets and props and encourage children to act out a story you read with them.	Gather props and act out *Goldilocks and the Three Bears* in the Dramatic Play area. Show the facial expressions of the troll as they retell *The Three Billy Goats Gruff*. Make up a puppet show for others to watch. Ask, "Guess who I am?" and then pretend to walk like an elephant.
Visual Arts (Using a variety of media to communicate; learning to use art materials; appreciating many forms of art)	Provide materials children can use to represent their ideas (e.g., markers, crayons, paints, paper, clay, collage supplies, wire, and wooden scraps). Talk about book illustrations and explain techniques such as torn-paper pictures, watercolors, and pastels. Provide materials in the Art area for children's exploration. Add mirrors to the Art area and encourage children to look at their own facial features when they draw people. Encourage children to draw pictures to show what they have learned. Display children's work attractively, prominently, and at children's eye level.	Create a torn-paper collage after looking at books illustrated by Leo Lionni. Use brightly colored paint at the easel. Try different ways to balance a mobile. Make a get-well card for a friend.

Objectives for Development and Learning in the Arts

Objective 33. Explores the visual arts

Objective 34. Explores musical concepts and expression

Objective 35. Explores dance and movement concepts

Objective 36. Explores drama through actions and language

Process Skills

When children learn content in literacy, math, science, social studies, the arts, and technology, they learn more than facts. They learn to communicate, think mathematically, do what scientists do, conduct social science research, create as artists, and use technology. These methods of learning, called *process skills*, are also discussed in chapter 1, "How Children Develop and Learn."

Children use process skills to learn concepts in each of the content areas. They observe and explore, make connections, solve problems, organize information, and communicate and represent their learning in many different ways. Process skills are part of the progression of development and learning for each of the content area objectives.

For example, **literacy** learning requires children to notice that some letters have curves and others have straight lines. They must also understand that letters represent sounds. This involves observing, making connections, organizing information so that they can recall it, and using this learning as they become emergent readers and writers.

Mathematics learning requires similar connections among numbers and numerals as well as constant problem solving. For example, as children learn that sets of objects can be separated and joined together and that shapes maintain their identities even when their orientations change, they have to observe and explore, remember information, organize the information, and solve problems.

For **science** and **social studies** learning, children use process skills as they investigate to find answers to their questions. These process skills are the investigative methods they use to learn about living things, the physical properties of objects and materials, and Earth's environment. They use the same skills to communicate information about themselves, to explore similarities and differences among people and how they live, to explore change, and to use simple geographic knowledge.

As children explore **technology** and **the arts,** they use process skills to experiment; to figure out what to do next; to solve problems of design, movement, color, sound, and language; and to communicate and represent their learning.

Integrating Learning Through Studies

If the objectives for development and learning are the backbone of *The Creative Curriculum® for Preschool*, then studies are the heart. Implementing a study well means bringing together all of the processes of learning with content knowledge and meaningful interactions. And studies of a science or social studies topic in a preschool classroom can be much more engaging and informative than you might think. Studies are an opportunity to really dig deep into topics that children already have some knowledge of and interest in. Working from children's everyday experiences, their observations in and out of the classroom, and the resources you have available, you can create a several-week study that challenges children to test predictions, find more information, represent their findings, and make conclusions.

In the past, the standard approach to tying content learning together was through the use of themes, which usually came from teachers' experiences, ideas shared by colleagues, or published guides and activity books. A common practice was to use the same themes year after year, whether or not the topic and experiences suited the interests and skills of the new groups of children. Although some themes worked well and teachers were able to implement them in a developmentally appropriate way, others were not appropriate for all classrooms. When teachers in Hawaii tried to use an autumn theme in October—even though the local temperature was a constant 80 degrees and the leaves on the palm trees outside did not change color or fall off—the material was not meaningful or relevant to children's experiences.

A more meaningful way to teach content is to build on children's knowledge and interests. We call this approach to integrating content *studies*. Educators Lilian Katz, Sylvia Chard, and Judy Helm use the term *project approach*. Much like a study, a project is

an in-depth investigation of a topic worth learning more about….The key feature of a project is that it is a research effort deliberately focused on finding answers to questions about a topic posed either by the children, the teacher, or the teacher working with the children (Katz, 1994 quoted in Helm & Katz, 2001, p. 1).

Whether you call it a *study* or a *project*, this approach involves organizing the daily program in a way that is both relevant and exciting for children. The strongest feature of a study is its support of children's dispositions to be curious, to explore the world, and to make sense of their experiences.

Throughout a study, you can observe and record children's comments and questions, their involvement with materials, their successes, and their confusion. Samples of children's work, photographs of their constructions, and photocopies of their writing can be collected and reviewed as you reflect on each child's learning. Using documentation and reflecting on children's progress helps you plan for the group and for each child.

Selecting a Good Study Topic

Studies begin with a good topic. Ideas may originate from any source: teachers, children, or families. The topic may center on something children are curious about (e.g., balls), a social concern (e.g., how recycling helps our environment), or an unexpected event (e.g., an invasion of ants in the classroom).

No matter where the ideas come from, good study topics excite the children and have enough aspects that can be investigated and explored. So what makes a good study topic? How can you know if you are on the right track? Here are some questions to ask as you decide the appropriateness of a topic:

- Does this topic address children's **interests** or potential interests?

  I have noticed that several children have been playing at the water table lately. They are really interested in some of the props and what they can do with them.

- Is this topic **relevant** to children's experiences, and is it **age-appropriate**?

  The children saw the water running out of the rainspout when they came to school this morning. We could make our own version of a gutter and rainspout that they can build on their own.

- Do enough of the children have **experience** with the topic so they can come up with questions to investigate and explore? Does the topic **build** on what children already know?

  Because the water table has been so popular lately, I think the children are starting to think of new ways to use the pipes, funnels, and other props.

- Can children **explore** the topic firsthand? Can real objects be manipulated?

  I bet we can find even more types of pipes to use with water if we look around the classroom. The children can look for pipes around the school, too.

- Are **resources available**, such as people to talk with, books to read, places to visit, and objects or living things to observe and explore?

  We could ask the plumber who fixed the bathroom sinks to come back and talk with the children.

- Can children do some research about this topic **independently**, without depending entirely on the teacher's assistance?

  It would be fun to have the children search for pipes at home. They might notice pipes at home that they've walked past many times and never noticed.

- Can the topic be explored in a variety of ways over an **extended period**?

  We can explore different materials used to make pipes and test them to see which work best. The children can use and observe the pipes over an extended period to find out which pipes hold up best.

- Will the topic permit children to use **literacy** learning and **mathematics** in real-life contexts?

  It would be fun to experiment with long and short pipes and see how fast the water goes through each. We could also use pipes of different diameters in our experiments. When we chart the results, we could save that information along with children's observational drawings to share with visitors at the end of the study.

- Will the topic encourage children to explore the important components of **science** and **social studies**?

  Having the plumber visit would be a great way for children to learn more about that important job and how it helps us. The plumber could also participate in some of our experiments.

- Can the **arts** and **technology** be incorporated readily into children's investigations?

  We can look online to find some really big water pipes. We could use tape to mark the area on the wall as big as the opening of the pipe.

- Does the topic lend itself to representation in a variety of **media** (e.g., dramatic play, writing, and constructions)?

  The children would enjoy constructing all kinds of pipe configurations for experiments. I could include props similar to the plumber's tools and see how the children decide to use them.

- Will you be able to communicate with **families** about the topic? Are family members likely to want to get involved with the project?

  Families might enjoy coming in to help with our experiments. I can also think of ways for them to use pipes at home with their children.

- Is the topic respectful of **cultural differences**?

  I will make sure to communicate to families the types of activities we will be doing so that I can address any concerns.

- Is the topic worth **studying**?

  I think this topic would really work well. It would be great for the children to begin to notice water pipes and how they are used everywhere. They can learn vocabulary and science concepts that would be applicable to other experiences.

Once you decide that a topic will work, you can begin figuring out how content might be addressed. Then you can collect resources and find appropriate experts and ideas for field trips. You will also want to consider how families can be involved.

The length of a study depends on many factors, including the children's ages and interests. Studies run on your program's momentum, not by a calendar. In general, a study should be able to sustain children's interest for 3–4 weeks.

Your Teaching Practice

You may want to brainstorm study topic ideas with other teachers and talk about whether or not those ideas can be turned into studies. Think about any themes that you currently teach or have taught in the past. Is there a way to take a favorite theme topic and expand it to become a meaningful study full of hands-on investigations? For example, an apple theme that includes cutting out and coloring paper apples could be a study in which children look closely at each stage of an apple's life cycle, compare and contrast different types of apples, learn whether or not they can grow their own apples, and discover what happens to an apple core after it is thrown away.

Using *Teaching Guides* to Plan and Implement a Study

Teaching Guides help you plan and manage your day while implementing studies. *The Creative Curriculum® for Preschool Teaching Guides* include detailed guidance about how to plan and implement a study as well as suggestions of what to do during all times of the day. Each of the *Teaching Guides* has been carefully organized so that the content area concepts and ideas are introduced in a logical sequence.

Planning for a study using a *Teaching Guide* does not mean that teachers need to make drastic changes to every interest area or go out and buy new supplies. Each *Teaching Guide* starts with what children already know about the topic and includes materials readily found in the classroom or at home. Sending out a letter at the beginning of the study to explain the topic and how families can help may be the only task needed to form a collection of relevant materials. And interest areas shouldn't change just because a new study topic is introduced. The *Teaching Guide* will suggest a few props or ideas for one or two interest areas as the study progresses. That means that a teacher's organized and engaging interest areas will stay the same with only slight modifications to allow for experimentation and further investigation of the topic.

The Three Parts of a Study

While studies are flexible and unique by nature, they are not without a structure. In fact, every good study shares common structural features. All of the teaching strategies we described earlier are used in engaging children in a study. Each study has three parts: beginning the study, investigating the topic, and celebrating learning. Each part has several steps.

Part 1: Beginning the Study

Select an appropriate topic. *The Teaching Guides* offer teachers a great way to begin a study. Or, teachers may have additional ideas that children are interested in. Topics do not need to be complex. Children show curiosity about so many things they encounter each day. After choosing a topic, use the questions from pages 125–127 to determine if the topic is ideal for a successful study.

Plan and conduct exploratory investigations. Your next step is to give children time to explore. For example, if you are implementing a study on balls, you would put out a variety of balls and give children time to play and explore their properties. As children investigate the materials, you observe, question, probe, and draw children's attention to different characteristics of the balls.

Obtain background information. The more information you have about a topic, the more creative you can be in planning meaningful experiences that address important concepts in science and social studies. In the *Teaching Guides*, we provide background information as a start. You can also learn more about a topic by talking to knowledgeable people, reading, and using the Internet.

Pause and reflect. Think about the level of interest and the curiosity children showed during their explorations. Revisit the questions on pages 125–127 and think about whether or not the topic is worth studying with your current group of children. If you can answer *yes* to most of the questions, you have found a good topic.

Discuss the topic with children. Find out what children know and record that information on a chart. Post the chart so you and the children can add to it as new discoveries are made. Ask children what they want to find out and what they wonder about. List their questions on another chart. This list will inspire the investigations that children conduct in the next part of the study. New questions will probably arise and can be added.

Create a web of important ideas. Creating an idea web is a way to think about the important ideas related to the topic that children could discover during their investigations. A web with space to record your ideas has been started for you in each *Teaching Guide* with space to record your ideas. If you are designing your own study, write down many topic-related words on small pieces of paper. Next, organize these words into groups on chart paper. Write a statement or a question that summarizes each group. These statements and questions are the important ideas that you want children to learn. For example, in a study about insects, the big ideas might include how insects move, what they eat, where they live, and how they help us. Return to the web throughout the study and highlight or circle what children have explored. That will give you a visual reminder of possible investigations.

Integrate content learning. Once you have explored the big ideas and concepts related to the topic and linked them to the content you want to teach, think about experiences to offer the children. What kind of investigations can you plan to enable children to discover the answers to their questions? How might you integrate this topic into classroom activities? How will you address early learning standards through the study?

Creating weekly plans. You can also add all of the "At-A-Glance" sections of each *Teaching Guide* to your weekly planning forms at once – this includes customizable activity content for every time of day, as well as suggested *Intentional Teaching* experiences that group children along the Teaching Sequence based on their latest preliminary or checkpoint rating in *GOLD®*.

Tell families about the proposed study topic. Involve families early in the study by sending home a letter describing the topic, inviting their participation and contributions, and suggesting things they might do at home in relation to the study. Let them know they will be invited to a special event at the end of the study so children can share what they did and learned. A sample letter about each of the topics is included in the *Teaching Guides*.

Part 2: Investigating the Topic

Investigations that enable children to find answers to their questions are the heart of a study. Each of *The Creative Curriculum®* studies includes four or five sample investigations that address the big ideas of the topic and are designed to engage children in finding answers to their questions. You can use these to get started, extend an investigation, and adapt or develop your own investigations. Investigating the topic includes multiple components intended to foster children's curiosity and support their learning of the topic.

Organize materials and plan experiences. Think about how children might investigate the topic in interest areas, during daily routines, and through group activities. Our *Teaching Guides* simplify this process and suggest the activities, experiences, and investigations you might use throughout the day.

Facilitate investigations. Use your group time to talk about which investigation questions children can work together to find the answers to. When interacting with children during choice time, ask open-ended questions to encourage further discoveries. Observe how children are investigating and suggest additional materials and resources. Decide whether you should teach particular content material directly. After investigating, bring the group back together to share findings and give each other ideas.

Document findings. Encourage children to document what they have learned by making representations (drawings, writings, diagrams, maps, graphs, collections, constructions, and the like) and displaying them throughout the room. You might also want to display some of this documentation in the classroom's entryway to share with families and school visitors.

Part 3: Celebrating Learning

When you see that children have investigated and found answers to most of their questions, think about a way to end the study enthusiastically. Some teachers have a celebration during which children share their investigations with others in the school and wider community and with their families. You can help children review and evaluate their work and think of imaginative ways to present their findings to others. The children's ideas and cues will lead you to the next study.

A Sample Study of Sand

To illustrate how a study comes to life in a preschool classroom, we show what each part looks like by using our imaginary class of children (ages 4–5) taught by Ms. Tory and Mr. Alvarez.

Part 1: Beginning the Study

Select an appropriate topic.

The children have been experimenting using their magnifying glasses to examine sand from the Sand and Water interest area. They have noticed that the grains of sand vary in size and color.

Plan and conduct exploratory investigations.

Ms. Tory and Mr. Alvarez provide close-up photos of sand, a collection of natural sand of different colors and texture, and contact paper to create sand specimens. For several days, Ms. Tory and Mr. Alvarez let the children independently explore the sand specimens in the Discovery area. During outdoor play, Ms. Tory and Mr. Alvarez point out sand in the play area and encourage children to notice how the sand's colors and textures vary

Discuss the topic with children.

At the next day's morning meeting, Ms. Tory brings the sand samples to the meeting area and encourages the children to examine and touch the sand if they want. She asks the children to comment on what they see or had seen outdoors. These are a few of the children's comments:

Jonelle:	This sand is so scratchy.
Dallas:	This one is so dark.
Crystal:	It sticks to my fingers.
Zack:	I see different colors.
Malik:	I saw sand on the playground. On the sidewalk, in the cracks.
Alexa:	I don't like the sand in the sandbox. It gets in my shoes.
Jonetta:	I saw sand at the beach. It was mostly wet.
Carlos:	Look how this sand is bigger than that sand.

After a discussion with the children about whether sand is a good topic for them to study, they talk about how they could learn about sand. Ms. Tory helps the children come up with a list of questions they would like to investigate:

Where does sand come from?

Why does sand stick to our hands?

Why is sand different colors?

How do people use sand?

Where can we find sand?

Why are there different sizes of sand?

Is sand like dirt?

At story time that week, Mr. Alvarez and Ms. Tory read books set in the desert and displayed close-up images of sand.

Create a web of important ideas.

They make a web of idea to help them decide whether sand would make a good study topic. By creating the web, they could see that many important ideas related to earth science could be explored

Integrate content learning.

They then explore whether a study of sand would address the academic content that they want to cover. They develop the following chart:

A Possible Study of Sand

Literacy	Look at informational books about sand	Learn new words related to sand (e.g., *grain, friction, dune, coarse*)
	Read storybooks related to sand (e.g., *Brian and Ron's Sand Pile Adventure* by Lori J. Parker)	Sing songs and do fingerplays as animals found in sand

Mathematics	Compare weight of dry and wet sand Measure and compare how high a ball bounces on pavement and in sand	Estimate how much sand is needed to fill a container and count the number of scoops used to fill the container
Science	Investigate how rocks, shells, or minerals become sand Use magnifying glasses to examine different types of sand up close	Compare sand from different places Observe how sand absorbs energy by jumping or bouncing a ball in sand
Technology	Use tools to explore the sand (e.g., magnifying glasses, a computerized microscope, etc.) Watch a video about rocks or shells being broken into grains of sand	Create a slideshow of close-up or microscopic images of sand
Social Studies	Find out where sand is found Invite a mason to lead the children in making mortar with sand	Learn how water and wind help break down materials into grains of sand Visit a construction site to see how sand is used

Making the chart enabled Ms. Tory and Mr. Alvarez to think about how to teach content knowledge and process skills during the study. Confident that they have a good topic, the teachers are ready to continue studying it with the children.

Tell families about the proposed study topic.

The teachers send a note home to families about the new study of sand and encourage them to think of ways in which they might become involved in the study. Tyrone's father, who works at a nursery where desert plants are sold, says he could come in and talk about sand. Jonetta's mother, who is a high school track coach will give children a tour of the long jump sand pit.

Part 2: Investigating the Topic

Organize materials and plan experiences.

Ms. Tory and Mr. Alvarez plan investigation options for interest areas and group times. Ms. Tory locates a number of Web sites that the children can use to study sand, and she makes sure there are magnifying glasses, contact paper to make sand specimens, containers to collect sand samples around the school, and other tools available for the children's investigations. She also asks the children's librarian to help her find books the children might want to check out.

Facilitate investigations.

Children are interested in investigating different questions, so the teachers help them form groups. One group studies where sand is found around the school. Another group researches the way sand looks. A third group explores how sand is used.

Document findings.

Over the next month, the children seek answers to their questions about sand. They make

drawings, gather samples, and use sand to create sand sculptures. They dictate stories about how sand is used in art and record videos of the children making sand from crumbly materials. The class takes a trip to a nearby construction site. The children interview Tyrone's father and experiment doing the long jump at the high school where Jonetta's mother coaches.

The children study sand for many weeks. They create a number of creations, homemade books, labeled sand collections, and murals to represent their findings. Throughout the study, Ms. Tory and Mr. Alvarez document the children's progress. They write observation notes and organize them in a class binder. They take photos of the children's creations and representations, and they keep copies of the children's books, drawings, writings, and audio clips for their portfolios. They use the documentation to help them track the children's progress with regard to objectives for development and learning.

Part 3: Celebrating Learning

Plan a special event to end the study.

When the children have answered many of the questions they chose to investigate, the study starts to lose momentum. The teachers decide to conclude the study. They ask the children to think about all of the work they have done and how they want to share what they have learned with others.

The children decide to hold a sand sculpture festival and to make an exhibit featuring their projects. Families, other classes, and the school staff are invited for a celebration of the sand study. Following the study, the class decides to keep the sand specimens in the Discovery area and the rock tumbler in the outdoor play area. The brick wall created with the mason becomes a part of the Block area.

A study of sand worked for Ms. Tory's and Mr. Alvarez's class that year. It appealed to the children because they wanted to know more about the substance they're drawn to in the classroom and in the sandbox outdoors. The teachers built on this interest and crafted a study that engaged children in meaningful investigations to find answers to their questions. The concepts children explored were related to science and social studies. They used skills in literacy, mathematics, the arts, and technology as they explored, made discoveries, and documented what they were learning. This is why studies are a powerful way to make learning meaningful for children and to integrate knowledge and skills in all content areas.

Conclusion

In this chapter we described appropriate content for preschool children and what teachers can do to help them learn it. We also explained the process skills children use as they work to master content knowledge and how engaging children in studying a topic over time enables teachers and children to integrate learning. With an understanding of content and how children learn it, teachers can expand the opportunities they offer children to acquire skills and understand concepts. They can make a direct link between the preschool curriculum and what children will learn in elementary school. When content is taught with children's developmental stages in mind, children are more likely to be successful learners who feel excited about and challenged by what they are learning. The next chapter defines the various roles of a teacher in *The Creative Curriculum*® classroom.

References

Consortium of National Arts Education Associations. (1994). *Dance, music, theatre, visual arts: What every young American should know and be able to do in the arts: National standards for arts education.* Reston, VA: Music Educators National Conference.

Hart, B., & Risley, T. R. (2010). *Meaningful differences in the everyday experience of young American children* (2nd ed.). Baltimore, MD: Paul H. Brookes Publishing Company.

Helm, J. H., & Katz, L. (2001). *Young investigators: The project approach in the early years* (p. 1). New York, NY: Teachers College Press.

International Society for Technology in Education. (2007). *ISTE Standards: Students.* Eugene, OR: Author.

National Council of Teachers of Mathematics. (2000). *Principles and standards for school mathematics.* Reston, VA: Author.

National Institute of Child Health and Human Development. (2007). *Report of the National Reading Panel: Teaching children to read: An evidence-based assessment of the scientific research literature on reading and its implications for reading instruction.* Washington, DC: Author.

National Research Council. (2013). *Next generation science standards.* Washington, DC: National Academy Press.

Tabors, P. O. (2008). *One child, two languages: A guide for early childhood educators of children learning English as a second language* (2nd ed.). Baltimore, MD: Paul H. Brookes Publishing Company.

Caring and Teaching

Caring and Teaching

The fourth component of *The Creative Curriculum®* framework addresses two aspects of your role that cannot be separated: caring and teaching. Everything you do to create a positive social environment in the classroom; to promote children's social–emotional skills; and to help them become competent, enthusiastic learners makes a profound difference in the way they experience school. Much recent research indicates that the way adults interact with children is the primary mechanism for child development and learning (Greenberg, Domitrovich, & Bumbarger, 2001; Morrison & Connor, 2002; Rutter & Maughan, 2002; Pianta, 2006). More than any other factor, the high quality of your interactions with children leads to positive outcomes.

This chapter discusses four aspects of the teacher's role in *The Creative Curriculum®* classroom:

"Creating a Classroom Community" addresses the social–emotional environment of *The Creative Curriculum®* classroom. Teachers purposefully create a classroom community by building a relationship with each child and helping children build positive relationships with each other.

"Guiding Children's Behavior" discusses the ways teachers involve children in developing rules for the classroom community, teach them the steps for solving social problems, and respond to challenging behaviors. Teachers guide children's behavior in ways that promote self-regulation and conflict resolution skills.

"Teaching Intentionally and Responsively" presents a range of approaches and strategies to support children's development and learning. Recognizing the many benefits of learning through play, we explain how teachers support children's learning in interest areas as well as during routines, transitions, and planned small- and large-group activities. It offers strategies for including all children.

"Assessing Children's Learning" explains how teachers track children's progress and plan instruction by using a systematic approach that is based on the objectives for development and learning. There are four steps in the assessment process: 1) observing and collecting facts; 2) analyzing and responding; 3) evaluating; and 4) summarizing, planning, and communicating.

Creating a Classroom Community

The Creative Curriculum® classroom functions as a community, a place where people feel safe, help one another, and consider themselves to be part of a group. A community nurtures social competence by helping children understand how to treat other people well and how they want to be treated by others. It also helps children learn to cooperate and negotiate, begin to understand friendship, and resolve problems and conflicts. As children learn to interact with peers and adults in complex ways, they become productive members of the group.

The Creative Curriculum® emphasizes community because the classroom is an important setting for developing the positive relationships that are the foundation for all learning (Pianta, 1999). In preschool, positive social relationships are the core of the classroom community. The social climate of your classroom is the most critical part of the learning environment because relationships with peers and teachers influence the way children feel in school and how they learn. When they feel secure and comfortable, children are free to do the work of learning. The relationships you develop with children and their families make more of a difference than anything else you do. Lasting positive results can be achieved through the supportive relationships you build with children—from the very first day—and the guidance you provide to help them work cooperatively and develop good relationships with their peers.

Preparing for the First Few Days

Plan carefully for the first few days of school so children can make the necessary transition and feel comfortable. Try to anticipate their needs and structure their arrival. Some children, especially those who have been in group settings previously, will have an easy time adjusting to a new classroom. Others will be having their first experience away from home or in a group. In either case, expect that the children are wondering about what lies ahead. If they could put their concerns into words, they might ask,

"Will I be safe?"

"Will my mommy and daddy stay with me?"

"Are my teachers going to like me?"

"Will my teachers be nice to me?"

"Will the other children like me?"

"What will I do here?"

In addition to the concerns children have, they are required to process a lot of new information in the first few weeks of a new program year. They have to learn

- the names of many strangers
- to trust adults they are meeting for the first time
- to interact with children they do not know yet
- what they may and may not do
- where things are located

- how to use and care for materials
- how to follow the sequence of daily routines
- what it means to make choices
- where to find and return materials

All of the strategies for setting up the classroom and planning each day help children feel comfortable and welcome. Even so, you may want to do a few things a little differently during the first few days. Here are some guidelines:

Keep groups small. Try to stagger entry dates so children can play and work in small groups as they get used to the classroom arrangement and routines. If you cannot have children begin on different days, have enough adults available to divide the class into smaller groups as you teach children about routines and practices.

Allow time for hellos and good-byes. At the beginning of the year, you can expect some children to have difficulty with separation. Make transitions from home to school easier by encouraging family members to stay for a few minutes and help children begin activities. Reminders of home can also be helpful. Invite children to bring a comfort item, such as a stuffed animal or blanket for rest time, or have family members record a favorite story, poem, or song.

Select activities that children can do independently. During the first few days of school, plan experiences in which children can engage successfully on their own or with a classmate. For example, put out simple puzzles, crayons and plain paper, props related to the children's homes, and self-correcting toys like pegboards with pegs. Teach children where to find materials, how to use them, and how to put them away.

Teach children your signal for getting their attention. Decide whether you will sing a special song, play an instrument, or hold an arm in the air until everyone pauses and stops talking. Whatever signal you choose, teach it to the children and practice it. Talk about why it is important to stop and listen. Explain that the classroom is a busy place that is often noisy. For safety reasons, having a way to get everyone's attention quickly is important.

Keep the first group meetings short. Bring the group together for an active and brief meeting (about 5–10 minutes). Remember that some children will not be ready to participate, so allow them to watch from a comfortable distance. Teach one or two simple songs or fingerplays. Incorporate the children's names and repeat them each day.

Take children on a tour of the classroom. Talk about the different interest areas and what children can do in each one. In the beginning, it is best to limit the number of activity choices. Explain that everything has a place and that the labels show where things belong.

Keep in mind that many children probably will not remember most of what you say. Be prepared to repeat your directions and explanations many times during the first days and weeks. *The Creative Curriculum® for Preschool Teaching Guide: Beginning the Year* offers detailed plans for the first 6 weeks with a new group.

Building a Relationship With Each Child

Each child is unique, but, to flourish, every child needs to feel accepted and appreciated. Your influence extends beyond the walls of your classroom and continues long after children move on to the higher grades. The quality of children's relationships with their preschool teachers is an important predictor of children's future social relationships and academic success (Peisner-Feinberg et al., 1999). In other words, the way children feel in your classroom is as important as how they think (Shonkoff & Phillips, 2000).

In *The Creative Curriculum®* classroom, teachers accept and respect every child, viewing all children as capable, competent learners. They convey the messages that exploring and experimenting are encouraged and that there is more than one solution to a problem. Mistakes are considered opportunities to learn. For these reasons, children experience a sense of belonging to a community, and that sense gives them the self-confidence to tackle new tasks and seek answers to questions.

Some children are easy to get to know and immediately form warm relationships with adults. Others are more difficult to understand, so it is harder for teachers to see their positive attributes and build positive relationships. Learning about children's unique qualities—what they like to do, how they learn best, what skills they are developing, what challenges they face, and with whom they like to be—can help you appreciate and respect each child. That appreciation becomes the basis for building the child's trust. Here are some steps for getting to know children and building supportive relationships:

Observe, observe, observe. The best way to get to know what is special about each child is to make purposeful observation an everyday practice. Document what you see and discuss your observations about children with other staff members. When you observe with an open mind, you find very useful information. Set yourself the goal of knowing every child in your classroom well enough to be able to answer the question, "How is this child special?"

Talk with children respectfully. Talk with each child just as you would talk with an adult. Avoid talking down or using baby talk. Use your best manners so children learn from your example. If you are not sure how you are doing, tape yourself one day and then listen to the way you sound. Ask yourself, "Would I talk this way to another adult?" You may be surprised at what you discover!

Be sensitive to children's feelings. Like adults, children want their feelings to be taken seriously, not ignored or belittled. Sometimes, in an effort to be reassuring, we make light of a child's pain or distress. We say, "Oh, that's not such a big problem," or "Where's your smiley face today?" Instead of making comments like those, use your eyes and ears to gauge how a child is feeling and then acknowledge what you see and hear.

Sometimes you can pinpoint a problem by observing and then make a specific, relevant statement: "It's hard when the person you want to play with is busy with someone else. It doesn't mean she won't play with you another time." At other times, you won't know what the problem is without asking. You will need to prompt, "You look as though something is bothering you. Do you want to talk about it?" When you listen to children and accept their feelings without making value judgments, you show respect and understanding. You also teach children how to manage their own feelings and interpret the emotional cues of others.

Validate children's efforts, accomplishments, and progress. Young children want approval, but adults have to be careful and thoughtful about making them too dependent on adult affirmation. Think about the message children receive when adults repeatedly say, "Good job. I like the way you did that." When praise is very general, children learn that they should seek and depend on adults for validation of their behavior and their work (Kohn, 2001). Praise involves judgments about a child's actions, so it can have an unintended negative effect. A child may think, "If I am praised, I could just as easily be criticized." The point is to promote children's confidence in their skills and in their ability to judge their work. You can help by being specific when you acknowledge a child's efforts:

"You put your coat on all by yourself!"

"That was a hard puzzle, but you did it! You didn't give up!"

"You figured out how to make the car go down the ramp faster."

Another alternative to empty praise is to ask questions that help children identify by themselves what they have accomplished:

"How did you figure it out?"

"What was the hardest part?"

"What helped you?"

However you phrase your responses to children, be sure that your words nurture their self-confidence and sense of competence.

Taking a step back and evaluating your relationships with the children you teach can be a challenging, but crucial, practice. Children's success in school depends largely on the teacher-child relationship. Remember to show interest in children's thoughts, feelings, and ideas. Use a tone of voice that communicates patience and acceptance instead of irritation and criticism. When reflecting on your observation notes for children, keep in mind how you interacted with them during those learning experiences.

It may be helpful to ask a coach or colleague to observe your class and give you feedback on your interactions with children.

Helping Children Learn to Work and Play With Others

Successful peer relationships are an essential part of social competence. Such relationships affect children's adjustment to school, academic success, and mental health (Berk, 2006). Most preschool children are eager to engage with other children. Their peer play has been developing since they were infants, and they are now ready to learn the skills needed to enter groups successfully and to sustain positive interactions with a small group of children. In addition to learning these necessary social skills, they begin to show preferences among their classmates and may play regularly with preferred children. As they gradually learn the skills needed to make and keep friends, they seek out particular children for certain activities.

Children who do not have successful peer relationships, who are rejected repeatedly by their peers, are in a cycle of rejection that they often cannot break on their own. They may approach other children in ways that invite rejection: showing off, acting silly, playing too roughly, or bullying or otherwise being aggressive. The more they are rejected, the harder they try to use the same behaviors that did not work in the first place. Some children simply withdraw.

To break this cycle, children need the help of a caring adult. The preschool years are a prime time to head off the negative consequences of unsuccessful peer relationships. The longer a child remains socially isolated, the greater the likelihood that he or she will behave in increasingly disruptive ways and academic achievement will suffer.

Children who are very shy also have trouble interacting with others. Because they are quiet and not disruptive, teachers might not notice their isolation (Rubin, 2003). Some children, such as those with limited English skills or with disabilities, may need extra help with positive peer relationships if they do not form them on their own. In a classroom community, the goal is for all children to relate positively with others and enjoy a special relationship with at least one other child.

Children need three types of skills to form successful peer relationships and friendships. They must know how to establish contact with another child, maintain a positive relationship, and negotiate conflicts (Kostelnik et al., 2009).

Establishing contact—To make contact, a child must use the behaviors that are required in their community and that are accepted by other children. These behaviors include smiling, asking questions, offering ideas, making positive comments, inviting someone to join him, or offering to share something. Children who are rejected at the initial stage of interaction often have not learned acceptable ways to establish contact with their peers. You can model the language they need to be more successful in their approach to others.

Maintaining a positive relationship—To form positive peer relationships, children must learn how to cooperate, share, show empathy, express affection, offer ideas, help, take turns, and express enthusiasm. Children who have these skills are acknowledged as members of their community, and they are viewed as reliable and fun to be with. The behaviors that cause trouble and isolation from the classroom community include aggression, unwillingness to cooperate, showing off, trying too hard to please, and acting in other ways that annoy others. By coaching and teaching intentionally, you can help children understand how their behavior causes them difficulties. At the same time, you can provide them with positive alternatives so they become full members of the classroom community.

Negotiating conflicts—Like all communities, classrooms are sites of disagreements. Because disagreements inevitably arise in any relationship, children must know how to resolve them. Children usually resort to either physically or verbally violent outbursts or withdraw from conflict entirely when they fail to maintain and deepen positive relationships with their peers. You can teach specific skills that help children learn how to negotiate conflicts peacefully and successfully.

Socially successful children express their ideas, explain how they feel, listen to others' points of view, and work out solutions to problems. As each child masters these skills, the whole community benefits.

Classroom Strategies That Support Positive Peer Relationships and Friendships

As you purposefully build a classroom community, you give children many opportunities to practice the skills they need to develop positive peer relationships and begin to make friends. It may also be necessary to take specific steps to overcome the rejection some children encounter. Here are some useful strategies:

Have discussions about making friends. One way to start a discussion about making friends is by reading a book on the topic. For instance, *Will I Have a Friend?* (Miriam Cohen) or *The Rainbow Fish* (Marcus Pfister and T. Alison James) can help you introduce the subject and begin a discussion.

Coach children. Both neglected and rejected children can have trouble entering groups. To help them, model language for asking questions, making positive comments, and offering help. Help children practice those skills. As children master them, coach them on how to offer trades, take turns, share, and converse. The more their overtures produce good results, the more children will risk trying to use those skills and the better the classroom community will function as a whole.

Pair children to work on a task. Partnering provides opportunities for children to work with someone they usually do not choose. Use opportunities to have two children who are not usually together share a job, such as helping you set up an activity. They may soon work together on their own initiative, and the classroom will be a more productive community.

Interpret children's actions. Children who have trouble entering a group and sustaining positive relationships often do not know what they are doing that alienates others. By describing their actions, you help them become more conscious of and therefore better able to change the behaviors that cause them problems. For example, you might coach a child, "Did you notice that when you sat down in the middle of the floor you were in the way of the block builders? Next time try asking the others, 'Where should I play?' Let's see if that works better." You may find that you need to stay with the child and continue to model language and appropriate behavior. The help you provide will contribute to a positive classroom atmosphere.

Point out the benefits. "Look at the smile on Crystal's face. You can tell she is happy because you shared the markers with her." A child who recognizes the positive consequences of a behavior is more likely to behave that way again, not because she is seeking praise from an adult but because the behavior pleased another child. That paves the way for becoming accepted more fully into the classroom community.

Minimize rejection. In any preschool classroom, rejection is a powerful and hurtful problem. One well-known teacher, Vivian Paley, noticed that some children in her class had all of the power and were excluding others. Feeling that this arrangement was unfair, she decided to put an end to the issue by establishing a simple rule: "You can't say you can't play" (1992). Paley discovered that having this rule was an effective way to minimize rejection and promote a sense of belonging to a community. At the same time, she helped less assertive children become more assertive.

As you observe children, you will usually find a reason why a particular child is excluded regularly. Find out what the underlying problem is and develop a plan to help the child. Your goal is for your classroom to be a community in which children relate to each other respectfully and where every child enjoys positive peer relationships.

Guiding Children's Behavior

Self-regulation involves being able to control impulses by not acting (behavioral self-regulation); planning and problem solving (cognitive self-regulation); and managing feelings (emotional self-regulation) (Riley et al., 2008). The ability to understand one's own feelings and the feelings of others, to regulate and express emotions appropriately, to control impulses, tolerate frustration, follow limits and expectations, and delay gratification are all critical to a child's success in school and in life (Bronson, 2000). Children learn how to manage their emotions, control their behavior, and plan ahead when teachers create a predictable environment and schedule and when teachers are consistent, trustworthy, and responsive to each child's strengths and needs.

Using Positive Guidance Strategies

You can do many things to promote self-regulation skills and help children experience the benefits of managing their feelings and behavior. These strategies involve learning to speak with children in particular ways as well as modeling the skills you want them to learn. You scaffold their learning by using particular language and other strategies:

Reflective statements show children that you are paying attention to what they are doing. Letting children know that you notice them can sometimes be enough to stop challenging behavior and encourage positive behavior. State your observation by saying, "I see. . ." For example, when you notice that a child has built a block structure, you might say, "Carlos, I see that you used all of the square blocks. You stacked them very high."

"I" statements explain what is happening, your feelings, and the reason for your feelings. They teach children that their actions affect others, and they support children's increasing empathy. As you label your own feelings, you also help children learn names for emotions: "I feel worried when you climb on the shelf. You could fall and get hurt."

"When…, then…" statements explain the expected sequence of behaviors. They let children know the appropriate next step and help children learn to plan: "When you put on your jacket, then you may go outside." "When you spill milk, then you get the supplies you need to clean it up."

Modeling specific language helps children understand what behavior is appropriate. Rather than say, "Good job," explain exactly what the child is doing and why it is appropriate: "You are sharing the crayons with Jonetta. That makes her happy because she wants to draw, too."

Modeling specific language also helps children learn how to handle conflicts verbally. Rather than say, "Use your words," when a problem arises, model the particular language they need in the given situation. For example, when a child tries to grab a truck from a child who is holding two trucks, you might coach, "Say, 'I want a truck, too, please.' Now you say it."

Offering choices supports children's independence and ability to make decisions. Choices give children control over what is happening. Limit choices to two. Make sure that both choices are acceptable to you and the child. Do not offer an unrealistic or unacceptable choice, such as staying alone on the playground. Instead, offer acceptable choices: "You may walk to the door by yourself, or you may choose a classmate to go with you."

Redirection provides a child with an acceptable alternative to unacceptable behavior. For example, if a child is throwing rocks on the playground, you might redirect her to throw balls instead. You would prompt, "I see that you are practicing your throwing skills. It's not safe to throw rocks because someone might get hurt. Here's a bag with balls of different sizes. You may choose which balls to throw."

Changing the environment can involve moving the child to a new location, adding or removing materials, or changing the time of day when something occurs. For example, after noticing that several children are climbing on furniture during choice time, you would talk with the children and designate a special time for small groups to practice climbing on the outdoor equipment. That will help children master the skills they need to climb safely.

Showing while telling involves talking to children about what they should do as you use gestures and other visual clues to show them. Focus on the positive—the "do" rather than the "don't"—and demonstrate the behavior you expect. For example, you would touch the jackets as you explain, "We need to put our jackets on before we go outside." You can also use this strategy to draw children's attention to other people's feelings. You would point to and look at Derek's face as you explain, "Look at Derek's face. His frown tells you that he doesn't like it when you poke him."

Developing Rules for a Classroom Community

Setting limits and explaining the consequences of behavior help children understand why rules are needed. Involving children in deciding the rules is a powerful way to encourage them to share responsibility for communal life in the classroom. Children are more likely to understand and follow rules they helped to establish. You will have to lead them through the rule-making process by first discussing why rules are needed and then helping them verbalize their ideas. Most children understand the concept of staying safe, and safety is the most important topic to address in a discussion of rules. Young children need clear, realistic limits, and they need adults consistently to communicate which behaviors are acceptable and which are not.

Before you meet with children about classroom rules, give some thought to which behaviors are absolutely essential to you. It may be helpful to think about categories before thinking about specific rules. Consider these categories:

- maintaining physical safety
- respecting the rights of others
- not hurting the feelings of others
- caring for the classroom

The following vignette shows how one teacher discusses class rules with children.

Ms. Tory:	*Our classroom has to be a safe place for everyone. I think we need some rules to make everyone feel safe here. Does anyone know what a rule is?*
Carlos:	*It's something you can't break.*
Ms. Tory:	*Tell us what you mean, Carlos.*
Carlos:	*It means you have to do it, what it says.*
Ms. Tory:	*So a rule is something that tells you what to do.*
Carlos:	*Yeah.*
Ms. Tory:	*What kind of rules make you feel safe? Take a minute to think.*
Tasheen:	*I don't like it when people hit me. It hurts.*
Ms. Tory:	*So, for Tasheen to feel safe, we would have a rule that says, "Be kind to others. We keep our hands to ourselves." Would that make anyone else feel safe?*
Zack:	*Yeah. No kicking either.*
Ben:	*And no biting.*
Ms. Tory:	*So everyone would feel safer if we were nice to each other. I'm going to write down your ideas on this chart to help us remember them. "Be kind to others."*
Susie:	*And no spitting. That's yucky!*
Ms. Tory:	*Okay. I think "No spitting" is included when we say, "Be kind." What happens when people run in the classroom? Is there a lot of room here for running?*

In this example, the teacher guides children to think about possible problems and to identify some important rules for the classroom. She restates children's ideas in positive terms so children know what to do, instead of focusing on what not to do. Children can grasp positive statements long before they understand negative statements. Additionally, emphasizing the positive sets a better tone. Limit the number of rules to about four and keep them simple:

- Be kind to others.
- Take care of our classroom.
- Be safe.
- Help each other.

Post the rules in the meeting area, where you can review them with the children. You will probably need to remind children of the rules regularly. Then use the "**big rule, little rule**" strategy in talking with children. Always pair one of the three or four big classroom rules with a very specific behavior you want to encourage (the little rule). For example, when children are not returning books to the proper shelf you would say, "'Take care of our classroom' is one of our rules. Books go on the shelf." If a child is tipping a chair, remind her, "Be safe. Keep all four of the chair legs on the floor when you are sitting."

When a rule is not working, ask children what they think the problem is. You may be surprised by how seriously they begin to approach problem solving when they are part of a community that respects their ideas.

Teaching Social Problem-Solving Skills

Conflicts are part of life. They occur frequently in every classroom. Because children get frustrated easily, it is tempting for adults to solve problems quickly by imposing solutions. However, quick solutions from adults do not teach children how to solve problems on their own. Rather, they encourage children to depend on adults to solve their problems. Therefore, in addition to having general rules, you need to teach social problem-solving skills directly. Using a problem-solving approach to conflicts among a few children and problems that involve the whole class is a powerful way to help children resolve conflicts increasingly on their own. Take the opportunity to teach problem-solving skills each time a conflict comes up.

Handling Problems Among a Few Children

1. Help the children calm down.
2. Identify the problem.
3. Help the children generate possible solutions.
4. Review the solutions and help the children choose one.
5. Check back.

Preschool children typically fight about actions or things. You will hear them say, "He took my book," or "She pulled my hair." Whenever possible, try to settle a conflict before it escalates. As soon as you hear voices rising, try to calm the situation by moving close to the children involved. Once a conflict has begun, the following steps can be taken to resolve it:

Help the children calm down. When children are upset, the first step is to defuse the situation. You might suggest a cooling-off time or describe what you think the children are feeling so they know that you listened to them and that you think their concerns are valid:

"I can see you're having a hard time waiting for your turn. It's difficult to wait. It makes you feel frustrated. Let's take a few minutes to calm down. Take a few deep breaths."

Many people think that batting a pillow is a good way to release anger, but the opposite is true. Hitting a pillow or punching bag encourages aggression. Other methods are better. Techniques for calming down include breathing deeply, counting slowly, and using positive self-talk: "Calm down. I can handle this." You can teach these techniques during group time when no one is angry and children are likely to be more receptive. Later, when stressful situations arise, you can remind children to use the techniques they learned in group time.

Another good approach is to establish a calm-down place in the classroom where children can go to relax or take a break. Such a place gives children a positive alternative to acting out or losing more control during a conflict. A calm-down place is not the same as a time-out chair in a corner. Rather, a calm-down place might be the classroom library, a loft, or a listening area. The designated area ideally will contain comfortable furniture, such as a rocking chair, beanbag chair, rug, covered mattress, or pillows. Just flopping onto a beanbag chair, curling up with a book, staring at tropical fish, or listening to a favorite tape can be calming.

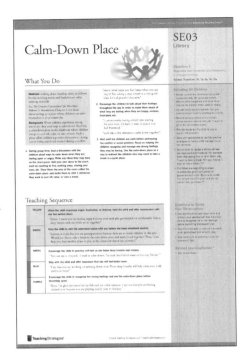

At first, you may have to guide children when they need to retreat and calm down. The goal is for children to recognize their own strong feelings and know when they need to take a break in a quiet space. In this way, children become increasingly responsible for their own feelings and behavior.

Identify the problem. Many childhood disagreements stem from confusion or misunderstandings. These can be addressed once children have calmed down. Let each child have a chance to speak. The goal is to have all of the involved children listen to each other. Like adults, children listen better when they think that they have been heard and understood:

"We need to be able to hear what both of you have to say. Tell us what happened, Leo. When you finish, then it will be Setsuko's turn to talk. . . Did you hear what he said, Setsuko?. . . Do you need to hear it again?. . . Do you have a question to ask him?"

Staying calm and neutral is important, even if you have strong opinions. Attend with your eyes as well as your ears. Repeat what you hear so children have a chance to correct any misunderstandings:

"You're saying. . ."

"You're feeling. . ."

"I hear you saying that. . ."

Have children restate what they heard. Then review each step of what happened, who did what, how each action made the other person feel, and what resulted. A light hug might reassure some children but not all. Open-ended questions encourage children to give their views of the situation: "What do you think happened? What made Kate upset?"

Some teachers identify a peace table in the classroom for conversations like these. Children know to go there to work out a problem together.

Generate solutions. Once children have identified their problem, encourage them to generate several possible solutions. You can start this process by asking questions: "What can we do about this? Do you have any ideas?"

If the same type of conflict occurred recently or you discussed a similar situation during group time or after reading a book, you can remind children of the solutions they generated then: "Remember when. . . Think about what you did then and see if that gives you an idea for solving your problem now."

If children are stuck, you might have to suggest some ideas or ask whether they would like help:

"What do you think would happen if. . .?"

"What do you think about. . .?"

"Would it help if we. . .?"

The goal is for children to come up with as many ideas as possible. One technique for encouraging a variety of solutions is to give neutral responses to children's suggestions by saying, "That's one idea. What's another?"

This approach also helps you avoid making premature judgments.

Review the possible solutions and choose one. Remind the children of their ideas and ask which one they think will work best. Begin by listing the ideas. Then ask, "What solution do you think would work best? Would that idea be fair to both (or all) of you?"

The goal is to arrive at a solution that each child can live with and for all involved children to think their needs have been met.

Check back. Once a solution is implemented, it is a good idea to check with the children to see how it is working. Of course, if the solution is not working well, they will probably let you know on their own! Explain that they are experimenting to find the best solution, just as scientists do. At a group meeting you might invite them to share what happened and talk about their decision.

Solving Problems That Involve the Whole Class

1. Discuss the situation.
2. Help the children generate possible solutions.
3. Encourage everyone to contribute ideas.
4. Help the children make a plan.
5. Assess the results.

In addition to problems that occur among a few children, there are problems that affect the whole class. These include fighting on the playground, excessive noise during choice time, and superhero play that gets out of control. Teachers sometimes think they have to solve these problems for children. In a classroom community, group problem-solving is a better alternative.

When the group is involved in solving problems, children begin to learn to manage the responsibilities required for community living, even if not every offered idea is helpful or even relevant. In addition, children will be more likely to accept and follow solutions they figure out, themselves.

The steps for group problem-solving are similar to the steps for helping a few children resolve conflicts (Levin, 2003):

Discuss the situation. Present the problem in simple terms without saying what you think the children should do. Share the reasons for your concern:

"I've been thinking about a problem, and I need your help in solving it. Lately, I've been noticing that there's a lot of superhero play in our classroom. It's a problem because it's very noisy and someone usually gets hurt. Remember, we said this has to be a safe place for everyone. What should we do to solve the problem?"

Invite children to offer their thoughts about the problem. Clarify and validate the children's ideas by restating what each child says: "So you think that. . ."

Help the children generate possible solutions. Summarize the problem and encourage the children to think of possible solutions. Let them know that there are several right answers, that many possibilities might work:

"Some of you think that superheroes only fight. Others think that superheroes can do different things, such as fixing items that get broken or giving out reminders when people forget our class rules. What are your ideas?"

Encourage everyone to contribute. Record their ideas and ask children to explain any that are not clear:

"Can you say more about that?"

"Tell us more about your idea."

Help the children make a plan. Review the list of solutions and ask children to choose the one they would like to try first. Explain how the solution would work and make sure everyone has the same understanding:

"A lot of children think that it's a good idea to have superheroes give out rule reminders. Let's think about what we need to do to make it work."

Let children know that not every possible solution to a problem will work. Explain that everyone will try the plan and observe what happens. Agree on a time to review the situation together.

Assess the results. Evaluate what happens. If the problem is not solved, review the children's other ideas or generate new possibilities. Encourage everyone to contribute and make a new plan. When a solution is working well, encourage children to think about why it works:

"Is giving reminders a good idea? What have you noticed?"

Establishing a classroom environment where conflicts are minimal and where children acquire the skills to solve social problems is part of building a community. A calm classroom helps children feel in control, understand that their feelings and concerns are respected, and know that together they can solve problems and create a peaceful place for everyone.

Responding to Challenging Behavior

The steps you take to organize the physical space, establish a clear structure for the day (as discussed in chapter 2), create a classroom community, and guide children's behavior will help most children develop self-regulation skills and function productively in the classroom. However, some children's challenging behavior might be so entrenched that you will have to address the problem very deliberately so that their behavior does not disrupt the class. The way you respond to these children sends a powerful message to everyone in the class.

Imagine how children feel when, day after day, they hear their teachers say,

"Haven't I told you a hundred times not to do that?"

"I don't care what happened. I'm angry with both of you."

"Don't you know better than that? You should know the rules by now!"

"Instead of going outside, you need to sit in the time-out chair and think about what you just did!"

"You know we have a rule about sharing. I'm going to put this toy away, and no one will get to play with it. I hope you're both satisfied!"

"You're making life miserable for all of us."

Statements like those make everyone tense and do little to help children change their behavior. Most likely they reflect a teacher's frustration at being unable to establish control in the classroom. The better alternative is to have a repertoire of strategies for dealing with challenging behaviors and establishing control in the classroom.

Common Challenging Behaviors

Testing limits, physical aggression, biting, temper tantrums, and bullying are among the most common challenging behaviors. Many caring teachers struggle with these behaviors every day. Unfortunately, our society glorifies aggression in many ways. Consider the television programs children watch and the toys marketed to children. Sadly, too many children experience violence or neglect, and their behavior shows the profound impact of these experiences.

Here are suggestions for responding firmly and positively to children whose behavior is challenging:

Testing limits is one of the ways preschool children discover how much power they have and the kind of authority with which they are dealing. Some children test limits repeatedly, and they need adults who understand children's need to do so. A clear framework for managing challenging behavior is helpful. Here is a framework recommended by Dr. Becky Bailey in her book, *There's Got to Be a Better Way* (2003, pp. 202–212).

1. **Acknowledge the child's feelings and wishes.** A child who feels acknowledged and understood is more open to hearing what you have to say. The first step is therefore to figure out what the child is trying to accomplish and verbalize what you think the child's intentions or feelings are: "You feel like climbing today," or "Those small beads are frustrating for you."

2. **State the limit clearly.** In simple terms, convey what behavior is not permitted. Be very specific and direct: "We use tables for our work and for eating. Tables are not for climbing." "You may string the beads. They are not throwing toys."

3. **Say what behavior is acceptable.** Give the child alternative ways to address a need or wish: "You may climb up to the loft or stand on the hollow blocks. Which one would you like to do?" "Let's pick up these beads first. If you want to throw something, you may throw beanbags. If you want to use beads, I will find some large ones that won't be so frustrating. What's your choice?" When children may choose between ways to address their needs, they are more willing to comply.

4. **Offer a final choice.** If a child is determined to test the limits, does not stop an unsafe behavior, and does not choose one of the acceptable options you have offered, that child needs your additional patience. Keep your message consistent and firm. The child must understand that the behavior must stop. "If you continue to climb on the table, you will have to leave this area and play in one without tables. It's your choice." If the child continues, lead him gently away, saying, "You are still climbing, so you will have to go to another area. I'll help you find a place to play safely. When we go outside, you will have a chance to do some real climbing." To the child throwing beads, you could say, "It looks like throwing is more important to you right now than stringing the beads. You may come back here when you are ready to string them. Right now, let's find something for you to throw safely."

The most important message to communicate is that the classroom is a safe place. Immediately stop any behavior that might injure someone. Keep in mind that challenging behavior of any kind is an opportunity to identify limits and clarify which behaviors are acceptable and which are not.

Physical aggression (hitting, scratching, kicking, and other behavior that hurts people) must be stopped immediately. Both the aggressor and the victim need immediate attention. Intervene by positioning yourself at the aggressive child's level. Clearly state the rule forbidding physical aggression. "Alexa, stop now! You may not hurt people." Involve the aggressive child in comforting the one who was hurt (if the hurt child permits this). This technique helps the aggressor understand the connection between his or her actions and the victim's pain: "Please get the ice pack from the freezer right away so Sonya can put it on her leg."

When a child is physically aggressive and loses control, you may need to hold her until she calms down. Ask a colleague to respond to the hurt child. Children feel scared when they lose control, and your firm arms can help that child feel safe because you have taken charge of the situation. A few minutes may be required, but the child will calm down. Then you can discuss what happened: "Do you want to talk about what made you feel so angry? I could see that you were upset." Reassure the child that you want to listen to her feelings. Let the child recover before discussing alternative ways to handle anger and frustration.

Biting, like other forms of aggression, requires an immediate response. Clearly state the rule about not biting. Involve the child who did the biting in comforting the one who was bitten, and talk about what caused the problem.

Refuse the idea that biting a child back teaches a child what it feels like to be bitten. That strategy only reinforces aggression. Instead, think of a way to redirect the child's energy and attention positively. When a child has great difficulty controlling the urge to bite, it may help to provide something that may be bitten (e.g., a clean washcloth) until the child learns to control this behavior.

If a child bites often, talk with family members to find out whether the child bites at home. Purposefully observe the child to see whether you can pinpoint when the behavior occurs and what might be the root of the problem. Develop a plan to stop it, for example, by intervening before the child reaches the frustration level. Observe, anticipate, and redirect biters before they reach their target!

Temper tantrums are a child's way of expressing frustration by screaming, kicking, and crying. Tantrums often occur when children have very strong feelings that they cannot express through words. When a child is having a temper tantrum, you have to act quickly to protect the child as well as other people and things. Some children calm down when you hold their arms and legs firmly. Others need you to be nearby and to hear your calm voice. Once a child relaxes, you can talk about what happened and what the child can do differently in the future:

"I could tell you were really mad. Your arms were going like this, and your face looked like this *(demonstrate)*. Your whole body was telling me that you were angry. You really wanted to play with the truck. Next time, try telling Juwan, 'Let me play with the truck when you are finished.'"

Many tantrums can be avoided by offering a developmentally appropriate and engaging program. Children who are tired or frustrated are more likely to have tantrums than those who are well-rested, fed nutritious meals and snacks before they get too hungry, and provided with age-appropriate materials and activities. Observe children to determine when and why they lose control. Learn to recognize the signs that a child is getting tired and frustrated. When a sign appears, direct the child to a soothing activity such as water play, sand play, or listening to music.

Bullying is a way some children exert control over others. Often the biggest bullies are the most fearful children. Their behavior has to be stopped and redirected. The longer children are allowed to bully others, the harder it is to change this behavior. When you see a bullying incident, be ready to step in. Help children verbalize their thoughts and feelings so they can learn to use language to regulate their behavior independently.

Bullies sometimes pick on particular children. They know which children will not stand up for themselves so bullies disrupt their play, grab their toys, and frighten them. Children who are victimized time after time as targets of aggression often suffer from low self-esteem. They learn to be helpless and to depend on adults to defend them, and the vicious cycle is hard to break (Slaby, Roedell, Arezzo, & Hendrix, 1995).

You can stop the bullying and teach victims to be assertive when an incident occurs or at a more neutral time such as a group meeting. For example, you might read a story about teasing and have children practice ways to respond. Involve children in practicing what to say if someone does something mean to them: "Stop pushing!" or "I'm still playing with it," or "Stop calling me that name."

Here is an example of how one teacher handles challenging behavior.

Derek grabs the truck that Jonetta is playing with and wheels it away. Mr. Alvarez notices that Jonetta just sits still as tears well from her eyes. Jonetta does not usually defend herself, so Mr. Alvarez steers Derek back to where Jonetta is sitting and says, "Hold on a minute. What happened here? Jonetta, you were playing with the truck. Tell Derek, 'No. I'm using the truck. You may not have it now.'" Then he continues to coach Jonetta, "You try it now." When she does not respond, Mr. Alvarez says, "Let's say it together first."

Determining the Causes of Challenging Behavior

Challenging behaviors are often cries for help. Children whose behavior is unacceptable may not know how to express their feelings in constructive ways. Focus attention on what the children need rather than on what they are doing. Try to imagine what a child might say if he or she could:

"I don't feel well." Health problems and conditions such as illness, allergies, lack of sleep, poor nutrition, or hunger can be causes of children's challenging behavior. If you suspect a physical problem, talk with the child's family and consider having the child evaluated by a health professional.

"I don't know what I'm supposed to do." Teachers often give children brief instructions: "Clean up." "Get ready." "Use the brush properly." When a child does not comply, the teacher might assume that the child is resisting on purpose. However, many young children do not understand what the teacher wants them to do. Vague words like *properly* have no meaning for the child, and he or she is not likely to ask what the strange word means. Children often need a teacher to show them what to do and how to do it, for example, how to hold a brush so the paint doesn't drip down the page or onto hands and clothing.

"I want you to notice me." Children need to feel important and valued. When they do not receive enough positive attention, they may seek negative attention. They have learned that, when they act inappropriately, adults notice them and spend time with them. Unfortunately, once children are successful in getting attention by misbehaving, they are likely to continue their unacceptable behavior unless the cycle is broken.

"I'm bored." Even in the most interesting and varied environment, some children are bored because they do not find new ways to use the materials and engage with other children. Make an extra effort to consider their unique characteristics and interests when planning activities, selecting new materials, and encouraging involvement.

"I want more control." Some children have very few opportunities to make decisions or to exercise control over their lives. When children are given choices, such as which materials to use, with whom to play, and alternative ways to express strong feelings, they feel more powerful and begin to develop self-regulation.

"I'm scared." Often the children who are aggressive toward others and challenge adults are fearful. To overcome fear, the children try to be powerful. To help them, try to find out what their fears are and what is causing them. Make a plan that will address their fears and reassure the children that they are safe.

Helping Children Regain Control

When children lose control, you can help them compose themselves by modeling calm behavior. This approach is not always easy because you need to manage your own frustration. Being human, you may get angry when a child's behavior is particularly challenging.

Keep in mind that you cannot help children develop self-control if you are out of control, yourself. Screaming at children, isolating them when they are out of control, and making them feel incompetent rarely produce positive results. These approaches only fuel the fire. Once you are in a power struggle with a child, you have lost the battle. Instead, keep the ultimate goal in mind: to help children develop self-control, not just to behave acceptably when adults are present because they fear the consequences of behaving otherwise.

It often helps to reframe the situation and talk yourself into a more positive way of responding. For example, suppose that a child is running around the room, screaming at the top of her lungs, turning over chairs, and throwing things. The interpretation you choose will affect the way you respond. You could think to yourself, "That's just what I would expect from her. I've had it! I'm going to show her who's boss." Instead you could think, "She is testing me. She needs my help. I need to be patient and consistent." The second choice can help you remain calm so you can respond constructively.

There are several steps to take in responding to challenging behaviors and helping a child regain control:

Intervene to stop dangerous behavior. Your job is to keep everyone safe. You cannot reason with a child who is out of control.

Establish a positive relationship with the child. A child who knows you care will be much more likely to respond to the help you offer.

Obtain more information by observing. Systematic observations over time reveal a great deal of valuable information about what triggers challenging behavior and which of the child's needs are not being met.

Talk with others who know the child. Family members can provide insight, as can other teachers and staff members who know the child. Multiple perspectives enable you to understand the child better.

Develop a plan. When a child's behavior is particularly challenging, meet with those who share responsibility for the child. In this way you are likely to come up with a plan that will be implemented consistently by all involved.

Implement the plan and evaluate its effect. The first plan may take time, and it might not be the best one. If it is not working, develop a new plan.

When you are dealing with challenging behaviors of any kind, remember that reasons underlie all behavior. Children whose behavior is challenging may not feel safe or connected to others. They may lack the foundation of trust necessary to experiment with constructive activities. They need adults who care about them, form positive relationships with them, and build their trust. They need opportunities to express their fears and anger appropriately through creative art, dramatic play, storytelling, and talking with caring adults. They need you to remain calm and to be helpful. Only then will they be ready to learn.

Teaching Intentionally and Responsively

Intentional teaching is complex. Teachers must keep many elements of practice in mind at the same time. They need to know *what, why, how, when,* and *where* to teach, and they need to know each child well. To be purposeful, teachers have to know *what* to teach, that is, what they want children to be learning. *The Creative Curriculum® for Preschool, Volume 6: Objectives for Development & Learning* provides guidance, and specific information about the content areas is offered in chapter 3, "What Children Learn." Teachers make learning meaningful for young children by using their knowledge of how children think and learn to determine *why* an experience or activity is likely to help children connect new experiences to what they already know and understand. The information in chapter 1, "How Children Develop and Learn" helps teachers understand child development so they can engage children actively in solving problems, using tools and materials, and interacting positively with others.

This section provides guidance about *how, when,* and *where* to teach. The *how* of teaching is the range of approaches and instructional strategies you use as you respond to children. What works to introduce, reinforce, and extend learning in one situation may be less effective in another. In addition, the various skills and concepts that children are to learn require different teaching approaches. Excellent, responsive teaching requires teachers to make decisions intentionally.

Because children have unique learning styles and needs, teachers also need to consider *where* and *when* to teach, that is, to determine the best setting or context for particular learning. Sometimes child-initiated learning in interest areas during choice time is best. Other skills require small- or large-group instruction. Still others can be supported or reinforced during routines and transitions. A skill or concept introduced during large- or small-group time can be practiced and applied during child-initiated experiences. This section also describes how learning occurs in interest areas, in large- and small-group settings, and during routines and transitions.

Using a Range of Teaching Strategies

As teachers work with children every day, they use a variety of teaching strategies individually and in combination in order to help children progress. The purpose of these teacher–child interactions is to scaffold children's learning. Scaffolding involves determining the level and type of support that will help a child become more competent.

Here are five basic ways in which teachers support children's development and learning:

Acknowledge and describe children's learning. This strategy begins with observing what children are doing and saying. Then teachers tell what they notice in order to validate what children are doing and saying. This strategy also helps children become more aware of their thought processes and actions.

"I see that you are making a tall tower. You used only long rectangular blocks."

"I notice that you are mixing yellow and blue paint. I wonder what new color you will create."

This strategy also helps children build their vocabularies.

"I heard you say that the fabric is rough. You described the texture of the fabric."

Sometimes you acknowledge initiative and independence from adults, and cooperation with classmates.

"You began cleaning up when you heard the signal, and I see that all the paint brushes were put in the bucket."

"You and Bryan worked together to clean up the blocks. It's much faster that way."

Coach children's efforts and make suggestions. This strategy involves scaffolding children's learning by encouraging them to attend, engage, and persist in the learning process beyond what they do on their own.

"You have been working hard for a long time, making that sign for your block fire station. You can find the word you're looking for in this book."

"That magnifying glass really makes the spider look big, doesn't it? I bet you can even see how many legs it has."

Sometimes coaching involves helping children use deliberate strategies.

"If you put your finger on each counter as you say the number name and move the piece to the side, it will be easier to keep track of which ones you have counted."

Coaching can also nurture imagination and flexible thinking as well as helpful peer relationships.

"You discovered a way to cut that heavy paper. Will you show Brenda how you used the scissors to do that?"

Extend children's thinking with open-ended questions, prompts, and conversations. Questioning children not only extends learning, it also gives you insight into children's thinking. There are two basic kinds of questions: closed and open. A closed question has one right answer. It can be answered *yes* or *no*, or with one or two other words. The teacher usually already knows the answer. Here are some typical closed questions:

What color is this?

How many are there?

What is this called?

What is the name of this shape?

Closed questions are easy to ask, and the answers give some insight into what a child knows. They are also appropriate when they are structured to encourage English-language learners to respond in English. Open-ended questions, however, require more thinking from a child and give teachers more insight. They usually require more than a one- or two-word response, and many answers are possible. Open-ended questions encourage critical thinking. If you ask a child, "What happened to the play dough? Why do you think that happened?" you are bound to gain far more insight about the child's thinking than if you were to ask, "Did the play dough get hard?" Here are some different types of open-ended questions that you can ask to extend children's thinking.

To encourage children to verbalize their ideas: "Why do you think the little boy in the story was afraid to sleep over at his friend's house?" (*Intentional Teaching Card* SE36, "You & Me Time")

To encourage observation: "What do you see? Hear? Feel? Smell? Taste? What did you notice?" (*Intentional Teaching Card* M07, "Ice Cubes")

To encourage predictions: "What will happen if you keep adding blocks to your tower?" (*Intentional Teaching Card* M84, "Ramp Experiments")

To encourage thinking about similarities and differences: "How are these two blocks the same? Why did you group these things together?" (*Intentional Teaching Card* M09, "Bigger Than, Smaller Than, Equal To")

To encourage children to apply knowledge to solve a problem: What can you do to keep paint from dripping on the floor? (*Intentional Teaching Card* SE27, "How Can We Help?")

To encourage abstract thinking: "What would happen if there were no cars, trucks, buses, planes, or boats? How would we get around?" (*Intentional Teaching Card* LL14, "Did You Ever See...?")

To encourage children to consider consequences: "What do you think will happen if you add more flour to the sticky dough? How much more flour do you need?" (*Intentional Teaching Card* SE23, "Related Consequences")

To encourage evaluation: "Why did you pick this book to read? What did you like best about the story?" (*Intentional Teaching Card* SE15, "Making Choices")

To encourage children to think and talk about feelings: "How would you feel if that happened to you?" (*Intentional Teaching Card* SE33, "Where Are My Feelings?")

Questions that ask children to consider consequences, make predictions, and apply what they already know to new situations are especially effective in building children's understanding. They challenge children's thinking, encourage children to make inferences and generalizations, help children differentiate important from irrelevant information, and lead to more meaningful learning.

While questioning is usually an effective strategy, too many questions or questions that are not responsive to what children are doing and saying can undermine your goals. Listen and observe children carefully first. When you do ask questions, provide enough time for children to think and respond. Remember that some children are quick to respond verbally; others need more time. Children who are developing skills in a new language and children with language delays or information-processing disabilities usually need extra time to process questions and respond appropriately.

In addition to questioning children, teachers extend learning by conversing with them. Conversations encourage children to talk about their work, make connections, solve problems, and reason. Here, too, it is important to allow children sufficient time to respond.

"I see you are using straws to make that. I wonder what made you decide to use them."

"Does that design remind you of something else?"

"What can you do to keep the tower from falling?"

Demonstrate effective learning behaviors. When teachers use this strategy, they talk about what they are doing and why they are doing it. They model a skill or behavior for children to imitate.

Teachers model ways to assist memory:

"I need to make a list of all the ingredients we need for our cooking project so I can remember what to buy at the supermarket."

They model ways to learn and use skills:

"This word begins with the letter *S*. That's the first letter of Suzie's name. It makes the /s/ sound."

"I'm going to use my hands to catch this ball against my body. Otherwise I might drop it."

They model ways to sequence and organize activities:

"The first thing we have to do before we begin our cooking activity is to wash the table. The second thing we'll do is wash our hands."

Modeling is also an effective way to teach the social skills that you want children to learn. For example, when you show respect to children, to other teachers, and to everyone else who enters your classroom, you show children what you mean by *respect*.

"Will you please excuse me for a minute, Tasheen? I need to answer Mr. Alvarez's question. I'll come right back to this table to continue working with you."

Give information to expand children's knowledge base and let them know what is expected of them. While teachers always want to help children make discoveries on their own, sometimes the most effective instructional approach is to provide answers or resources to satisfy children's curiosity quickly and enable them to move to the next level of a learning progression. For example, children who are learning to recognize numerals and the letters of the alphabet need to hear the names of the symbols.

"Yes, Carlos, that letter on our bucket of counters is the letter *c*. It is a small, or lowercase, *c*. The *c* on the bucket it is not the beginning of a person's name, so it is smaller than the *C* in your name."

These interactions with children support their learning in interest areas, during small- and large-group times, routines, and transitions.

Supporting Learning in Interest Areas

You teach intentionally every day as children play in interest areas and outdoors. The choices you offer children about where to play, which materials to use, how to use them, and whether to play alone or with others enable them to engage in child-initiated, or child-guided, learning. In these situations, children take the lead. They control the use of materials and create their play scenarios. They make discoveries as they explore and experiment, try their ideas, and observe the results. Here are two examples:

Dallas experiments with objects at the sand table, pouring sand from one container to another. He fills a small container with sand twice, pouring it into a larger container. Then he adds water to the sand, packs it down, turns it over, and says, "I made bread! Who wants some?"

Setsuko calls Kate on the toy phone in the Dramatic Play area and says, "Dr. Kate, my baby is sick."

Kate responds, "Come quickly so I can check her."

Setsuko brings her baby over to Kate, who uses a stethoscope to listen to the baby's heart. "She needs medicine," announces Kate. She takes a pad and pen, writes, and hands a page of the pad to Setsuko. "Take this 'scription to the drugstore right now."

In both instances, the children are developing understandings about concepts through self-initiated play. Dallas is learning about measurement (math) and what happens to sand when water is added (science). Setsuko and Kate are learning about jobs (social studies), the use of different tools (technology), and human bodies (science). They are recalling past experiences, and the girls are applying literacy skills. The teacher observes carefully and makes decisions about how to build on these explorations immediately or later. For example, she might decide to scaffold Dallas' learning by engaging him in a conversation and using comparative words (e.g., *more, less, the same as*). She might also add more measuring tools to the sand table. She might find out what ideas Kate and Setsuko have about how a doctor examines a patient and the various tools doctors use. She might begin by describing what they are currently doing. Then she could add props to extend their play and provide some coaching about how to use the props.

Take an active role as children play in different interest areas. Continually decide when your involvement will be helpful, how much support is needed, and what type of guidance to give. For example, you might add notepads and writing tools to the Dramatic Play area so children can make menus and take orders in the restaurant they have created. Another time, you might describe what children are doing and offer a challenge as they engage in an activity: "I see you decided to play with the tubes we added to the water table. Can you figure out a way to use the tubes to make the water go from one container to the other?" On another occasion you may decide to model a skill or behavior, for example, by showing a child how to use a balance scale to weigh rocks and compare them. When teachers talk with children about what they are doing and ask questions that challenge their thinking, they promote children's learning.

Child-initiated learning in interest areas is not a matter of chance. It occurs when teachers think about children's development and their knowledge of content to prepare an interesting and rich environment that offers children choices. All of the considerations about the environment outlined in chapter 2 must be addressed so that children can explore the concepts and practice the skills teachers want them to focus on that week. Child-initiated learning is supported by the arrangement of furniture and selection of materials, and by carefully planned daily routines and schedules. Effective teachers create extensive opportunities for children to make discoveries and initiate learning.

Supporting Learning Through Small- and Large-Group Instruction

While children learn many things through their play and through your interactions with them in interest areas, some skills and concepts require more deliberate teaching. Such instruction requires thinking about how to teach a concept or skill; the materials needed; and whether it is best taught to an individual child, to a small group, or to the whole class. For example, suppose that you want children to begin using woodworking materials and tools. Because safety issues are involved, you cannot let children explore these materials without specific instruction on how to proceed safely. You therefore show children in small groups how to handle the tools safely, and you discuss the rules that must be followed in the woodworking corner. With clear instructions, children learn how to put on safety goggles and use a hammer and saw safely.

Learning the alphabet is another example for which small- and large-group instruction is appropriate. While children explore magnetic letters and play with alphabet puzzles, they need someone to tell them the names and sounds of the letters. You display the alphabet at children's eye level in the classroom and use some morning meeting time to discuss various letters. You organize some small-group times for children to work with you and use magnetic alphabet letters. As children arrange the letters to spell their names, you teach the names and sounds of the letters.

Small-Group Times

In the course of each day, teachers conduct a variety of planned small-group activities. These activities are designed with particular learning objectives in mind. Each activity has a purpose.

Each child in a small group may be at a different level in terms of particular objectives. Your knowledge of each child's development with regard to the various objectives will help you determine how to conduct the activities. *The Creative Curriculum® for Preschool, Volume 6: Objectives for Development & Learning: Birth through Third Grade* gives you the developmental progression for each objective that you will be assessing formally. This information helps you think about individualizing activities for different children. *Intentional Teaching Cards*™ also show you how to adapt activities appropriately.

The following example shows how a teacher might guide learning during a small-group activity. It is the beginning of the year, and she chooses to use a material that invites exploration and enables her to observe children's use of a variety of math skills.

A Small-Group Activity

During choice time, Ms. Tory invites five children to join her on the rug for a small-group activity. She brings a collection of bottle caps and asks each child to take a pile to explore. Ms. Tory has a set of caps as well. As she begins using caps, she observes how the children are using theirs, and she listens to what they say. She remarks, "Leo, you put all the red caps, blue caps, yellow caps, and orange caps together. I'm going to do that with mine."

Leo points out, "You have more blue caps than orange."

Ms. Tory responds, "You're right, Leo. I have more blue caps."

Janelle draws Ms. Tory's attention to her caps. "Look, I made a pattern! Red cap, white cap; red cap, white cap; red, white; red, white; red, white."

Ms. Tory says, "I wonder what will come next. Blue? Yellow?"

Janelle laughs, "No, red will come next!"

Ms. Tory notices that Janelle has become very skilled at making patterns and does so each time she works with collectibles. Ms. Tory says, "I'm going to start a pattern, and I bet I can trick you! Watch this." Ms. Tory lines up her caps as follows: red, blue, yellow, red, blue, yellow, red, blue.

Janelle touches each one, names the color, and then exclaims, "You can't trick me! I know what comes next. Yellow!"

While Janelle makes patterns with her caps, Ben watches and says, "Look Ms. Tory, I can make a pattern, too!"

Kate organizes her caps into a long line and begins counting them. She counts to ten correctly, but then she gets confused about which caps she has already counted. Ms. Tory asks, "May I count them with you?" Carlos, who has been stacking his caps, wants to join in, too. "One, two, three. . ."

Ms. Tory moves each cap aside as they count together.

Ms. Tory announces to the group that cleanup time will be in a few minutes. Then she makes a game of cleaning up. "Find all your caps that have writing on them and put them into the bucket."

Carlos says, "I want to try. Find all the caps that are black and put them in the bucket."

Janelle takes a turn. "Find all the caps with bumpy sides and put them in the bucket."

The children continue taking turns until all of the caps are put away. While the children finish cleaning up, Ms. Tory takes a few minutes to write notes about her observations of the children in the small group.

This small-group activity was successful for many reasons:

- The activity was short (10–15 minutes).
- The teacher modeled use of the materials.
- All children had materials to use.
- Children played at their own developmental levels.
- The teacher observed how the children used the materials, and she offered additional challenges.
- The children observed each other and shared ideas and problem-solving strategies. They learned new ways to use the materials by watching each other.
- Skills related to multiple objectives were addressed during this activity: patterning, counting, classifying, and problem solving.

You can design your own small-group activities and get ideas from *Intentional Teaching Cards*. For example, you might choose the card "Which Has More?" The activity focuses on Objective 20, "Uses number concepts and operations." You gather the materials: ice cube trays or clean egg cartons; resealable bags; and collections of similarly sized objects such as counters, coins, and colored chips. Prepare five bags, each with a different type and number of objects. For example, put one counter in a bag, two coins in a second bag, and three colored chips in a third bag. Invite a small group to join you, display the bags for them to explore, and pose different challenges to different children. Here are some suggestions:

• Have a child select two bags and ask the group to predict which bag has more. Ask, "Which bag has more? How do you know?" Encourage children to use the ice cube tray or egg carton to count the items in each bag and compare the totals.

• Ask a child to select three bags and tell you which bag has the most or fewest objects. Ask the child to tell you how many more objects are in the larger group. Then continue, "You're right, there are more colored chips than coins. How many more chips are there? How many coins would we need to add to have the same number of chips and coins?"

Pose different levels of challenge according to what you know about each child's skill development. The *Intentional Teaching Card* shows the teaching sequence, so you know how to adapt the activity appropriately. Continue as long as the activity interests the children. Then put the bags and trays in the Toys and Games area for use during choice time.

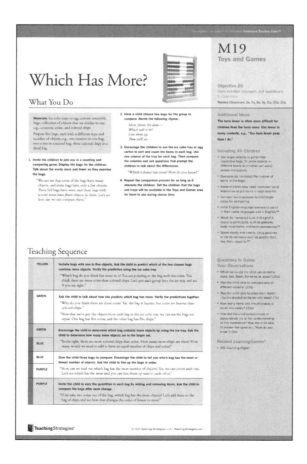

Large-Group Times

You also gather all of the children together several times each day. The first and last meetings of the day are two examples. At other times, the whole class may be together to listen to a story, to participate in a music and movement activity, or to discuss a topic the children are studying. These meetings enable children to learn to be part of a large group as well as to learn particular information.

In the following example of a large-group meeting, Mr. Alvarez wants to teach the children how to use and care for materials. He knows he cannot assume that children know how to do this and recognizes that they must be shown.

Introducing Materials to the Class

Mr. Alvarez decides to introduce unit blocks to the class. He structures the meeting in a way that will encourage children to explore blocks freely. He brings a selection of blocks to the meeting area and invites each child to choose and play with several of them.

Mr. Alvarez:	*What do you notice about these blocks?*
Ben:	*Smooth. They're smooth.*
Mr. Alvarez:	*Ben noticed how smooth the blocks are.*
Carlos:	*Pretty heavy.*
Mr. Alvarez:	*They're kind of heavy, aren't they?*
Kate:	*Mine have points.*
Mr. Alvarez:	*Kate noticed that her blocks have points, or corners, on them.*
Sonya:	*I have a triangle.*
Leo:	*Two little ones fit on this long one.*
Mr. Alvarez:	*Yes, Leo. If you run out of long rectangular blocks, you can use two of the smaller rectangular blocks to make a long one. That's a good thing to know.*

He then invites the children to think of ways to use the blocks, and he comments on what they build. After several children have shared their ideas, he concludes the discussion.

Mr. Alvarez:	*In our classroom, you may use the toys in many ways. You just saw that we can do a lot of things with unit blocks. These blocks will be here every day. During choice time, the Block area is one of the areas you may choose, and you may make whatever you want with the blocks. When you are finished, there's a special way to tell where the blocks go on the shelf. Who can figure out where this long unit block belongs? Can you show us, Janelle? When we put blocks away in their right places, children know exactly where to find them when they want to use them.*

When you introduce materials at the beginning of the year and each time you put out something new, you have opportunities to talk about how to use them properly and where they will be kept. You and the children can also brainstorm creative uses. Introducing materials in this way generates interest and often motivates children to try activities they might otherwise ignore or avoid. You can also take the opportunity to reinforce the idea that cleaning up is everyone's responsibility.

Sometimes a large-group meeting takes place spontaneously because the teacher wants to take advantage of a teachable moment. In the following example, Ms. Tory decides to bring the group together because there is an opportunity for intentional teaching. She and the children have just returned from a walk in the neighborhood. They want to talk about what they saw, so Ms. Tory pulls the group together.

A Teachable Moment

Ms. Tory:	*We saw many things on our walk. Let's make a list so we remember them. I'll write down what you say.*
Crystal:	*We saw a digging machine.*
Ms. Tory:	*That's right, Crystal. It's called a* bulldozer.
Derek:	*And a big bus.*
Juwan:	*And lots of bugs!*

Ms. Tory writes the words *bulldozer*, *big bus*, and *bugs* on chart paper and asks everyone to say each word with her as a group as she points to it.

Tasheen:	*Hey, those all start the same.*
Ms. Tory:	*They sure do:* bulldozer, big bus, bugs. *She draws a line under each* b *and says, "They all start with the letter* b. *I'm thinking of something else we saw on our walk that starts with the /b/ sound. It sounds like utterfly."*
Children:	*Butterfly!*

Whenever you want to teach a skill or concept directly, it makes sense to consider whether it is best to work with children in a small group, in a large group, or individually.

Supporting Learning During Routines and Transitions

Routines and transitions are also opportunities for intentional teaching. These times often involve waiting, for example, while getting ready for lunch, lining up to go outside, getting outdoor clothes on, or getting everyone settled for a read-aloud time. Sometimes teachers plan to teach particular skills and concepts during these times. Activities should relate to specific objectives for development and learning. You can invent your own brief activities or use the *Mighty Minutes®* cards. Each *Mighty Minutes®* card lists primary and related objectives, and directions for what to do and say. It also suggests variations so that you can conduct the activity in different ways at different times, sometimes changing the primary objective.

Some *Mighty Minutes®* activities involve songs or chants. For example, "This Old Man" focuses on Objective 15, "Demonstrates phonological awareness, phonics skills, and word recognition." Teachers introduce the song with motions for each line. They emphasize the words that rhyme with the numbers in the song.

Other *Mighty Minutes®* activities require particular materials. For example, "Sorting Syllables," which also focuses on phonological awareness, involves using three hula hoops labeled with the numerals *1*, *2*, and *3*. Each child selects a small object and says its name. The children indicate the number of syllables in the object's name by clapping. Then they put the object in the corresponding hula hoop circle.

Including All Children

Teachers often think that they have to do something dramatically different in the classroom to accommodate children with special needs. This is not usually the case. As you develop relationships with children and use a variety of teaching strategies, you will be able to judge how children respond and which strategies work best in which situation. In the following sections we offer additional guidance about meeting the strengths and needs of children who are advanced learners, those with disabilities, and children who are English-language learners.

Teaching Children Who Are Advanced Learners

The teacher's role is to provide all children with appropriately challenging and stimulating experiences. Advanced learners are often eager to explore a topic in greater depth and approach studies that interest them with a high level of enthusiasm and intensity. Here are a few suggestions for meeting the needs of advanced learners:

Stock interest areas with interesting and challenging materials. Create an environment that promotes curiosity, experimentation, and independent exploration.

Follow the child's interests. When a child has a keen interest, such as in dinosaurs or helicopters, help him explore it by providing books and other resources. It is not necessary to involve the entire class in exploring the topic, but do include others who share the interest.

Teach to the child's strengths. For example, if a child already recognizes numerals, there is no need to keep repeating their names to her. Find out what else the child knows about mathematics and offer challenging problems to solve. Boredom can be an advanced learner's greatest enemy.

Have realistic expectations. Keep in mind that being talented in one area of development does not mean that a child is advanced in all areas. A mathematically advanced child might not be advanced in terms of physical, social–emotional, or language skills. You need to individualize your approach to match each child's unique profile of skills.

If a child can read, find books that are at or slightly below his reading level for pleasure reading. For instructional purposes, find books that are slightly above his reading level. The important point to remember in selecting books for this child is that, while he may read, he is still a preschooler. The content of books written for older children may not appeal to or be appropriate for a 3- to 5-year-old child, so you will have to choose thoughtfully.

Remember that advanced learners are children first. Keep in mind that these children sometimes feel different and have special social–emotional needs. They need adults to accept their differences and help them feel understood and supported.

Teaching Children With Disabilities

Thoughtful planning can help you address the needs of children with disabilities so they are included fully in the program. Think about your environment, how your day flows, and what obstacles keep children from participating and feeling competent. As you observe the children in your classroom, think about what you can do to help them participate fully. In order to take part in classroom routines and activities, children must understand what to do, be able to access materials easily, and communicate their ideas and feelings. Here are some ways to promote the involvement of all children. Many children in your class will benefit from these planned supports.

Here are strategies to help children understand and participate in routines and activities:

Use visual and tactile cues.

- Provide color-coded cubbies or cubby labels with children's pictures and names to help them understand where to put their belongings when they arrive.
- Create placemats with outlines of a plate, fork, spoon, napkin, and cup. Use potholders to designate places for large bowls, serving plates, and so on. These cues tell children how to set the table.
- Use multisensory ways to present stories, fingerplays, and songs so children have more than one way to get information and to participate.
- Use plastic bins with picture and word labels to help children know where to find and return toys and other materials.

Use picture sequences.

- Use photos or drawings to illustrate the events of the day on a written schedule.
- Review the schedule with children upon arrival and at various points during the day.
- Post the steps of routines such as handwashing.
- Help a child identify the completed step and point to the next step on an illustrated poster of the routine.

Prepare children for transitions.

- Provide auditory cues, gestures, and other visual cues when you want children to change what they are doing.
- Give children 5-minute, 2-minute, and 1-minute warnings about transitions.
- Establish consistent closing routines so that they are predictable and promote independence.

Use peer buddies.

- Identify children who have strengths in different areas and build peer-mentoring capabilities.
- Assign partners to work together to complete tasks and follow routines.

Help children communicate.

- Provide pictures or objects so that children can indicate choices by pointing. For example, a child can point to a block to indicate his choice of going to the Block area. Start with two choices and gradually increase the number.
- Label spaces, objects, and materials with photos or simple drawings and with writing.
- Anticipate the words and phrases children might use during choice, group, and story times. Record these responses on a child's communication device and label each response with a picture.

Here are suggestions for helping children use toys and materials:

Select materials that are easy to use.

- Provide toys and materials with large parts that require little physical effort.
- Use writing and drawing tools with large, built-up handles.
- Use special equipment and assistive technology when appropriate.

Keep materials within children's reach.

- Provide a table or another work area with a nonslip surface that helps keep materials in place.
- Make sure each child is positioned comfortably and securely and within reach of the materials.
- Provide large or bright materials that are easy to see and reach.

Provide a variety of materials.

- Provide a variety of materials with a range of sensory features (e.g., visual, auditory, tactile). They should interest the children and have varying levels of complexity.
- Limit the number of materials, parts, or toys, and give them to a child one at a time.

Simplify the activity.

- Explain the steps of an activity. Provide pictures of each step.
- Adjust the number of steps according to the amount of task analysis a child can manage.
- Pace directions according to the amount of information a child can handle at one time.

Evaluate the effectiveness of your teaching strategies. You may find that you want to continue some but also try other approaches. With the support provided by your intentional teaching, children with disabilities can thrive in *The Creative Curriculum®* classroom.

Teaching English-Language Learners

As outlined in chapter 1, children who are learning English as a second language follow a developmental progression as they learn English. You can support them by using teaching strategies that meet their needs and help them build on what they already know. Here are some suggestions:

Learn some words in the children's home languages and use them as you speak with children and make classroom labels. Seeing and hearing their home languages make children feel welcome and safe in an environment where people are speaking a new language.

Use objects and gestures to communicate with children who are at the nonverbal/ observational level. Remember that they are still actively learning, observing, and making sense of what is going on around them, even though they are not speaking in the classroom. Make them feel included in the classroom community.

Use objects and hands-on experiences to support children's comprehension of language and content area concepts, and to help children transition from nonverbal communication to using a few words. Focus on the children's intent, and extend or repeat what they say.

Offer encouragement as children feel more confident and begin conversing in English. Avoid correcting the children's grammar, but model correct language in your conversations.

Use pictures and gestures that help children grasp the complexities of English, especially when they begin to use more formal language.

In addition to these strategies, you can use general strategies to help all children improve their communication skills. These include the following practices (Tabors, 2008; De Houwer, 1999):

Establish a classroom community in which everyone assumes responsibility for helping others and in which children practice language skills together. Explicitly teach them how to help one another.

Create a language-rich environment in which materials are labeled in English and the children's home languages (see chapter 2). Stock interest areas with high-quality books and other print materials in children's home languages as well as in English. Children need to have ongoing experiences in both languages.

Use lots of repetition, running commentary, and actions as you talk (e.g., "Now I'm putting the block on the shelf."). Describing what children are doing helps to enlarge the children's vocabularies and increase knowledge of syntax.

Establish a predictable sequence of daily routines so children know what comes next in the schedule. Discussing the schedule also helps children learn the names of events (e.g., *choice time, lunch, rest time, group meeting*).

Encourage children's sociodramatic play. Provide background information, introduce props, and explain roles. Sometimes children whose first language is not English need scripted dialogue to enter and sustain play.

Be patient. Give children time to express themselves. Do not rush them.

Choose predictable books for story time. These books tend to repeat phrases and are written in simple language. Bring props and act out the story as you read. Read the same books to children many times. Encourage children to "read" to one another and to retell familiar stories.

Involve families by encouraging them to continue speaking their primary languages at home and when they visit the classroom. Invite them to record books on tape or help make signs and books for the classroom in their home languages.

Keep in mind that your attitude is very important. If you appreciate the value of bilingualism, all children will benefit, not only those who do not yet speak English.

Assessing Children's Learning

In early childhood education, assessment is the process of gathering information about children in order to make decisions. Assessment has at least four purposes (Bowman et al., 2001, p. 234):

- to support learning
- to identify special needs
- to evaluate programs and monitor trends
- to respond to program and school accountability requirements

While programs need information for all of these purposes, the purpose that is most important to the everyday work of teachers is to support learning. A process for ongoing assessment enables teachers to gather information about each child in order to plan instruction and ensure that every child is making progress. Curriculum and assessment go together. The link between them is especially strong for teachers who use both *The Creative Curriculum*® and the *GOLD*® assessment system. While designed to be used by any developmentally appropriate program serving children birth through kindergarten, that assessment system uses the same 38 objectives as *The Creative Curriculum*®.

If you are using a different assessment system, it should be compatible with *The Creative Curriculum® for Preschool* objectives for development and learning. Whatever system you use, there are four steps in the assessment process: 1) observing and collecting facts; 2) analyzing and responding; 3) evaluating; and 4) summarizing, planning, and communicating.

Step 1. Observing and Collecting Facts

In your work, you observe young children every day. You watch what they do, listen to what they say, and decide how to respond. This process happens so quickly, you may not even be aware of its importance. Ongoing observation is an essential part of connecting curriculum and assessment, and it is the basis for effective teaching. Excellent teaching depends upon observation. When you observe to find out what is unique and special about each child, you have a basis for building a positive relationship with each and for planning experiences that will enable him or her to flourish. As Jablon, Dombro, and Dichtelmiller state, "There is always something new to learn about a child—even a child you think you know well" (2007, p. 14). To help you remember and use what you learn from your observations, you need to set up a system that works for you.

Setting Up a System

A system is an organized way to keep track of your observations, make sure that you have documented each child's development and learning, and store samples of work. If you are using *GOLD®,* the system for organizing and storing observations notes and digital samples of children's work is already set up. Each child has a *Child Assessment Portfolio* for storing information either online or on paper. You can enter documentation directly into children's online portfolios, or you can upload documentation from the *GOLD®* Documentation app. If you are using another assessment system, you can organize a notebook by each child's name. Samples of children's work can be stored in large envelopes, clean pizza boxes, cardboard magazine holders, accordion files, or hanging files. You may also need a system to name and organize digital photos as well as audio- and videoclips.

Because observing is your method for learning what each child knows and can do, you need ways easily to record what you see. It is best to make notes during or immediately after an observation, so you will want to have some convenient ways to do so. You can add more detail to your notes later. Here are some ideas for recording your observations:

- Use mailing labels or sticky notes to write what you see and hear. Each day, place on a clipboard three or four notes or labels with the names of the children whom you want to observe. Keep some extras handy in case you want to write a note about another child.

- Keep sticky notes or file cards in your pocket or readily accessible in each interest area.

- Use a digital pen to write notes if you are using an online assessment system that includes this feature. Some even have voice recorders so you can interact with a child while the pen is recording.

- Develop your own system of shorthand to record brief notes and phrases that will help you recall what happened.

Documenting Your Observations

Observation notes are most accurate and useful when they are objective and factual. When your notes include words like *shy, aggressive, upset, hyperactive,* or *angry,* they reveal your impressions, interpretations, or assumptions rather than the facts about what a child did or said. These judgmental words may or may not tell an accurate story. Interpretations, impressions, or assumptions include

- labels (e.g., *shy, vivacious, creative*)

- intentions (e.g., *wants to*)

- evaluations and judgments (e.g., *good job, beautiful, sloppy*)

- negatives (e.g., *didn't, can't, won't*)

Objective notes include only the facts about what you see and hear. Factual observations include

- descriptions of an action

- quotations of language

- descriptions of a gesture

- descriptions of a facial expression

- descriptions of a creation

Compare the following two examples of observation notes about a child at the water table.

Example 1

Carlos is being mischievous today. He splashes water on the floor and other children on purpose. He checks to see whether I am watching him and then laughs at other children.

Example 1 is not an objective note. It uses a label (*mischievous*) and makes judgments ("He splashes water...on purpose"). The teacher speculated about Carlos's intentions ("checks to see whether I am watching him. . . laughs at the other children").

Example 2

Carlos plays with the waterwheel. Some water falls on the other children's shoes. He looks at me and then at the other children and begins to giggle.

Example 2 is an objective note. It includes only the facts of what Carlos did ("plays with the waterwheel"), what happened ("Some water falls on the other children's shoes"), and his reaction ("He looks at me and then at the other children and begins to giggle"). Accurate notes include only the facts about what a child did and said, and they are recorded in the order of occurrence.

Writing objective notes takes practice. The more aware you are of what objective notes include, the more skilled you will become at writing them.

Here are two examples of objective observation notes.

Ben   10/27

Draws some lines and curves and says, "I'm writing a story about helicopters."

Jonetta   10/16

Points to printed name on cubby and says, "That's my cubby."

Other Forms of Documentation

In addition to observation notes, documentation can take many different forms. Here are some examples:

Photographs—Take pictures of a child's work, such as a block structure, artwork, and a pattern or other design made with table blocks. Be sure to label and date each photo and write a brief description of what the child did and said.

Audio- and videoclips—Try to record activities without intruding on what children are doing. Be selective about what you film or tape.

Samples of children's work—Select similar samples over time (e.g., at the beginning, middle, and toward the end of the year). Collect writing samples, drawings, stories the child dictated and illustrated, computer print-outs, graphs, and screen capture print-outs from a tablet or other mobile digital device.

Checklists, participation lists, frequency counts—Systematically record such things as which interest areas a child chooses, the letters a child recognizes, physical skills, and so on.

Each sample of a child's work reveals a great deal of information about that child's development and learning. While you do not need a great many samples of work in a portfolio, you do need enough variety to give a complete idea of the child's development and learning. In collecting a child's work for a portfolio, take time to write observation notes about the contexts in which the child was playing and clip the notes to the back of the samples. Be sure to include the date of each sample.

To show progress, collect similar samples over a period of time. For instance, comparing a child's attempts to write her name throughout the course of the year is an excellent way to document writing development. It would be hard to document development if you were to try to compare to each other a writing sample, a painting, a photograph of a block structure, and a dictated story. At the beginning of the year, think of two or three types of samples (e.g., writing samples or paintings) that would be good for documenting development in particular areas. Collect examples of those types 3–5 times throughout the year.

Also refer to the discussions of development in each chapter of *The Creative Curriculum® for Preschool: Volume 2: Interest Areas*. Collect samples of children's work or photographs that show children's skills as they progress. For example, the *Volume 2* chapter on the Block area outlines the developmental stages of block building. A series of photos of a child building towers and roads, then building bridges, and finally building elaborate constructions is an excellent way to show development and learning over time.

Observing With the Curricular Objectives in Mind

The objectives for children's development and learning presented in chapters 1 and 3 of this volume and in *Volume 6* are a guide for making the observation process systematic and meaningful. You are more likely to collect objective, factual observation notes if you are familiar with the objectives and the particular indicators of the widely held expectations for the children you are observing. That way you are likely to focus your notes on the information you will need later when you are ready to evaluate progress. For example, instead of recording, "Counts tiles while walking across room," a more valuable note would be, "Counts 16 tiles accurately while walking across room."

A small-group activity will often yield information about multiple objectives. For instance, if the children are following a picture recipe, you can note which children are able to count the number of cups and tablespoons (Objective 20), note who demonstrates awareness of particular features of print in a recipe (Objective 17), and record the number of exchanges that take place during a conversation (Objective 10). Keep some file cards or sticky notes handy so you can record what you see and hear immediately.

The Creative Curriculum® for Preschool, Volume 6: Objectives for Development & Learning presents indicators for all of the objectives related to social–emotional, physical, language, cognitive, literacy, and mathematics development and learning. Indicators are behaviors that you are likely to see in your daily observations of children. However, to get the information you need about some objectives (particularly those for literacy and mathematics), you may need to conduct additional activities during which you focus your observations on particular skills. The *Assessment Opportunity Cards* included in the *GOLD®* assessment system present activities designed for that purpose.

A chart of the 38 objectives for development and learning are included in *Volume 6*. Keep the chart handy so you can refer to it often. You can also obtain from Teaching Strategies a colorful poster that shows the objectives at a glance. Displaying it in your classroom will help you as you observe children, and it will help family members understand what their children are learning.

Keep in mind that you do not have to write an observation note about every child, every day. However, do try to select a few children to observe each day and write three or four brief notes about them. For some objectives, it is sufficient to see a child use a skill once or twice (e.g., a physical skill). You may record such accomplishments on a checklist; an observation note is not usually necessary. Other objectives require more evidence and documentation. No set number of observation notes or amount of other documentation is required for each objective. Use common sense to determine what is needed.

Step 2. Analyzing and Responding

The information you gain by observing children and thinking about their skills is the basis for responding to each child and supporting each child's learning appropriately. Knowing what each child can do in relation to the objectives helps you decide such things as how much support a child needs, how many directions a child can handle at a time, whether the classroom routines and rules are working, how well a child plays with others, and a child's level of persistence and curiosity. All of this information will help you decide when to teach, what to teach, and how to teach it. You can offer experiences that challenge children rather than frustrate them.

If you use *GOLD®*, you can analyze your observations by tagging objectives and dimensions while adding documentation. If you use *GOLDplus®*, you can refer to the Teaching Sequence on each *Intentional Teaching* experience to respond appropriately to children in the moment of instruction.

In your daily work with children, you continually observe, reflect on what you see, and respond to each child. You respond as you observe and use what you learn as you plan experiences to extend children's learning. The following chart gives examples of how this analysis and response take place throughout the day.

Observe	Reflect	Respond
Arrival Crystal announces, "Ms. Tory! Guess what? I got a new puppy, and his name is Sparky! He's white with some black spots, and he licks my face."	Crystal is very excited about her new puppy and talks in detail about what he looks like. *(Objective 9, Uses language to express thoughts and needs)* How can I use her interest in her new puppy to strengthen her oral language and literacy skills?	Engage Crystal in conversations about her new puppy and introduce new vocabulary. *(Objective 9)* Show her books about puppies. *(Objective 18, Comprehends and responds to books and other texts)* Suggest that she draw and write about her puppy. *(Objective 19, Demonstrates writing skills; Objective 33, Explores the visual arts)*
Group Meeting Setsuko sits still and looks at the other children, who are singing and marching. She looks down without speaking when other children ask her why she does not join in.	Setsuko is not interacting with others in the group. *(Objective 2, Establishes and sustains positive relationships; Objective 3, Participates cooperatively and constructively in group situations)* She is not benefitting fully from music and movement experiences. *(Objective 34, Explores musical concepts and expression; Objective 35, Explores dance and movement concepts)* Would she feel comfortable exploring music and movement with just one other child?	Observe Setsuko in other settings to better understand her relationships with peers. *(Objective 2, Establishes and sustains positive relationships)* Invite her to participate in a different way, such as turning on the CD player or beating a drum. *(Objective 34)* Provide additional opportunities for her to explore music independently or with one other child. *(Objective 34)*

Observe	Reflect	Respond
Choice Time Derek pretends to be a police officer who is writing a ticket. He says, "You're going too fast," as he scribbles on a piece of paper from left to right and top to bottom.	Derek recruits others to join him in playing police officer. *(Objective 14, Uses symbols and images to represent something not present; Objective 36, Explores drama through actions and language)* He attempts to write to convey meaning and follows the way print is written conventionally on a page. *(Objective 17, Demonstrates knowledge of print and its uses; Objective 19, Demonstrates emergent writing skills)*	Continue to observe Derek's play. Enter into the play without interrupting its flow. Ask, "What's the speed limit, Officer? I don't want to break the law. Maybe we need to make a sign so we'll know how fast to drive." *(Objective 2, Establishes and sustains positive relationships; Objective 10, Uses appropriate conversational and other communication skills; Objective 36)* At group time, talk about what police officers do and why. Invite a police officer to visit the classroom. *(Objective 30, Shows basic understanding of people and how they live)* Take a walk in the neighborhood to find and interpret traffic signs *(Objective 4, Demonstrates traveling skills; Objective 18, Comprehends and responds to books and other texts)*

Observe	Reflect	Respond
Snack Time Zack counts the number of children at his table and says, "We need five straws." He gets the straws and gives one to each child.	Zack uses his knowledge of numbers in a purposeful way: to count the children at the table accurately and distribute the straws. *(Objective 20, Uses number concepts and operations)*	Acknowledge Zack's helpfulness. *(Objective 3, Participates cooperatively and constructively in group situations)* Plan an *Intentional Teaching* experience such as *Intentional Teaching Card*™ M89, "Dig It!" Following the guidance for the green and blue color bands on the teaching sequence and observe how he counts more than five objects. *(Objective 20a)* Challenge Zack to count larger quantities (e.g., "Will you please get seven paintbrushes for the easel?"). *(Objective 20)*
Outdoor Time Tasheen tells Kate, "Let's play 'Follow the Leader.' You follow me." She walks along the edge of the sandbox, hops to the fence, and crawls through the tunnel.	Tasheen leads others in play. *(Objective 2, Establishes and sustains positive relationships)* She uses gross-motor skills. *(Objective 4, Demonstrates traveling skills; Objective 5, Demonstrates balancing skills)* How can I help her extend her physical skills?	Challenge Tasheen physically by suggesting more complex tasks (e.g., balancing on a beam or walking backwards). *(Objectives 4 and 5)* Challenge her to move her body in different ways around the environment (e.g., "Can you jump *over* the mat?" or "Run *up* the hill and then crawl *through* the tunnel," or "Stay *between* the two lines as you hop down the path.") *(Objectives 4, 8b, 21a)*

Observe	Reflect	Respond
Story Time Tyrone asks me to read *The Hungry Thing*. When the Hungry Thing asks for "feetloaf" to eat, Tyrone says, "He wants meatloaf!"	Tyrone selects a favorite story and then participates actively in story reading. *(Objective 18, Comprehends and responds to books and other texts)* He plays with sounds to figure out what the Hungry Thing wants. *(Objective 15, Demonstrates phonological awareness, phonics skills, and word recognition)*	Offer Tyrone food props from the Dramatic Play area so he can retell the story on his own. *(Objective 18 and Objective 36, Explores drama through actions and language)* Read other books that involve playing with language, such as *Jamberry* or *Alphabite: A Funny Feast from A to Z*. *(Objective 15)* Teach songs, rhymes, and chants that promote phonological awareness. *(Objective 15)*
Small-Group Time/ Choice Time A small group of children is sorting a collection of toy cars. Leo takes all of the red cars and lines them up. Then he takes the green cars and puts them in a line.	Leo participates in small-group activities and is able to share materials. *(Objective 3, Participates cooperatively and constructively in group situations)* He comes up with an idea and completes the task. *(Objective 11, Demonstrates positive approaches to learning)* He groups cars by color. *(Objective 13, Uses classification skills)*	Observe Leo closely and ask questions or make statements that will extend his thinking (e.g., "Why did you put this car on the end?"). *(Objective 11 and Objective 9, Uses language to express thoughts and needs)* Challenge Leo by inviting him to think of additional ways to sort the red cars, such as cars with two doors and cars with four doors. *(Objective 13)* Use other opportunities throughout the day for sorting, classifying, and arranging objects in a series. *(Objective 13)*

Observe	Reflect	Respond
Rest Time Sonya wiggles on her cot, hums a song, and tickles another child who is beginning to fall asleep.	Does Sonya understand the rules for nap time? *(Objective 1, Regulates own emotions and behaviors; Objective 3, Participates cooperatively and constructively in group situations)* Perhaps Sonya does not need to rest as much as the other children. How can I meet Sonya's need to be active and still respect other children's need to nap?	Place Sonya and other wakeful children away from children who need to rest. Give them the opportunity to rest for a short period of time. *(Objective 3)* Offer her quiet materials (e.g., books and a magic slate) to use on her cot. *(Objective 18, Comprehends and responds to books and other texts* and *Objective 7, Demonstrates fine-motor strength and coordination)*
Closing/Departure While discussing the day, Juwan says, "Me and Tasheen dug a hole outside and found a bug. It's like the one I found yesterday but bigger. We're gonna find that bug again tomorrow."	Juwan recalls past events and can recognize a particular type of insect. *(Objective 12, Remembers and connects experiences* and *Objective 25, Demonstrates knowledge of the characteristics of living things)* Although his grammar isn't perfect, he uses complete sentences. *(Objective 9, Uses language to express thoughts and needs)* How can I support Juwan's language development? How can I build on Juwan's and Tasheen's new interest?	Rephrase some of Juwan's language, modeling correct grammar (e.g., "Oh, you're going to dig again tomorrow. Do you think that bug will be in the same place? Carlos and I will want to know where you find it."). *(Objective 9)* Provide tools (e.g., shovels, a magnifying glass, or a bug catcher) to help with their explorations *(Objective 28, Uses tools and other technology to perform tasks)* Offer a book about insects to help the children identify those they find. *(Objective 18, Comprehends and responds to books and other texts)*

Step 3: Evaluating

Evaluating children's progress means deciding which indicator of an objective best describes the child's skill level. By systematically analyzing and evaluating your observation notes and portfolio samples, you will be able to determine each child's level of development in relation to each objective. You can organize your observation notes as well as the information in children's portfolios by regularly asking yourself, "What does this mean?" If you use *GOLD*®, you can evaluate each child's progress while entering documentation and while finalizing your checkpoint ratings. If you use *GOLDplus*®, you can also evaluate progress during each *Intentional Teaching* experience. Refer to the chart of objectives to decide which apply and note the numbers right on the note or on the back of the work sample.

For example, suppose you have a writing sample and an observation note about Ben.

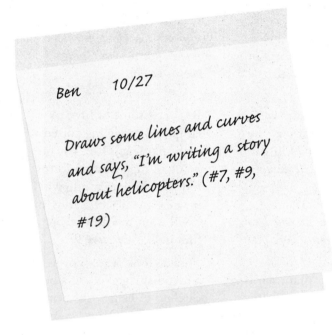

This writing sample and observation note about Ben clearly relate to more than one objective. His experience involved physical development (*Objective 7, Demonstrates fine-motor strength and coordination*); literacy (*Objective 19, Demonstrates writing skills*); and language (*Objective 9, Uses language to express thoughts and needs*). You can use this note to evaluate Ben's development and learning on various dimensions of these three objectives.

Volume 6: Objectives for Development & Learning shows the developmental progression for each of those objectives, so you can pinpoint Ben's level for each objective. Let's see how this works for Objective 19. Looking at this note, at your other observation notes about him, and at his portfolio items, you decide that Ben makes mock letters or letter-like forms. That is the indicator for level 6. He writes segments of letters (lines and curves) but is not yet making letters accurately.

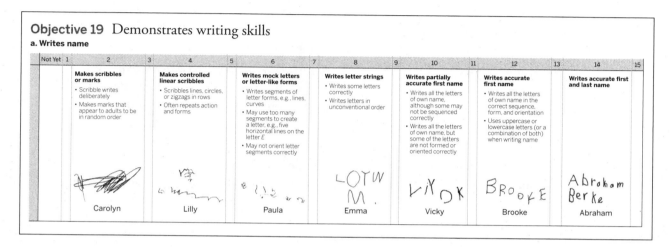

Objective 19 Demonstrates writing skills
a. Writes name

In the same manner, you can make determinations about all of the other objectives, using the documentation you have gathered for Ben.

Step 4: Summarizing, Planning, and Communicating

This last step in the assessment cycle involves summarizing what you know about each child, developing plans for individual children and the group, and communicating your findings to families and others to whom you report. With assessment information you can plan routines, transitions, and activities and change the environment appropriately.

Summary Form

Most assessment systems recommend that you summarize children's development and learning at least three times during the year. If you are using the *GOLD*® assessment system, you can use the forms specifically designed for this purpose. Teachers who use a different assessment system also need a way to summarize the information they have collected and to prepare reports.

Because *Objectives for Development & Learning* describes widely held expectations for children birth through third grade, it can be used with all children, those developing according to expectations and those who are advanced, have a developmental delay, have a disability, or lack experience in an area. You cannot expect every child in your program to progress to the highest levels for each objective. Over the course of the year, however, you would hope to see evidence that every child is making some degree of progress.

Planning for Individual Children

The wealth of information you have about each child is only meaningful if you link it to teaching decisions. It can help you plan for children individually and for your group as a whole. Here are some examples of decisions you might make on the basis of assessment information:

- Jonetta is now aware that text is meaningful and can be read (*Objective 17, Demonstrates knowledge of print and its uses*). She is noticing print in the environment. To help her learn more about print concepts, I will read with her and call her attention to the way I read from left to right and from the top of the page to the bottom.

- Setsuko is beginning to initiate brief conversations (*Objective 10, Uses appropriate conversational and other communication skills*). She seems very excited about having a guinea pig in the class. We can build on this new interest to promote her language and literacy development. We will read books about guinea pigs and encourage her to talk about what the guinea pig does.

- Leo likes to measure the plants in our garden. To do so, he has been using multiples of the same unit, such as interlocking blocks, string, and his hands (*Objective 22, Compares and measures*). Tomorrow I'll put out some rulers, a measuring tape, and a yardstick and observe what he does with them. I may need to introduce those tools to him and show him how to use them.

- Alexa engages with materials for brief periods of time but only if a teacher offers suggestions and stays with her (*Objective 11, Demonstrates positive approaches to learning*). She might really like to work with play dough if rolling pins and cookie cutters are available, so I will put those materials in the Art area. I will see if she can sustain her interest and involvement a little longer.

Planning for the Group

Another important use of the information you collect during the assessment process is to plan for the group. When you review the progress of the class as a whole, you may find that focusing on particular skills could benefit everyone.

Think about when and where to teach particular skills. You will teach some in large- and small-group settings. As an example, let's take a look at Objective 15, "Demonstrates phonological awareness, phonics skills, and word recognition." Imagine a classroom of 20 children aged 4–5 years. Suppose there are

- two children who join in rhyming songs
- ten children who fill in the missing rhyming word
- seven children who can decide whether two words rhyme
- one child who can generate a group of rhyming words

Reflecting on this information, you conclude that most of the children are still developing the skill of noticing and discriminating rhymes. You decide to make Objective 15 a group focus and to try these strategies:

- Stock the Library area with recordings of poems and chants with lots of repetition and rhyming words. Encourage children to listen to them on their own.

- Gather a small group of children who are at a beginning level of understanding rhyme. Lead them in singing some fingerplays and simple songs.

- Play rhyming games during transitions (e.g., say, "You may get a book if your name rhymes with *eater*. Right, Peter, it's your turn.").

- Encourage children to rhyme nonsensical "words" with meaningful words (e.g., *apple, papple, bapple* and *car, bar, mar, dar, far*).

- Read aloud books that contain rhyme and repetition (e.g., *Brown Bear, Brown Bear, What Do You See?* by Bill Martin, Jr. or any of the Dr. Seuss books). Omit some of the rhyming words as you read and encourage children to fill them in.

On the basis of what you learn from your review of children's development and learning, you can identify which children would benefit from more focused instruction and practice. This information will help you to plan individual support and small-group activities, and it will help you decide how to respond when unplanned teaching opportunities arise.

Communicating

The progress of the children in your class interests others as well as you. Families want to know how their children are doing, and they have valuable information to share. In many programs, administrators want to review reports, and some funders require reports to verify that their investments are leading to positive results.

Most programs schedule conferences with children's families several times during the year. It is important to prepare for these conferences and to have a form on which to summarize the information you want to share with families. The "Family Conference Form" that is part of the *GOLD*® assessment system serves that purpose. Review the samples of the child's work and the child's levels of development for the various objectives. Think about what information and evidence is most important to the child's family in each of the areas of development and learning. Write a brief description of the child's strengths and give examples of what the child can do in each area. Identify a few learning goals you have in mind for the child. In chapter 5, we discuss how to prepare for and conduct family conferences.

If you are using the online system for *GOLD*®, the process of creating reports is streamlined for you. Data collected on all of the objectives can be aggregated and disaggregated to generate a range of individual and group reports.

Conclusion

Caring and teaching are inseparable. To teach all children effectively, you must get to know every child well and develop positive relationships that let children know you care about them and are genuinely interested in their success. The year begins by purposefully creating a classroom community where all children feel safe, accepted, and competent. Teachers help children learn important social skills and guide children's behavior in ways that promote self-regulation and the ability to resolve conflicts when they arise. They guide children's learning intentionally, whether they are supporting child-initiated experiences or teacher-planned activities. They also know how to individualize instruction to include all children. Excellent teaching is based on purposeful observation, so teachers use an ongoing assessment system to learn about each child and to plan instruction. Teachers are most effective in their work when they develop partnerships with children's families, so we explore partnerships in the next chapter.

References

Asher, S. R., & Coie, J. D. (Eds.). (1990). *Peer rejection in childhood*. New York: Cambridge University Press.

Bailey, B. A. (2003). *There's got to be a better way: Discipline that works!* (Rev. ed.). Oviedo, FL: Loving Guidance.

Berk, L. E. (2006). Looking at kindergarten. In D. F. Gullo (Ed.), *K today: Teaching and learning in the kindergarten year* (pp. 11–25). Washington, DC: National Association for the Education of Young Children.

Bowman, B. T., Donovan, M. S., & Burns, M. S. (Eds.). (2001). *Eager to learn: Educating our preschoolers*. Washington, DC: National Academy Press.

Bronson, M. B. (2000). *Self-regulation in early childhood*. New York: Guilford Press.

De Houwer, A. (1999). *Two or more languages in early childhood: Some general points and practical recommendations* (No. EDO-FL-99-03). Washington, DC: ERIC Clearinghouse on Languages and Linguistics Center for Applied Linguistics. (ERIC Document Reproduction Service No. ED433697)

Greenberg, M. T., Domitrovitch, C., & Bumbarger, B. (2001). The prevention of mental disorders in school-aged children: current state of the field. *Prevention and Treatment, 4*.

Jablon, J. R., Dombro, A. L., & Dichtelmiller, M. L. (2007). *The power of observation: Birth to age 8* (2nd ed.). Washington, DC: Teaching Strategies, Inc. and National Association for the Education of Young Children.

Kohn, A. (2001). Five reasons to stop saying "Good job!". *Young Children, 56*(5), 24–28.

Kostelnik, M. J., Whiren, A. P., Soderman, A. K., & Gregory, K. M. (2009). *Guiding children's social development*. Clifton Park, NY: Delmar.

Levin, D. E. (2003). *Teaching young children in violent times: Building a peaceable classroom* (2nd ed.). Cambridge, MA: Educators for Social Responsibility and Washington, DC: National Association for the Education of Young Children.

Morrison, F. J., & Connor, C. M. (2002). Understanding schooling effects on early literacy: A working research strategy. *Journal of School Psychology, 40*(6), 493–500.

National Research Council, & Institute of Medicine. (2000). *From neurons to neighborhoods: The science of early childhood development*. (J. P. Shonkoff & D. A. Phillips, Eds.). Washington, DC: National Academy Press.

Paley, V. G. (1992). *You can't say you can't play*. Cambridge, MA: Harvard University Press.

Peisner-Feinberg, E. S., Burchinal, M. R., Clifford, R. M., Culkin, M. L., Howes, C., Kagan, S. L., et al. (1999). *The children of the cost, quality, and outcomes study go to school: Technical report*. Chapel Hill: University of North Carolina at Chapel Hill, Frank Porter Graham Child Development Center.

Pianta, R. C. (1999). *Enhancing relationships between children and teachers*. Washington, DC: American Psychological Association.

Pianta, R. C. (2006). Teacher–child relationships and early literacy. In D. Dickinson & S. Neuman (Eds.), *Handbook of early literacy research* (Vol. 2, pp. 149–162). New York: Guilford Press.

Riley, D., San Juan, R. R., Klinker, J., & Ramminger, A. (2008). *Social & emotional development: Connecting science and practice in early childhood settings*. St. Paul, MN: Redleaf Press and Washington, DC: National Association for the Education of Young Children.

Rubin, K. H. (2003). *The friendship factor: Helping our children navigate their social world and why it matters for their success and happiness*. New York, NY: Penguin Group.

Rutter, M., & Maughan, B. (2002). School effectiveness findings, 1979–2002. *Journal of School Psychology, 40*(6), 451–475.

Slaby, R. G., Roedell, W. C., Arezzo, D., & Hendrix, K. (1995). *Early violence prevention: Tools for teachers of young children*. Washington, DC: National Association for the Education of Young Children.

Tabors, P. O. (2008). *One child, two languages: A guide for early childhood educators of children learning English as a second language* (2nd ed.). Baltimore, MD: Paul H. Brookes Publishing Co.

Partnering With Families

Partnering With Families

Home and school are a young child's two most important worlds. Children must bridge these two worlds every day. If home and school are connected in positive and respectful ways, children feel secure. When the two worlds are at odds because of adults' apathy, lack of understanding, or an inability to work together, children suffer. Teachers can build partnerships when they truly value the family's role in a child's education and recognize how much they can accomplish by working with families.

Developing partnerships enables you to work together with families to support their children's healthy development and learning. Start by acknowledging the fact that families are already involved. They have been rearing their children since birth. They demonstrate a commitment by enrolling their children in your program and getting them to your classroom each day. This chapter will help you build positive relationships with families by addressing the following topics:

Getting to know families—recognizing differences among families, making the most of initial contacts to learn about each family, and learning about families over time

Making families feel welcome—creating a welcoming environment, introducing your program to families, building trust, and reaching out to all members of a child's family

Communicating with families—taking advantage of informal daily exchanges and more formal methods of communication to share information and keep families up-to-date about your program

Involving families in the program—offering a variety of ways for families to participate, involving families in the program, and conducting conferences to discuss children's progress and to plan together

Responding to challenging situations—recognizing when families are experiencing stress, dealing with misunderstandings, and handling differences that are based on strongly held philosophical and cultural beliefs

Getting to Know Families

Just as you get to know each child and develop a relationship that helps each develop and learn, you begin building a partnership with each family by getting to know and appreciate each one. Every family is different. If you try to relate to all families in the same way, you will reach only the families who respond to that approach. By contrast, if you vary the ways you communicate with families and involve them in the program, you will be more likely to reach every family.

One obvious difference among families is their **structure**. The traditional family—two parents and their children—is not as common as it once was. Many children are growing up with one parent. Some are being reared in foster homes or by grandparents or other relatives. Other children live with two mothers or two fathers. To appreciate differences among the families you serve, begin by keeping an open mind about what constitutes a "family." Remember that however nontraditional a family may seem to you, children's families are the most important people in the world to them.

Families also have different temperaments. Some families are easy to get to know. They feel comfortable in school environments, and they are eager to communicate with their children's teachers. Others are uneasy or shy in school situations. They may have unhappy memories of their own school experiences and are unsure of how to relate to their children's teachers. Regardless of these differences, you can convey to all families that you value them and that your classroom is a safe place for them to visit.

Life experiences such as level of education, socioeconomic status, health issues, and length of time in this country also account for differences among families, and they influence the way families relate to their children's teachers. Some parents not only care for their children but also care for elderly or ill family members. Some face challenging circumstances such as unemployment, substance abuse, unstable or unsafe housing, depression, or lack of access to a phone or transportation. Your sensitivity to life circumstances can go a long way in helping you accept and appreciate all families.

Cultural differences are sometimes less obvious but no less important than structure, temperament, and life circumstances. Culture includes the beliefs, values, and practices we learn from our families, either through example (watching what others do) or through explicit direction (being told what is expected). Culture affects the way people communicate and interact with others and their expectations about how others will respond. Because every culture has its own set of rules and expectations, different cultures interpret what people do and say differently. To appreciate how and why families respond as they do, it is helpful to be aware of your personal experiences and how they influence your thinking and actions.

Gaining Self-Awareness

Think about the messages you received while you were growing up and the experiences you had in your own family and community. The following questions may help you begin (or continue) your own process of becoming self-aware:

- How did you become aware of your personal identity (your nationality, culture, ethnicity, and so on)?

- What early messages did you receive about other groups?

- How did you define *family* when you were growing up? Is your definition different now?

- What messages did you receive about your family's socioeconomic status?

- Were girls treated differently from boys in your family? What do you think your family's expectations were for you?

- How and when were you encouraged to express your ideas and feelings?

- Was it acceptable to be noisy and active in your home, or were children expected to be quiet?

- How was discipline handled?

- Was independence encouraged?

If you were to share your experiences with someone from a similar background, you would probably find many similarities in beliefs and practices, but also many differences. You might not want to be labeled as belonging to the same group as that person. For this reason, it is not helpful to try to generalize about any group's characteristics. Labels only perpetuate stereotypes and are often inaccurate. It is far better to learn as much as you can about and from the families in your program than to depend on stereotypes that might be entirely wrong. Consider the many factors that influence the practices and values of an individual family, including the family's country of origin, its social class there and here, the parents' educational background, and whether extended family members live in the home.

Using Initial Contacts to Learn About Families

Initial contacts with children's families are opportunities to get to know a little about them. Depending on your program's procedures, your first contact with families may be at enrollment or during a home visit. Because initial contacts make a strong impression, use them to learn about families and to begin building positive relationships.

Think about what makes families feel comfortable right from the start. How can you convey that you are eager to get to know them and their children? Ask yourself whether it is appropriate to serve something to eat or drink. Do you need to arrange for someone who speaks the family's home language to be present? Be guided by the idea that in these initial contacts you want to make families feel comfortable with you.

Enrollment

Most programs have an enrollment form with questions about the child's history and about the family. If you have any doubt about how to pronounce the child's name correctly, find out before meeting with the family. During enrollment, explain how the information on the form will be helpful to the program. Try to leave time to speak informally with families about their children. You will probably gain valuable insights by asking open-ended questions:

- What would you most like us to know about your child?
- What are your child's favorite activities?
- Does your child have a favorite toy?
- What are your child's greatest strengths?
- Are there any concerns about which we should know?
- What are your hopes and dreams for your child?
- What do you most want your child to learn in our program?

Enrollment is also a good time to conduct a home-language survey so that you can begin to identify English-language learners and to find out in what languages families prefer to communicate with you. A form for such a survey is included in *Volume 6: Objectives for Development & Learning.*

If appropriate, you might use the enrollment process to learn a little more about each family's culture and values because it is easy to misinterpret what families do or say if you do not understand something about their values. However, you also must avoid assigning cultural labels to families. Rather than making assumptions about cultural influences, it is better to keep an open mind and consider the beliefs behind each family's practices. Seek to discover answers to questions such as those that follow, keeping in mind that not all families are comfortable with direct questions. Observe how family members interact with their child, and be selective about the kinds of questions you ask each family.

- Are there any special traditions, celebrations, or songs that are especially important to your family and your child?
- How would you like us to support your family's values and culture at school?
- How can I learn more about your heritage and culture?
- Are you willing to share something about your family's heritage with the program?

You may find that you are collecting a lot of information by speaking informally with families during enrollment. To keep track of what you learn, you might create a web for each child (see the section "Integrating Learning Through Studies" of chapter 3). In the middle of a piece of paper, write the child's name. As family members respond to questions and as the discussion evolves, write down a few representative words in a web format. Share the web with the child's family at the end of the session and explain how you will use the information to get to know and teach the child.

Enrollment also might be an appropriate time to explain how much you value the involvement of families in your program. Talk about ways you intend to communicate with and involve family members. Find out what special talents and interests families would be willing to share with your class.

Home Visits

One of the best ways to get to know children and families is to make home visits before the school year begins. Families are often more comfortable in their own settings than at school. Home visits are an excellent way to build a bridge to school for children who have never been in this kind of environment.

Here is a true story about how one teacher learned the power of home visits:

As I approached Gabriel's house, I saw a motorcycle in the side yard. Close by were two child-sized, motorcycle-like wheeled riding toys, and there was a collection of toy motorcycles on the patio. Before parking my car, I already knew that one way to engage Gabriel was to include motorcycle activities in my classroom. I made a mental note to put toy motorcycles in the block center and a motorcycle book in the book center.

Gabriel led me to the back of the house to see his room. I noted the stuffed animals on his bed and the toys he'd been playing with. I knew I could refer to them in class. Before I left, his parents proudly announced that Gabriel would have a new brother or sister in 6 months. Now I had another piece of information that might lead him to talk to his classmates and me. In a 10-minute visit, I learned more about this child and his background than I had learned previously about some children in an entire year as their teacher. Since that time I've made a commitment to visit every child's home before each school year.

Parents benefit from home visits, too. They receive information about the beginning of school, the school's discipline policy, my classroom management techniques, field trips, and class routines. Many of the parents I work with were once poor students in school, and some were school dropouts. Their memories of school and teachers aren't pleasant, and they have bad feelings about sending their own children to school. They associate family–teacher conferences with bad news and school problems, but they realize I'm visiting because I'm interested in their child's success.

Children benefit most from the visit. Taught to be wary of strangers, students meet me in their own homes and with their parents present. When they walk in the classroom door, my face is familiar. The snapshots I took of them and their families are on the bulletin board. Because I've met every child, I can greet each one by name.

If you've never made a home visit, I urge you to try it. You'll find it to be one of your most valuable teaching tools (Backer, 2001).

Before making a visit, send a welcoming postcard or call the child's family to let them know that you would like to visit. Then set up a time. Go with the intention of getting to know each family and building a relationship, not judging. Invite families to talk about themselves by responding to your open-ended questions. Briefly share a personal story if you think that will put families at ease.

Just as you might bring flowers or a gift to a friend's house when you are invited for dinner, consider bringing something from the classroom, such as a book or paper and crayons for the child or a guide to the program for parents. If possible, bring something that the child may keep until the first day of school. It will serve as a concrete connection to the program and make entering the classroom easier.

You might also bring a camera so you can take a picture of the child alone and one of the child with family members. You can use both pictures in classroom displays. Some teachers bring an instant camera so the family can take and keep a picture of the child with the teacher. These snapshots, often displayed on the family's refrigerator, are a meaningful way to connect home and school.

Visiting all children at home is not always possible. When it is not, make an effort to talk with families by phone before their children come to the program, or try to meet at a neutral public place, such as a coffee shop or a park. These options often work well when parents are intimidated by school settings. No matter where you first meet with family members, they can teach you a great deal if you are genuinely open and eager to learn from them. The insights you gain will help you to build a relationship with each child and family and to be a better teacher.

Making Families Feel Welcome

Everything you do to get to know families will help you welcome them. Families who feel welcome in your classroom are likely to return and to become involved in the program. The classroom environment you create and the ways you introduce the program can make families feel that they belong and that you appreciate their role in their children's development and learning. Over the course of the year you can build trust through the ways you reach out to and communicate with all family members.

Creating a Welcoming Environment

The most important message families can receive when they enter the building and your classroom is that this is also a place for them. The environment can carry positive messages.

Take time to assess continually whether your environment conveys the messages you intend. Let families know that their ideas and contributions are always welcome.

Introducing Your Program

When children first enter the program, their families are likely to be especially interested in finding out what their children will be learning and what each day will be like. Make them feel welcome by responding to their interests. Some programs develop a **booklet** that introduces their philosophy and goals for children, describes the kinds of experiences children will have, and outlines policies and procedures.

Take families (and children) on **a tour of the classroom**. Talk about how you have set up different interest areas, what the day is like, where children place their belongings, and what to expect on the first day of school. This might be a good time to invite families to bring something from home to display in the classroom.

Ways to Make Families Feel Welcome

Make the **entranceway** attractive, neat, and inviting. Include decorative touches, such as plants, pictures, and displays of children's work.

Provide a **message box** for each family. To help you sort messages by language, color-code the mailboxes according to the families' home languages.

Incorporate **family items** into your displays, such as handmade quilts, weavings, musical instruments, masks, and other contributions.

Provide **places for family members** to hang their coats and store their belongings during their visits.

Keep a **bulletin board** with up-to-date information about program activities, meetings, and interesting community events.

Place a **suggestion box** in a prominent place, and provide paper and pens.

Make an attractive display of **photographs** of the children in your class and their families. Place it at the children's eye level.

Place an **adult-sized rocking chair** in the Library area.

Have a **sign-in sheet** for families to check their children in each morning. Provide a separate sheet for children to sign their names.

Display **books and pictures** that respect the diversity of your program.

Offer **resources** that family members may read and check out.

Post **signs** throughout the classroom that show what children are learning in each interest area and how adults can support what children do.

You also can consider holding an **open house** for families at the beginning of the year. You can describe your program briefly, distribute and go through a family booklet, and explain what a typical day is like for the children. Start by having everyone sit in a circle to demonstrate circle time. Welcome each person by name. Go over a typical schedule and then explain the purpose of choice time. Invite each person to select an interest area and explore the materials you have set out. As people do so, move from one area to another. Comment on what people are doing and explain what children learn from the same activities.

Another way to share what and how children learn is to create an attractive **display** at the entrance to your classroom or school. Take photographs of children engaged in meaningful play. Display the photos with samples of children's work and brief descriptions of what the children were doing and what they were learning.

Building Trust

For families to feel welcome, you and they need to establish mutual trust. Trust between teachers and families develops over time and is based on many positive and respectful experiences. Some family members may be uneasy in a school environment and unsure of how they will be treated. You can build trust by conveying positive messages to families. Here are some suggestions:

Conveying Positive Messages to Families

To convey this message to families...	You can...
They are welcome at all times during the program day.	Greet each family member by name and say something positive about the child, the family, or the program.
They are invited to contribute to the program.	Find a way to discover each person's special skills and interests and invite each to share them with your program.
They are competent.	Acknowledge the expert insights and information family members have about their children and how valuable these are to you as a teacher. Avoid the use of jargon in both written and spoken communication.
Their ideas are valuable, and they have an important role to play.	Find out what topics are of interest to parents. Create a relaxed atmosphere, share information about children's strengths, invite family members to share ideas about their child's progress, and make conferences a joint planning time.
They understand what is happening in the classroom.	Explain how and what children learn through play. Especially if your classroom is different from what families expected, assure them that research confirms that children in your program learn important content and process skills.

All families have expectations for their children's education. Some are positive, some are negative, and some are neutral. Responding to families in a positive and respectful manner will help them trust you enough to engage in open exchanges.

Chapter 5 **Partnering With Families**

Reaching Out to All Family Members

Parents are not the only family members who should feel welcome in your classroom. All members of a child's family can be involved in the program, and their involvement can make a big difference. Grandparents, for example, may have more free time to share than parents and often (although not always) a great deal of patience. Their participation in the classroom can be valuable: reading to children, playing games, assisting with special activities, and more. Schools that have partnered with senior citizen homes or groups such as Foster Grandparents find that intergenerational programs benefit both older people and the children.

You will probably need to make a special effort to welcome and involve men, who sometimes feel uncomfortable in early childhood settings where most of the adults are women. There are substantial benefits to fathers' involvement in their children's lives at school. Research has shown that young children whose fathers are involved in their education do better in school (U.S. Department of Education, 2015). Moreover, the children of involved fathers are more likely to enjoy school and are less likely to be expelled or suspended than children whose fathers are not involved in their schooling. By *father* we do not always mean the child's biological father. A father figure may be another male who is a steady influence in the child's life: the mother's partner or husband, an uncle, older sibling, grandfather, another relative, or a family friend. Once male family members discover that their presence and contributions are appreciated by the program staff and are important to their children, they are more likely to take an active role.

The most important thing to keep in mind is that all children need caring adults who take an active interest in their learning. Find out which adults are important in a child's life and think about how you can welcome them. Learn about their interests, their jobs, any special hobbies that might be tapped, and what they would like to share with the children. Describe what others have contributed to the program. Some adults are more likely to come to an activity that involves the whole family than to come to one that is designed specifically for parents. You may also be successful if you create special projects or events to interest different family members. For example, you might invite grandparents or special friends to read or tell stories, and ask those interested in construction projects to help during a "fix-it" day. You might ask family members about topics of interest to them and arrange for a special speaker or activity.

The steps you take each day to make all families feel welcome in your program and classroom set the stage for a partnership with each. You can build on this foundation by communicating regularly with all families so they have current information about their children's lives at school.

Volume 1: The Foundation 201

Communicating With Families

Good communication is essential for building partnerships. Families want to know what their children are experiencing at school and what you have learned about their children. Often they have information to share as well. Daily exchanges are just as valuable as the formal methods you may use to communicate with families. When young children observe respectful and genuine interactions between their families and teachers, they see that their two worlds— home and school—are connected.

Daily Exchanges

In most programs serving preschool children, teachers have opportunities to communicate with family members every day. Make it a point to note something a child has done during the day and jot it down so it doesn't slip your mind at the end of the day. Here are some suggestions for making the most of daily exchanges with families:

Make families feel welcome. Greet each person by name. Tell each family about something their child has done or comment on your plans for the day.

Have something specific to say to each family: "Good morning, Ms. Lewis. I know Derek wants to show you the clock he's been taking apart in our Discovery area."

Share information about an event or something the child has done recently: "Let me tell you about the building Janelle made with blocks yesterday. It was pretty amazing."

Solicit family members' advice about their child: "We've been encouraging Tyrone to try new foods at lunch, but he is still very reluctant. Is there anything he particularly likes that we should know about?"

Give support to families when needed: "It's hard for Leo to say good-bye to you today. Can you think of a reason? Perhaps he just needs an extra hug. I know he'll be fine once he gets busy. We have a lot planned for today."

Be a good listener. Active listening skills convey that families' concerns and ideas are taken seriously. For example, you might say, "I understand how upset you are about the biting incident. I can assure you that we are taking steps to prevent more biting."

Talk about what children are learning. The end of the day can be a perfect time to talk with a family about what their child has done that day and to explain its value. You might explain, "We saved the design Kate made with pattern blocks to show you. Her ability to discover and create patterns is an important skill in every content area."

Clarify messages. Confirm your understanding of what a family member tells you. You might say, "Let me see whether I'm hearing you correctly. What I heard you say is. . ."

Formal Communication

In addition to family conference forms, there are many ways to tell family members what is happening in your program. As always, try to communicate in a language that the family will understand. If some family members are not readers, speak with them directly.

Ways to Communicate With Families

Daily or weekly bulletins—A brief note about what took place at school each day (or week) is one way to keep families connected. Write a short message and reproduce it for each family. That could be as simple as entering interesting information on a form that says, "Ask me about...," at the top. Bulletins give families topics to discuss with their children when they talk about school.

Telephone calls—Set up a schedule to call each family monthly to say hello and tell them something positive about the child's progress. Call to convey your concern when a child has been out sick. Some teachers offer their home phone numbers and encourage families to call any time. Others limit their availability for phone calls at home.

E-mail—More and more families and programs have access to e-mail. Sending e-mail is an excellent way to stay in touch. You can also update families through a list server, which is an electronic mailing list.

Internet—Introduce families to the online communication tool your program uses. Partnerships are enhanced when families can use a family-to-family message board, view their child's portfolio, add comments, and upload pictures.

A class Web site—You, a colleague, or a family member can build a class Web site. If you have a digital camera or a scanner, you can include photos of the children and their work. A Web site is a good way to keep families informed about long-term studies and class events.

Thank-you notes—Each week, send brief thank-you notes to a few families, telling them that you appreciate their contributions to their children's lives at school.

Journals—Provide each family with a journal that travels between home and school. Families and teachers can share information by writing entries.

Notices—There are times when you send a written notice so that every parent gets the same information quickly. Some examples might be a policy change, a special event, or the contagious illness of a child or staff member.

Telephone tree or electronic messages and text messages—With an automated phone messaging system, you can send a message to everyone's phone about any topic.

Whatever methods you adopt, it is important to have a variety of ways to communicate. Choose manageable approaches that keep you in touch with the children's families.

Involving Families in the Program

Families have been teaching their children since birth, so they are already supporting their children's development and learning. You have much to gain by recognizing their role and including them as partners in the education of their children. Numerous studies have documented the academic benefits to children of a family–school–teacher partnership. When family members are involved, children do better. These findings hold true regardless of the educational background of the parents or their income level (Henderson & Berla, 1994).

To partner effectively with families, you need to get and keep them involved. But what exactly do we mean by *family involvement*? Traditionally, it meant having parents attend meetings at school, volunteer in the classroom, and help with fund-raising. Success was measured by the number of family members who attended an event, helped in the classroom, or assisted with a special activity.

Today most parents work full-time. Some have more than one job, and others work at night. They are not always able to participate in their children's school programs. Teachers therefore need to think about family participation in new ways.

Involvement can take many forms, from contributions that family members can make from home to volunteering in the classroom. It always means sharing information about children's progress. Through the process of partnering, teachers learn a great deal about children and how to teach them. Families come to appreciate how much they have already taught their children. The biggest winners of all are the children, who thrive on the cooperative relationships between their families and teachers.

Offering a Variety of Ways to Be Involved

Although the strengths and talents of parents and other family members may not be evident immediately, every family has something positive to offer. Try to discover the special interests and abilities of all family members and think of ways to encourage their participation in the program. Ask yourself, "What does this person bring to our relationship that enhances our ability to work together?" The more options you provide for families to contribute to your program and to be involved with their children at school, the more likely you are to succeed in reaching every family.

Early in the year—during a home visit, at enrollment, by phone, or at an open house—let families know how helpful it would be to have them involved in the program and how much their involvement would mean to their children. Ask family members what they enjoy doing with their children, what interests them, and what they are most comfortable doing. Explain that there are many ways to contribute.

Ways for Families to Be Involved

Making things for the program—Family members can do projects at home that will benefit all the children in the program. They can help collect "beautiful junk" to be used in the art area (such as fabric scraps, ribbons, yarn, and pieces of soft wood), objects for sorting and classifying (such as buttons, shells, keys, and bottle caps), or props for dramatic play. Families may be willing to make things for the classroom, such as matching games, doll clothes, or curtains, or to record stories for the Library area.

Sharing their culture—Families who are willing to share aspects of their cultural heritage can enrich the program greatly. They might lend tools and art, and talk with the children about their significance, how they were made, and how they are used. You might invite a family member to cook a traditional dish with the children, teach them dances or songs, tell stories, or share photographs. Family members who cannot come to the classroom during the day might tape songs or stories.

Sharing a talent or job—Once you learn about their special talents, interests, and work, you can invite family members to share their knowledge and experiences with the children. The possibilities are endless: playing an instrument, keeping a garden, teaching children about insects or other animals, using carpentry skills to build something for the program, and so on. .

Participating in a study—Families can be a great source of information and ideas when they are knowledgeable about the study topic. You might send home a note describing what you will be studying and inviting families to be part of the planning. They might join you on a field trip, contribute materials (such as old shoes for a study of shoe stores), or participate in special activities related to the study.

Families can enhance your program in many different ways. The size of their contribution is not important. What families learn by contributing and the positive message their involvement conveys to children are what count most.

Sharing Information and Parenting Tips

Sharing aspects of the curriculum and related resources with families can really help them understand the value of the experiences you provide in the program and how to support their child's learning and development at home more effectively. These two resources will be helpful:

1. At the end of each chapter of *Volume 2: Interest Areas*, you will find a "Letter to Families" that describes what children do when they play in the area, how teachers support their learning, and how families can help at home. You can send these letters home over a period of time—perhaps one every few weeks—so that families do not feel overwhelmed with too much information at once. Alternatively, you can distribute the appropriate letter at a meeting during which you are talking about a topic, such as block building or art experiences.

2. Another valuable resource you can offer families is a set of activities called *LearningGames*®. These activities were originally developed for the Abecedarian project, one of the most frequently referenced projects that worked with families of children birth to age 5 and that produced long-lasting, positive results. Some of the positive benefits for the children were improved performance in math and reading, a reduction in grade retention, and increased college attendance.

Two books of *LearningGames* activities are for preschool children: one for children 36–48 months and a second for children 48–60 months. Each book contains directions for a series of games that are arranged in approximate order of increasing difficulty, a checklist to track which games you have given to each family, and an overview of development for that year of life. Each game is presented on the front and back of a full page, which is perforated so it can be removed easily and given to a family. An engaging photograph shows an adult playing the game with one or more children. The brief text on the front page describes the main idea and how the game supports children's development.

The back of each page has four sections:

- "Why this is important" explains how the activity supports a child's current and future development and learning. This is an excellent way to explain the benefits of playing the game.

- "What you do" gives step-by-step instructions for playing the game. Embedded in the instructions are examples of what a family member might say to and ask a child as they play the game together as well as other ways to respond to the child.

- "Ready to move on?" and "Another idea" present a slightly more challenging variation of the game to try after the child has mastered the original version.

- The last section suggests a children's book related to the topic of the game.

Programs that can provide these resources for families will need one *LearningGames* book for each child and a system for keeping track of which games have been sent home for each family. There is also a *Teachers' Guide* to help you use *LearningGames* to support your work with children and their families. (See TeachingStrategies.com for more information.)

Making Classroom Participation Meaningful

Some families will be able to participate in your usual daily classroom program. Doing so enables them to see firsthand how you work with children and promote learning. There are also many benefits for children. Seeing their families in their classroom is exciting and a source of pride for the children, and an extra adult in the room means more individual attention for all children.

Assure family members that you do not expect them to be teachers when they are at school. Explain that your primary goal is to give them opportunities to find out what goes on in the classroom and that their assistance will be very helpful. Prepare them for the possibility that their child will want their full attention at first. Explain that this is to be expected.

Talk with families ahead of time—at a group meeting or individually—about ways in which they can work with children, e.g., playing with a group in an interest area, playing or reading one-on-one with their child or another child, leading a small-group activity, giving a demonstration, or sharing their expertise on a topic. Some teachers have found it helpful to post in each interest area signs or posters that explain what children do there and what they are learning. When you need special assistance with an activity or in an interest area, contact the assisting family member in advance so he or she will have the opportunity to ask questions, make suggestions, or make the necessary preparations. However, during choice time also allow family members to select the areas that interest them.

In general, families can participate in ways that apply to all interest areas and activities. Think about developing a short, one-page flyer with the following tips for family members:

- Observe what children do and show that you are interested by describing what you see: "I noticed that you put all the red pegs in a row."
- Follow children's lead without taking over: "I'm trying to make the waterwheel turn just the way you did."
- Ask open-ended questions to find out what a child is thinking: "How many ways can you use this?" "What will it do?" "How does it feel?" "What do you like best?" "What do you think will happen next?" "Why did you do it that way?"
- Offer assistance when it is needed.

The following chart offers suggestions for telling families about the importance of each interest area and what they might do when they participate.

Interest Area	What You Can Tell Families About Each Interest Area	What Families Might Do When They Participate
Blocks	Blocks are designed in proportional units. Children's building skills develop in distinct stages. Children create designs and build what they see around them, e.g., roads, houses, and other buildings.	Talk with children about different shapes and how many blocks they need. Help children find and return blocks to their designated places. Suggest props a child might like to use.
Dramatic Play	Pretend play helps children make sense of their experiences. Children take on roles and pretend about a situation, use props, and play with other children.	Pretend with children by taking on a role. Help children find and return the props they need. Suggest ideas to extend make-believe play.

Interest Area	What You Can Tell Families About Each Interest Area	What Families Might Do When They Participate
Toys and Games	These materials teach math, support eye–hand coordination, and promote small-muscle skills. Some are self-correcting, and some are open-ended.	Play games with children. Help a child who is having trouble completing a task (e.g., putting a puzzle together). Comment on the pattern a child makes.
Art	Children need opportunities to explore and experiment with various art materials. Art is a way for children express their ideas and feelings. Adults should not impose their own ideas about art on children. Children's artistic skills develop in predictable stages.	Encourage children to experiment with paint, markers, clay, dough, and collage materials. Help with a special activity (e.g., making play dough). Help children write their names on their artwork. Write the captions and stories that children dictate about their artwork.
Library	Children develop valuable literacy skills and a love for books. It is a quiet place to get away and enjoy books. To a child, the most important letters are those in his or her name.	Read and enjoy looking at books with children. Encourage children's writing and take dictation. Tell stories and listen while children retell stories.
Discovery	This is an area where children can explore materials firsthand. Adults can encourage and share a sense of wonder with children.	Be curious about children's discoveries. Help children take apart an old, small appliance (e.g., a clock or a tape recorder).

Interest Area	What You Can Tell Families About Each Interest Area	What Families Might Do When They Participate
Sand and Water	These materials usually calm children. Children build understandings about scientific and mathematical concepts as they play with sand and water.	Show children how to keep the sand and water in the table or tubs. Offer props and talk about what children are discovering. Help with a special activity (e.g., blowing bubbles or testing what floats and what sinks).
Music and Movement	Children develop physical skills by moving and learn concepts through songs, dance, and musical games. They develop listening skills and an appreciation of different kinds of music.	Play an instrument, sing, share recorded music, or teach children a dance. Explore the sounds of different instruments. Participate in group activities.
Cooking	Children learn literacy and math skills by following recipes. Children make scientific discoveries while cooking. Preparing and eating food is very satisfying. There are safety rules and procedures.	Help collect the necessary equipment and ingredients. Assist children in following recipe cards. Prepare a favorite dish with the children. Remind children of the safety rules.
Technology	Computers and tablets are increasingly a part of everyday life. High-quality apps and computer programs engage children in active learning. Children can work together on the computer and on the tablet.	Assist children in following the procedures for using tablets and computers. Help children find and use the apps and programs that interest them. Participate in playing a game on the tablet or the computer.

Interest Area	What You Can Tell Families About Each Interest Area	What Families Might Do When They Participate
Outdoors	Outdoor time is important for children's health and well-being. Children can learn about nature firsthand. Children develop motor skills, balance, and coordination.	Help supervise children at play. Play a game with children. Take an interest in children's discoveries (e.g., watch a caterpillar and collect leaves together). Share a special skill or interest (e.g., woodworking, gardening, basketball, or ring toss).

When families have positive classroom experiences, they are likely to come again. A meaningful role in supporting their child's learning has a far greater effect than tasks such as washing paintbrushes or preparing snacks. Be sure to let family members know how much you appreciate their help and how important it is to their children. It is always nice to follow up with a brief note or phone call to thank them again.

Meeting With Families to Share Information and Plan

Most programs hold conferences with families several times a year to share information and discuss the children's progress. In the next chapter we explain how teachers individualize the program by observing and documenting children's progress on each of the objectives for development and learning. Families will be interested in finding out what you know about their children. In turn, you can learn a great deal about children by listening to and talking with their families.

Involving families in planning for their children is a powerful way to convey that this is a true partnership. Here are some of the benefits you can expect:

- You obtain richer, more accurate ideas about a child's development by exchanging observations with families.
- You gain valuable insights about a child's background, interests, and temperament that will aid you in planning appropriate experiences.
- You have a shared vision of a child's strengths and challenges.
- You agree on which objectives are important for the child and which teaching strategies are appropriate.
- You have shared expectations for the child's development and learning.
- You encourage family members in their role as their child's first and most important teachers.
- Children are more likely to receive common messages at both school and home.
- Education becomes a team effort.

Try to schedule a planning meeting with each child's family at least three times a year or whenever you report to families.

Preparing for a Conference

The more you are prepared for a conference, the more positive the experience will be for both you and child's family and the more you will be able to accomplish. In our discussion of assessment in chapter 4, we explain the value of maintaining a portfolio for each child and tracking children's progress by using an ongoing system such as the *GOLD*® assessment system.

Before meeting with families, make sure the *Child Assessment Portfolio* is complete and up-to-date. What evidence have you collected about the child's social–emotional development? Physical skills? Language development? Cognitive development? Identify the information and work samples that best document the child's progress and any areas of concern so you are prepared to discuss them with family members.

Before you meet with the family,

- review the child's portfolio
- consider the family's interests and values
- identify and summarize in writing the information that will be of most interest to the child's family
- decide which areas of development, objectives, and strategies you particularly want to discuss with the child's family

Many programs use a family conference form that teachers begin to fill out by summarizing the child's developmental progress during a particular period. The rest of the form is completed during the conference as the teacher and family together decide next steps. Think about what each family wants most for its child, what behaviors are important, and how the family views its role in the child's education. Keep the family's educational goals and priorities in mind as you prepare for a conference so you can emphasize the child's progress in those areas first. For example, some families value social–emotional skills more highly than physical skills. Knowing that, you can begin your conference by explaining the child's progress in the area of social–emotional development and learning.

A final step in preparing for a conference is giving some thought to the areas of development, particular objectives you plan to focus on, and the strategies you will discuss with the child's family. Ask yourself, "How can I help this child move to a higher developmental level in terms of those objectives? What new skills is this child ready to learn? How can I build on this child's interests and strengths?" You will not have all the answers before meeting with families, but you will have some ideas to offer as a starting point.

Conducting a Conference

A good way to begin talking with families about their child's progress is by sharing examples of the child's work. Pictures of block structures the child has made, writing samples, drawings, and dictated stories are concrete evidence of a child's accomplishments. Explain a little about each example and what it shows about the child's interests and strengths. Share something positive that shows you really know what is unique and special about the child. Starting a conference this way can put families at ease.

Next, share your summary of the child's development. Highlight the child's strengths as well as any areas of concern, and give specific examples from your observation notes or the child's work.

Invite families to share their observations. Questions such as the following encourage families to share their perspectives:

- What does your child like most about the program?
- Has your child expressed any concerns?
- What changes have you seen?
- What are your child's special interests?
- What would you like your child to experience at school this year?

After listening to what the family says, talk about some particular objectives you want to focus on with the child and invite family members to identify those that are important to them. Explain several strategies that you will be using and ask the family what they might enjoy doing at home with the child. Discuss next steps for school and for home. Write down the plan that you develop together and provide the family with a copy so it becomes a blueprint for supporting the child's development and learning. (Your administrator might also want a copy.) The next time you meet, you and the family can talk about how the plan worked, review new evidence of the child's progress, and revise the plan together.

Review what you have written about the child's development.

Invite families to share their own observations and identify objectives important to them.

Discuss specific objectives on which you want to focus.

Share work samples and offer positive comments.

Provide families with a copy of the plan.

Responding to Challenging Situations

Despite all of the positive steps you take to build a positive relationship with each family, you will still encounter challenging situations that work against a partnership. Some families are coping with basic needs and ongoing stress that make it difficult for them to be available to their child, much less to participate actively in the program. Others choose not to get involved, thinking that their child's education is a professional matter only. As always, it is important to understand what is causing a challenging situation so you can address the issues.

Families Under Stress

Teachers deal increasingly with families under stress. Many families are headed by single parents who must find employment or job training without knowing who will be caring for their young children when they are not at school. Ongoing and unrelenting stress can be caused by other factors as well. Here are just a few:

- living in a community plagued by violence

- unemployment

- long commutes or a job that does not allow flexibility in work hours to accommodate family needs

- meeting the daily needs of a family member with a disability or chronic illness

- domestic and/or substance abuse

- adapting to a new culture and/or language

- substandard, overcrowded housing or living in a shelter

- depression that has not been diagnosed or treated

- lack of health insurance

Families who are under stress from these or other life situations do not always have the emotional energy or physical resources to provide nurturing care for their children—sometimes even to meet their children's most basic needs. They may not be able to solve problems, communicate with their children, or give them the attention and affirmation they need. Their discipline may be inconsistent, overly punitive, or nonexistent. For children in these circumstances, life is unpredictable and dangerous, and their confusion may show itself in anger, withdrawal, or fearfulness in your program.

What Can a Teacher Do?

First, do not think that you need to solve families' problems by yourself. Begin by recognizing when a family is under stress. Avoid adding to the stress by being impatient or overly critical (e.g., when a parent has forgotten to bring boots for her child in spite of several reminders) or by reporting a problem you are having with their child if you can wait for a better time. Let the family know that helpful resources are available and that you can ask your supervisor or colleagues for advice if the family wants you to do so. Your program might have social services and family support workers who can conduct a family needs-assessment to learn about the family's situation and then help them find resources. At a minimum, every program can put together information for families. This might include

- an up-to-date list of community agencies and hotlines for referrals
- brochures and resources for families to borrow
- a list of support groups that deal with the issues families face

Rearing children is one of the most important jobs in the world, but there is very little training for this critical role. Family members who were fortunate enough to have caring, nurturing experiences during their own childhoods have a solid foundation for becoming good parents, themselves. Those who had less constructive experiences still want the best for their children and are doing what they think is needed. Although family members will sometimes do things that distress you—or otherwise fail to meet a child's needs—hold to the belief that most are doing the best they can. Learn as much as you can about the strengths and needs of each family so that you have realistic expectations and can individualize your approach to the partnership. What works for one family will not necessarily work for another.

Dealing With Misunderstandings

If you work with families who share your values and beliefs and who have similar life experiences and characteristics, you are more likely to interpret what they say and do accurately. But if you work with families who are very different from you—and if you know little about their beliefs and practices—miscommunication and misunderstandings can easily take place. Understanding and respecting practices that are different from your own help you build positive relationships with all families and involve them in your program.

The following chart illustrates how miscommunication between family members and teachers can occur. It shows differences in perspectives about particular situations.

Situation	The Teacher's View	The Family's View
Sonya's teacher reports how pleased she is that Sonya has begun to speak more in class and share her ideas. Her parents do not say anything about that before they leave the conference.	Talking in class is an important goal for all children. Initially, Sonya rarely spoke in a group, so the change is an exciting development. She will learn more if she participates actively and verbalizes what she knows.	Speaking up in a group means Sonya is boasting, and we do not approve of this behavior. We want our daughter to be respectful and quiet so she can learn.

Situation	The Teacher's View	The Family's View
After conducting a workshop on ways that families can help their children learn at home and after providing written suggestions, teachers find that several families do not follow through.	Parents who don't spend time on activities with their children at home just don't care very much about their success at school. The more families are involved, the better children do in school.	It's the teacher's job to teach my child, not mine. I don't know how to do what the teacher is asking.
After careful observations over time, a teacher is concerned that a child's language is delayed, so she suggests an evaluation. The family does not make an appointment with a specialist.	If a real problem exists, it should be identified as early as possible. Parents should want to get all the help they can get for their child.	Some children start speaking later than others. My child is fine.
Carlos's mother unzips his coat and hangs it in his cubby along with his mittens and boots. The teacher says, "Carlos, you can unzip and hang up your own coat, can't you? Tomorrow, show your mom how you can do things for yourself."	Self-help skills and independence are important objectives for children. Carlos's mother treats him like a baby.	Helping my child is one way I show him how much his family loves him. I want to care for him, especially just before I have to say good-bye for the day. There's plenty of time for him to learn to take care of himself.
Setsuko looks up reluctantly and glances away quickly when the teachers asks her to look her in the eye as she explains the rule about running in the classroom.	I can't be sure that Setsuko is listening to me if she is not looking at me when I speak to her.	We have taught our child that looking into an adult's eye when being spoken to is a sign of disrespect. Doing so goes against what we have taught her.

Families who do not understand what their children's teachers want—or who think that their values and goals for their children are not respected—cannot be comfortable and involved with their children's lives at school. When the values and skills children learn at home are not respected or understood at school, children become confused about what to do. Identifying most strongly with their home culture, children may reject the school culture because it is unfamiliar. In doing so, they also reject the goals and values of the educational system, feel alienated, and often eventually drop out of school. The opposite can happen as well: Children may identify more with the school culture and reject their own heritage, becoming increasingly isolated from their families and communities.

You can avoid making children feel as though they have to choose between the behavior they learn at home and expectations at school. Sometimes this means accepting what a child does. For example, knowing that a child has been taught not to look directly at an adult who is giving directions helps you appreciate why it would upset and confuse the child if you said, "Look me in the eye when I am talking to you." You would understand the child's behavior and perhaps check her attention to you by suggesting a way for her to demonstrate that she understood what you told her.

In other situations you may need to find a compromise that shows respect for the family's values without following their practices at school. For example, when you know that some families consider it a sign of love to do things for a child even if he is capable of doing them independently, you can validate a mother's practice of unzipping, removing, and hanging up her son's coat. At the same time, you might explain to the mother that her son is learning to care for himself when she is not available and that your program considers self-care to be an important life skill.

Another example is the situation of the family that resists the recommendation to have the child's language development assessed by a specialist. Here you may be more successful if you first acknowledge the family's point that children develop and learn at an individual pace. Confirm that, while this is true, it is also true that many problems can be overcome if they are identified early. Once an agreement has been reached, you can find out what would be most comfortable for the family. Perhaps offer to have someone from the program go along when they take the child to a specialist. Perhaps the child can be observed at the program.

Addressing Differences Constructively

Some differences are hard to reconcile but must be addressed directly because they go against your program's philosophy and your own strong beliefs. One common example is spanking. Some families want you to spank their children for misbehavior. They firmly believe that hitting is good for children: "Spare the rod, spoil the child." "If you hit your child, society won't." They may tell you, "My parents hit me, and I turned out okay." However, spanking a child goes against what we know from research on the negative effects of corporal punishment. Physical punishment is also against the law in most states, and it has no place in *The Creative Curriculum®* classroom, where teachers strive to create a peaceful classroom community by guiding children's behavior in positive ways.

In situations where a family's wishes and values conflict with those of the program, the following steps may be helpful in resolving differences constructively:

Seek first to understand the family's position. Ask open-ended questions and listen to the family. You might begin a conversation by prompting, "Tell me a little about the concerns you have for your child. What would you like your child to learn here?" These questions can help you understand the family's requests. More than likely, they want their child to behave well and develop self-regulation.

Validate the family's concerns and wishes. To let the family know that you are listening and to be sure that you understand what they are saying, restate what you hear: "I hear you saying that you want to be sure your child learns how to control himself and how to behave. That is an important goal for us as well. We spend a lot of time building children's skills in this area."

Explain how your program addresses the family's concern. Acknowledge that there are different points of view on any topic. Without negating their request, talk about your shared vision for children. You both want to help children learn how to behave in acceptable ways and relate to others in a caring and respectful manner. You might begin by sharing the objectives that relate specifically to emotional and behavioral regulation. (These objectives are included under social–emotional development.) Explain the practices in your program that support children's acquisition of self-regulation skills. If possible, share research on topics of concern to the family.

Plan to communicate with one another to assess progress. Assure the family that you will monitor their child's progress and stay in touch. Let them know that their concerns will remain on your mind and be addressed.

In some situations, you may decide that a compromise is the best solution and that you should put aside your own beliefs in order to accomplish something more important. An example is the issue of a graduation ceremony at the end of the year before children leave the program. You may think that a graduation celebration is not developmentally appropriate, particularly if it means a formal ceremony in which children perform, wear caps and gowns, and receive diplomas. Family members, many of whom had negative school experiences and never graduated themselves, may attach special significance to a graduation ceremony. To them, the ceremony might represent the fact that their child's experiences in school have been better and the hope that this is the first of many graduations. You may therefore decide to have a modified graduation celebration, a party to which all families are invited and at which they share food. The compromise conveys respect for families' wishes and enables everyone to enjoy a celebration.

By suspending judgment, you can convey to families that you are eager to learn from them and gain a deeper understanding of what they want and value. With the information that families share, you can try an approach that suits them and gains their trust and respect without violating the values, goals, and principles of your program.

Conclusion

Building partnerships with families and ensuring that they have a role in their children's education is a crucial component of *The Creative Curriculum*. Together, the five components—how children develop and learn, the learning environment, what children learn, caring and teaching, and partnering with families—will help you provide all children in your class with meaningful and engaging experiences that promote their development and learning. In *Volume 2: Interest Areas*, we show how these components, which are the foundation of a high-quality preschool program, enable you effectively to support children's learning in each of the 10 classroom interest areas and the outdoors.

References

Backer, B. (2001, January 28). Home visits. Message posted to ECENET-L@LISTSERV. UIUC.EDU (First appeared in *First Teacher* magazine, September/October 1994). Retrieved February 14, 2002, from http://www.awod.com/gallery/rwav/bbacker/articles/homevisits.html

Henderson, A. T., & Berla, N. (1994). *A new generation of evidence: The family is critical to student achievement.* Columbia, MD: National Committee for Citizens in Education.

U.S. Department of Education, Office of Educational Research and Improvement, National Center for Education Statistics. (2015). *The condition of education 2015.* (NCES 2015-144). Washington, DC: U.S. Government Printing Office. Also available from http://www.nces.ed.gov

Appendix

Weekly Planning Form

TeachingStrategies®

Weekly Planning Form

Week of: _____ Teacher: _____ Study: _____

	Monday	Tuesday	Wednesday	Thursday	Friday
Interest Areas					
Large Group					
Read-Aloud					
Small Group					

Outdoor Experiences:

Family Partnerships:

Wow! Experiences:

Weekly Planning Form, continued

"To Do" List:

Reflecting on the week:

Individual Child Planning